The Cyborg Experiments

TECHNOLOGIES:
STUDIES IN CULTURE & THEORY

Editors: Gary Hall, Middlesex University, and Chris Hables Gray, University of Great Falls

CONSULTANT EDITORS

Parveen Adams, Keith Ansell-Pearson, Jim Falk, Steve Graham, Donna Haraway, Deborah Heath, Manuel DeLanda, Paul Patton, Constance Penley, Kevin Robins, Avital Ronell, Andrew Ross, Allucquere Rosanne Stone

Technologies is a series dedicated to publishing innovative and provocative work on both 'new' and 'established' technologies: their history, contemporary issues and future frontiers. Bringing together theorists and practitioners in cultural studies, critical theory and Continental philosophy, the series will explore areas as diverse as cyberspace, the city, cybernetics, nanotechnology, the cosmos, AI, prosthetics, genetics and other medical advances, as well as specific technologies such as the gun, telephone, Internet and digital TV.

BOOKS IN THE SERIES

The Architecture of the Visible: Technology and Urban Visual Culture	Graham MacPhee
The Cyborg Experiments: The Extensions of the Body in the Media Age	Joanna Zylinska (ed.)
Transductions: Bodies and Machines at Speed	Adrian Mackenzie

THE CYBORG EXPERIMENTS

The Extensions of the Body in the Media Age

edited by

JOANNA ZYLINSKA

continuum
LONDON • NEW YORK

CONTINUUM
The Tower Building, 11 York Road, London SE1 7NX
370 Lexington Avenue, New York, NY 10017-6503

First published 2002

British Library Cataloguing-in-Publication Data
A catalogue record for this book is available from the British Library.
    ISBN 0-8264-5902-1 (hardback)
    ISBN 0-8264-5903-X (paperback)

Library of Congress Cataloging-in-Publication Data
The cyborg experiments: the extensions of the body in the media age /
edited by Joanna Zylinska.
      p. cm. — (Technologies)
    Includes bibliographical references and index.
    ISBN 0-8264-5902-1 — ISBN 0-8264-5903-X (pbk.)
    1. Human–machine systems. 2. Cyborgs. 3. Robotics—Social
aspects. I. Zylinska, Joanna, 1971- . II. Technologies (London,
England)
  TA167 .C93 2002
  303.48'3—dc21

Typeset by CentraServe Ltd, Saffron Walden, Essex
Printed and bound in Great Britain by MPG Books Ltd, Bodmin, Cornwall

Contents

Notes on Contributors

John Appleby is a doctoral student in the Department of Philosophy at the University of Warwick, UK, pursuing research into methodologies of anti-humanist contagion, and consequent materialist explanations of new technology.

Rachel Armstrong is a writer and former medical doctor. She works as a collaborator with artists on projects that are a hybrid between art and science. She is a part-time lecturer at the Bartlett School of Architecture, London, and has edited two publications: *Sci-Fi Aesthetics* (1998) and *Space Architecture* (2000). Her fiction novel *The Gray's Anatomy* was published by Serpents Tail in 2001.

Fred Botting is Professor of English Literature at Keele University, UK. He has co-edited (with Scott Wilson) *The Bataille Reader* and *The Bataille Critical Reader* for Blackwell and has published (also with Scott Wilson) two books: *Bataille* (Palgrave, 2000) and *The Tarantinian Ethics* (Sage, 2001).

Julie Clarke is a digital artist and writer who completed her undergraduate studies at RMIT, Melbourne, Australia. She completed her Honours year at the University of Melbourne, being awarded a Postgraduate Diploma in Fine Arts (Art History). She gained her Master's Degree in Fine Arts, Art History by research thesis in 1997 at the University of Melbourne, where she is currently a candidate for a Ph.D. Her poetic prose and articles have been published in Australia, the United Kingdom and Norway (in translation). She co-won the inaugural Faulding Award for writing for multimedia at the Adelaide Festival of the Arts in 1998, later exhibited at 'Lovebit', Staffordshire.

Chris Hables Gray, Ph.D., is an associate professor of the Cultural

Studies of Science and of Computer Science at the University of Great Falls in Montana. He is also part-time core faculty in the Graduate College of the Union Institute and University. He is the author of *Cyborg Citizen* (Routledge, 2001) and of *Postmodern War* (Guilford/Routledge, 1997), and editor of *The Cyborg Handbook* (Routledge, 1995). Currently he is working with others on a collection about contemporary anarchism and with another collective on a radio play about an Irish demi-god. Alone, he is writing a book about information technology and peacemaking and another about human–machine integration in space exploration (*NASA and the Cyborg*, Athlone/Continuum, forthcoming).

Gary Hall is Senior Lecturer in Media and Cultural Studies at Middlesex University, London. As well as general co-editor of the Technologies series, he is also founding co-editor of the electronic journal *Culture Machine* <http://culturemachine.tees.ac.uk>. His work has appeared in numerous books and journals, including *parallax*, *Surfaces*, *Angelaki* and *The Oxford Literary Review*. He has just completed a book on cultural studies, deconstruction and new technology entitled *Culture in Bits* for Athlone/Continuum.

Meredith Jones is a doctoral candidate at the University of Western Sydney, where she is writing a dissertation about cosmetic surgery, anti-ageing technologies, cyberspace and notions of immortality. She teaches media studies at Sydney's University of Technology.

Orlan is a French multimedia and performance artist who lives and works in Paris. Her projects have involved poetry, drama, painting, photography and, famously, installations with trousseau fabric stained with sexual fluids which were intended to challenge the splitting of the female image into the 'madonna and whore' dichotomy. In the 1990s Orlan embarked on a sequence of surgical operations – performances by means of which she self-mockingly modelled herself on selected mythological figures. The operating theatre became the artist's studio in which Orlan literally 'gave her body to art'. The surgeries were precisely staged and recorded in order to be shown in art galleries and other public spaces all over the world. Orlan's most recent project,

Refiguration/Self-Hybridation, involves the production of digital photo-images and interactive video installations dealing with body transformations in Maya and Olmec cultures.

Orlan's Web site: <www.orlan.net>.

Mark Poster is Director of the Film Studies Program at the University of California, Irvine, and a member of the History Department. He has a courtesy appointment in the Department of Information and Computer Science. He is a member of the Critical Theory Institute. His recent books are *What's the Matter with the Internet: A Critical Theory of Cyberspace* (University of Minnesota Press, 2001), *The Information Subject* in *Critical Voices Series* (Gordon & Breach Arts International, 2001), *Cultural History and Postmodernity* (Columbia University Press, 1997), *The Second Media Age* (Polity and Blackwell, 1995) and *The Mode of Information* (Blackwell and the University of Chicago Press, 1990).

Jay Prosser is Lecturer in American Literature at the University of Leeds. He is the author of *Second Skins: The Body Narratives of Transsexuality* (Columbia University Press, 1998). He is currently completing a book on photography and autobiography.

Edward Scheer lectures in performance studies in the School of Theatre, Film and Dance at the University of New South Wales and is a freelance arts writer. He is the editor of *100 Years of Cruelty: Essays on Artaud* (Sydney: Power Publications and Artspace, 2000) and *Antonin Artaud: A Critical Reader* (Rouledge, forthcoming), and is secretary of the board of directors of The Performance Space in Sydney.

Zoë Sofia (a.k.a. as Zoë Sofoulis) lectures in humanities at the University of Western Sydney and writes on the irrational and corporeal dimensions of our relations to high technology. Her publications include *Whose Second Self? Gender and (Ir)rationality in Computer Culture* (Deakin University, 1993), *Planet Diana: Cultural Studies and Global Mourning* (Research Centre for Intercommunal Studies at UWS Nepean, 1996), for which she was a contributing co-editor, and various papers on feminism, technology and contemporary art. She is currently working on a book about different kinds of container technologies.

Stelarc is an Australian artist who has performed extensively in Japan, Europe and the USA – including new music, dance festivals and experimental theatre. He has used medical instruments, prosthetics, robotics, virtual reality systems and the Internet to explore alternative, intimate and involuntary interfaces with the body. He has performed with a THIRD HAND, a VIRTUAL ARM, a VIRTUAL BODY, a STOMACH SCULPTURE and EXOSKELETON, a six-legged walking robot. In 1995 Stelarc received a three-year Fellowship from the Visual Arts/Craft Board of the Australia Council. In 1997 he was appointed Honorary Professor of Art and Robotics at Carnegie Mellon University. He was Artist-in-Residence for Hamburg City in 1998. In 1999 he was reappointed as a Senior Research Scholar for the Faculty of Art and Design at Nottingham Trent University, UK. He is now Principal Research Fellow in the Performance Arts Digital Research Unit at Nottingham Trent University. In 2001 he was awarded an honorary law degree by Monash University in Melbourne. His art is represented by the Sherman Galleries in Sydney.
Stelarc's Web site: <www.stelarc.va.com.au>.

Scott Wilson is Director of the Institute for Cultural Research at Lancaster University and Managing Editor of *Cultural Values*. He has co-edited (with Fred Botting) *The Bataille Reader* and *The Bataille Critical Reader* for Blackwell and has published (also with Fred Botting) two books: *Bataille* (Palgrave, 2000) and *The Tarantinian Ethics* (Sage, 2001).

Joanna Zylinska is Senior Lecturer in Cultural Studies at the University of Surrey, Roehampton. She is the author of *On Spiders, Cyborgs and Being Scared: The Feminine and the Sublime* (Manchester University Press, 2001). Her work on feminist ethics, women's fiction, cultural studies and new technologies has appeared in numerous journals, including *Women: A Cultural Review*, *parallax* and *J_Spot: Journal of Social and Political Thought*. She is book reviews editor for *Culture Machine*, an international peer-reviewed journal of cultural studies and cultural theory <http://culturemachine.tees.ac.uk>.

Acknowledgements

First of all, I would like to thank the editors of the Technologies series, Chris Hables Gray and Gary Hall, as well as Tristan Palmer of Continuum/Athlone, for their interest in – and support of – this project. My heartfelt thanks go to Stelarc, for his generosity, humour and unlimited assistance in putting this collection together, and for providing photographs of his performances. I am also grateful to Orlan for our correspondence, and for allowing me to include her 'Le virtuel **et/ou** le réel . . .' piece here. My most sincere thanks go to Diane Morgan for translating the latter. I am extremely grateful to the Faculty of Humanities at Bath Spa University College for providing me with research time and financial assistance which helped me to complete this collection. Last but not least, I would like to express my thanks to all the contributors to this collection for their interest, enthusiasm and extreme efficiency.

Extending McLuhan into the New Media Age: An Introduction

Joanna Zylinska

> [T]he need to understand the effects of the extensions of man becomes more urgent by the hour. (Marshall McLuhan, *Understanding Media: The Extensions of Man*)

> We should expect to be surprised. (Peter Menzel and Faith D'Aluisio, *Robo sapiens*)

When Marshall McLuhan was writing *Understanding Media* in the 1960s, he realized he was standing at the brink of a new age. After three thousand years of explosion 'by means of fragmentary and mechanical technologies', the world, according to McLuhan, began to implode, bringing together, in hitherto unforeseen ways, multiple geographical locations, nations and identities. As a result of these transformations, people of different nationalities, races and cultures found themselves living in an 'electrically concentrated' village. Moving beyond the mechanical age in which their bodies had been extended in space, humans approached

> the final phase of the extensions of man – the technological simulation of consciousness, when the creative process of knowing will be collectively and corporately extended to the whole of human society, much as we have already extended our nerves and our senses by various media. (McLuhan, 11)

While unable to decide whether the extension of consciousness he was predicting would be an unquestionably 'good thing', McLuhan nevertheless concluded that the world's implosion left us with a deeper sense of responsibility for others 'now involved in our lives . . . thanks to the electronic media' (13). McLuhan's aspiration for 'wholeness, empathy . . . depth of awareness' and 'the ultimate harmony of all beings' sounds idealistically old-fashioned. It has been discredited not only by later developments in global transnational economy, the strengthening of corporatism and the rise of anti-corporatist movements but also by the more sceptical discourses of postmodernism, postcolonialism and multiculturalism, which have put in question the desirability, or even feasibility, of such harmony. And yet it is worth pointing out that his by now abandoned 'global village' was not entirely dissimilar from the urban spaces of the 'new media age'. McLuhan's global village was not as unified as it is sometimes presented today: it remained open to the contradictory forces of both globalization and fragmentation which are now associated with the condition of postmodernity (see Harvey, 240–59), a state of events that has led to the radical redefinition of our position in the world, our self-perception, sense of belonging, and identification with other species and life forms. This perception of technologies as 'extensions of man', of our 'inner selves' (see McLuhan, 253), has allowed for a rethinking of the inner/outer distinction that was supposed to separate man from 'his' technologies. It is in its problematization of the boundaries between the self and the world that McLuhan's idea of the 'extensions of man' is particularly relevant for us.

Robotics is one area in which this process of 'extending' human identity by means of technology has been extremely prominent today. As Peter Menzel and Faith D'Aluisio explain in their book *Robo sapiens*,

> Today's robots are more than factory workers . . . Our mechanical destiny is not to be denied, and the questions arising from the creation of these creatures are ones that will shape the future of humanity, in whatever form it eventually assumes. (19)

For the past two decades, a number of high-tech companies, in Japan and the USA particularly, have been committed to developing humanoid robots that can perfectly emulate not only human bodily functions (such as gait, sight and responsiveness) but also our appearance. What we are witnessing here is a process in which the human is extrapolated onto an external agent which is supposed to be both a replacement for 'man', and 'his' perfect simulation. But while most scientists are still struggling to produce 'six degrees of freedom' robots that can perform basic human functions – like standing straight or walking up the stairs while being able to avoid colliding with other objects – there is no doubt that experiments of this kind 'shape the future of humanity'. By raising fundamental questions about the nature of the human (What would a humanoid robot be like? What functions would it need to perform? Could it dream of electric sheep?), these performances of McLuhanian 'extensions' contribute to the development of a new discourse of identity, one that goes beyond McLuhan's own humanism.

This new discourse, described by Chris Hables Gray, Steven Mentor and Heidi J. Figueroa-Sarriera as 'cyborgology', focuses on the exploration of 'intimate human–machine relationships' (2). It recognizes that the 'extensions of man' must be analysed not from a human point of view but from a position of inbetweenness, as the very process of 'extending humanity' undermines the inviolability of the boundaries of the human self and the non-human, machinic other. Rather than talk about the 'extensions of man', we are faced with a discourse that articulates the inherently prosthetic character of human identity. As Samuel Weber argues in *Mass Mediauras*, instead of telling the story of the individual Self, we need to focus on its highly divisible Settings. He suggests that 'the *being* of human beings has had more to do with *setups* and *sets* than with *subjects* and *objects*, unified in and through self-consciousness' (4). That is to say, the identity of the human is always already relational; it has to be seen as remaining in relation with alterity (this relation can take the form of immersion, connectivity, or separation-as-difference). The discourse of 'cyborgology' as developed by Gray *et al*. does not proclaim the story of the original purity of 'man' that was later polluted by technology. It is nevertheless historicized by its rootedness in the events and processes occurring in the information age and predominantly related to the development of new warfare techniques. As Timothy W. Luke writes, in the post-McLuhanian *new* media age,

[t]he boundaries dividing fact and fiction waffle and warp, a new lifeform – the cyborg – emerges, which is that hybridised organism

that (con)fuses man and organism, animal and apparatus, physical matter and non-physical information. . . . However, we must recognise how the cyborg materialises, in part, out of things, but also, in part, out of us, creating a new order that makes 'thoroughly ambiguous the difference between natural and artificial, mind and body, self-developing and externally designed, and many other distinctions that used to apply to organisms and machines'. (40)[1]

The idea that these emergent life forms are absolutely novel is therefore problematic. Even though it responds to recent changes in the world economy and the production of information, the cyborg is created, as Luke has it, in part 'out of us', and thus points to the legacy of this new hybrid life with the man of McLuhan's 'media age'. What perhaps distinguishes the cyborgian discourse of identity from some of the earlier discourses of human destiny – be they religious, scientific or science-fictional – is the withdrawal of the possibility of knowing in advance what 'the future of humanity' will bring. The future of humanity, of the cyborg and of technology, has to remain open. Otherwise, as Jacques Derrida points out, we would be replacing the idea of the future with what he terms a 'programmable tomorrow' (387), a moment in time that we attempt to control by foreclosing it to the possibility of surprise, bewilderment and even horror. The fatalistic scenario that foregrounds *only* horror in its forecasts as to the future of human–machine interactions has therefore to be seen as reductive, as it is based on the maintenance of radical boundaries between the human self and the robotic other and, therefore, on a disavowal of the future. In such cases, the fear of technology, of change, of what the future might bring, is projected onto the robot, whose being is then amputated and presented as intrinsically other: not as part of the human, but rather as humanity's competitor and enemy. This kind of identity extrapolation represents the foreclosure of a cyborgian future. The contrasting rhetoric of progression and rationalization that has frequently been applied to describe the transformations effected by technology poses us with exactly the same problem. In his Introduction to *The Critique of Pure Modernity*, David Kolb provides us with an example of how this logic of new technologies operates in post-industrial societies by arguing that 'Technological production,

4

bureaucratic administration, and other modernising factors bring about an economy that is efficient but also encourages the spread of an atomising and calculating style into other areas of our lives' (8). But the story of technology does not solely inscribe itself in the discourse of utilitarianism. It is always possible to tell a different narrative, foregrounding the working of an economy that is not based on direct gain, or on the equal balancing of investments and losses. This narrative is being developed today not only by netizens and cyber-artists but also by roboticists embarking on the seemingly impossible tasks of teaching their creations to smile, kick a ball or even dance.[2]

The impossibility of knowing the future in advance does not mean that we will not attempt to approach or even construct it. Cyborgology can thus be described as a performative discourse in an Austinian speech-act sense: it constitutes itself only through articulation and reiteration, participating in the constant redrawing of discursive boundaries. Rather than position a cyborgian future as the unknowable 'other' of the present, it blurs the boundary between the two by enacting and repeating the old *in* the new. Even if the future is to remain unpredictable and open, it will still provoke attempts to foresee, envision and perform it.

The Cyborg Experiments is one such attempt to perform the future. It consists of a series of experiments and interventions that attempt to trace current developments in science, technology and art. Its various chapters highlight some of those instances in which technology is taken *beyond* atomization and calculation, and enters into unprecedented couplings and unforeseen liaisons. Focusing on the work of two performance artists – the Australian artist Stelarc and the French artist Orlan – the book goes beyond the particularities of the work of Orlan and Stelarc to discuss wider issues regarding bodily extensions in cyberspace. By analysing some of the challenges technology poses to corporeality, *The Cyborg Experiments* also explores how humanism, and the idea of 'the human', have been brought into question by new developments in science, media and communications. Referring to Stelarc's and Orlan's reworking of the concepts of proximity, intimacy and distance, the book analyses the interactions between human and machine and asks whether this opening of the sacrosanct space of the flesh can be seen as a 'shift from the human to the post-human'.

One way in which *The Cyborg Experiments* attempts to deliver what its title promises is by staging an encounter between more traditionally 'academic' and 'discipline-oriented' essays and styles of writing, and those that can perhaps be seen as more experimental and cross-disciplinary. Such an arrangement is intended both to 'mimic' the hybridity of Orlan's and Stelarc's projects and to initiate still further links and connections between different artists, theorists and approaches. The result, I hope, is a complex and polyvocal debate, presented from a number of theoretical and critical perspectives, thus providing multiple interpretative possibilities of human–machine inter-actions in the 'new' media age.

The chapters of Part 1, 'The Cyborg Links', investigate some of the connections between technology and its alleged 'others': nature, humankind and biological life. Focusing on liminal, borderline states of being such as human–machine, dead–undead and premodern–postmod-ern, the authors put into question the Aristotelian conception of technology that has dominated Western thought for almost three thousand years. In this view, technology is positioned only as a tool which is applied to nature, 'an instrument . . . that happens to have been used well or badly' (Clark, 238). The horror narrative of technology that comes to life in today's scare stories about genetically modified food, cloning or plastic surgeries is thus only the inverse of this conception, leading to a conclusion that 'the instrument has taken control of its maker, the creation control of its creator (Frankenstein's monster)' (Clark, 238). Mark Poster's chapter 'High-Tech Franken-stein, or Heidegger Meets Stelarc', which opens both Part 1 and the volume as a whole, challenges precisely such an instrumental view of human–machine interaction. Revisiting Heidegger's influential 1955 essay 'The question concerning technology', Poster argues that the focal point of Heidegger's argument is modern humanity's way of being, which consists of 'bringing itself forth' while simultaneously concealing this process (i.e. its 'technology'). In this context, tech-nology is understood as a way in which the world is set up, or brought forth, and not a mere object. However, Heidegger's approach does not allow us to distinguish between different and constantly evolving technologies and technocultures; nor does it take into account the nature of postmodern technology-as-information processing, storage and dissemination. The 'real' question of technology today, as Poster argues, concerns the nature of the cyborg, or what he calls 'the new order of humachines', whose nature we can barely foresee. The question of how technology allows us to ask anew what it means to be human is developed further by Julie Clarke. In 'The Human/Not Human in the Work of Orlan and Stelarc' she explores the relationship between monstrosity, liminality and pollution in the work of these two artists. Interrogating the nature of the prefix 'post' in the term 'post-human', Clarke discusses a number of other less bounded and more connected models of human identity. Meredith Jones and Zoë Sofia are in turn interested in temporal connections between contemporary body and carnal art as represented by Stelarc and Orlan, and the medieval bodily practices of the mystics who embraced suffering for the sake of holiness. They interpret Orlan and Stelarc's work as staging 'baroque modern' forms of embodiment involving interchange between image and flesh, and thus opening themselves to the social world in ways similar to the rituals of mystics, visionaries and flagellants in the Middle Ages. Jones and Sofia argue that these two artists do not aspire to a holy communion with the Church but rather aim for a secular embrace with technoscience. Stelarc's pneumatic projects, which he describes in the final chapter of Part 1, provide an example of just such an intimate embrace with technology. His most recent Hexapod walking robot initiates a compliant coupling of human and robot in which 'the robot would be more than an extension of the body. And the body becomes more than a brain for the machine.'

Such bodily couplings are not inconsequential for our sense of identity and self-knowledge. Stelarc takes this conclusion further when, in an interview with Paolo Atzori and Kirk Woolford, he claims that 'it's *only through radically redesigning the body* that we will end up having significantly different thoughts and philosophies' (non-pag., emphasis added). Part 2 of the book, 'The Obsolete Body?', explores some of the ways in which redesigning the body can change the way we think and philosophize. It also explores different possibilities of understanding Stelarc's claim that the body has now 'become obsolete'. In 'What Does an Avatar Want? Stelarc's E-motions', Edward Scheer analyses Stelarc's work in the context of performance art. Posing the question 'What moves us?', he investigates the parallel mechanisms that regulate physical and emotional processes in the human. Scheer dismisses claims that Stelarc's performances are focused on the overcoming of the human body. Instead, he argues that in Stelarc's work the body functions as an interface between technologies, delineating a prosthetic model of human identity in which agency is dispersed into the world. What emerges is a connected model of the human which opens a gap in our thinking between motion and e-motion, without supporting a radical mind–body split. Applying Deleuze and Guattari's concept of 'rhizomatics', John Appleby expresses his disappointment with what he sees as Stelarc's straightforward teleological narrative of human evolution and optimization manifested in his theory of bodily obsolescence. He argues that Stelarc's pronouncements are not as radical as they are often presented as being, because they do not manage to escape the Cartesian dualisms that Stelarc claims to repudiate. And yet Appleby admits that even if Stelarc's performances do not necessarily point towards a 'post-human condition', they 'do indeed create interesting possibilities for rethinking the way in which we interact with the world'. In my interview with Stelarc, conducted together with Gary Hall, the artist reveals his concern over certain dualistic readings of his work which lead to the prioritization of his performances (often described as interesting, creative or promising) over his writings (sometimes seen as banal, contradictory or problematic). Resorting instead to the image of prosthesis, which has defined his artistic projects such as the Third Hand, Exoskeleton or Parasite, Stelarc describes his work as being situated in the liminal spaces *between* performance and writing, 'between the actual and the virtual', where the human is born out of the relationship with technology and where transformed environments necessitate the restructuring of the bodily design. Gary Hall's 'Para-Site', intended as a 'viral infection' of Stelarc's own official Web site, is itself an experiment devised to test the possibilities and limitations of new digital technologies. Through the use of hypertext links translated here into the paper medium, Hall 'performs' the idea of prosthesis as it is enacted in Stelarc's performances and texts, not only 'augmenting, extending, and modifying' but also 'invading, disturbing and contaminating' the 'original' material. This allows him to investigate the forms of knowledge facilitated by technology as well as to address the question of the ethics of reading, or interpreting, the projects actuated by it.

Part 3, '*Self*-hybridation', focuses specifically on the work of Orlan. The essays included here explore some of the ways in which experiments in medicine and plastic surgery allow us to reconceptualize the notion of 'embodiment' and its relation to knowledge. In 'Morlan', Fred Botting and Scott Wilson argue that the processes of surgical (re)construction Orlan undertakes inscribe themselves in an economy of excess which can be associated with what Jean-Joseph Goux calls 'postmodern capitalism'. Analysing the relationship between art and business, between artistic production and technological reproduction, they apply a Lacanian framework to trace the floating of lack and desire in post-industrial consumer societies. Here, Orlan's parodic femininity becomes yet another item of capitalist expenditure. Orlan's own piece is an attempt to question what she describes as a Manicheanism of our Western culture, which always makes us choose *between* two options. Explaining her artistic strategy as a refusal to be limited by such decisions, Orlan describes her projects as belonging to both nature *and* technology, the real *and* the virtual. Rachel Armstrong's 'Anger, Art and Medicine' provides an autobiographical reflection on her experience as Orlan's assistant, helping her with the promotion of her operations in the UK. A medical doctor disappointed with the disintegration of the UK's National Health Service, Armstrong confesses that the strength of Orlan's ideas matched the strength of her anger against the medical profession and its unreasonable demands. Both bemused and repulsed by the commercialization of medical care, which 'could be specifically customized to meet a single patient's every need, provided the funding was secured', Armstrong's solidarity with the artist wavers in the prospect of Orlan's final operation, intended to create 'the largest [nose] that could be possibly made for her face'.

The obsolescence of the body and a simultaneous reluctance to abandon it are thus two of the key problems explored throughout this collection. Significantly, a number of robots currently devised by Japanese and US technological institutes and laboratories are intended to be perfect simulations of the human. But it is not only external human features that are emulated in these experiments. One of Japan's

JOANNA ZYLINSKA

most respected roboticists, Shigeo Hirose, believes that 'any robot engineered to be intelligent could be engineered to be moral. Robots could be saints. . . . We could build them to be unselfish, because they don't have to fight for their biological existence' (Menzel and D'Aluisio, 19). However, what underlies these developments is a celebration of the human as both a physical and a spiritual model (i.e. not only is the human body emulated to construct the most perfect robot, which could 'pass' as human, but also human(ist) morality is seen as a desirable ideal). But what remains unaddressed in these experiments is what a number of theorists of cyberspace, including Chris Hables Gray, author of the controversial 'The Cyborg Bill of Rights', call 'the progressive cyborgization of our society'. The question that we should ask is not how we can teach robots to behave *like humans*, but rather what forms of ethics and politics will emerge as a result of the transformation of humanity through its coupling with technology. Gray continues his reflection on 'cyborg society' in his chapter 'In Defence of Prefigurative Art', which opens Part 4 of the book, 'Aesthetics and Ethics: Technological Perspectives'. He argues that the art of Orlan and Stelarc can be read as a direct attempt to shape, or prefigure, our cyborg future. Commenting on these two artists' engagement with medical discourses and technologies, he concludes that their art not only delineates new aesthetic boundaries but also changes ethical and political norms regarding the ownership of our bodies and the wider societal practices that regulate them. Jay Prosser's 'Ph/autography and the Art of Life' investigates the relationship between art and ethics as organized by technologies of representation such as photography and video. Interrogating a series of oppositions between reality and artifice, depth and surface, self and other, and participation and detachment, Prosser applies the Lacanian notion of the Real as 'a thing of trauma' to comment on a number of contemporary artistic practices intended to represent 'real life'. By comparing the work of such artists as Orlan, Cindy Sherman, Del LaGrace Volcano and Nan Goldin with the video installations of the British artist Gillian Wearing, he traces the boundaries of what he describes as 'ethical realism'. This final part of the book, on the relationship between aesthetics and ethics as outlined by new technologies, closes with my chapter '"The Future . . . Is Monstrous":

Prosthetics as Ethics'. Taking recourse to the concept of prosthesis – one of the 'nodal points' of this book – I look at different ways in which the self negotiates its relationships with alterity and exteriority. Prosthetics thus stands for me for an ethical way of thinking about identity and difference. Combining this newly emergent view of the human as always already 'intrinsically other' – that is, existing in relation to, and dependent on, its technology, with Emmanuel Levinas's ethics of respect for the alterity of the other – I explore ethical moments in the artistic practices of Stelarc and Orlan. Even though it is not necessarily through art that fixed identity can be challenged, I conclude by arguing that artistic practices of this kind foreground the broadly enacted performativity of identity, as well as preparing the grounds for the rethinking of identitarian relationships in our culture.

NOTES

1. Luke's passage incorporates a quotation from Donna Haraway's celebrated *Simians, Cyborgs and Women: The Reinvention of Nature*. New York: Routledge, 1991. Haraway's book, and especially her 'Cyborg Manifesto', which is included in it, famously inscribed the concept of the cyborg in a clearly articulated political discourse.
2. A nameless 'robot with a female head' developed by Hara-Kobayiashi Lab at the Science University of Tokyo is designed to 'show emotion' – that is, to articulate facial expressions which people will be able to recognize. The Honda robot, in turn, even though designed primarily for walking, can also kick a soccer ball or open a door. The achievements of DB, the Dynamic Brain robot developed by the Japanese research centre ATR, are not any less amazing: DB can both dance and juggle! (See Menzel and D'Aluisio, 43–79)

WORKS CITED

Atzori, Paolo and Kirk Woolford. 'Extended body: interview with Stelarc'. *CTheory*, 6: September (1995), <www.ctheory.net/text_file.asp?pick=71>.

Clark, Timothy. 'Deconstruction and technology'. In *Deconstructions: A User's Guide*. Ed. Nicholas Royle. Basingstoke and New York: Palgrave, 2000. 238–57.

Derrida, Jacques. 'Passages – from traumatism to promise'. In *Points . . . Interviews, 1974–1994. Jacques Derrida*. Ed. Elizabeth Weber. Stanford, CA: Stanford University Press, 1995. 372–95.

Gray, Chris Hables. 'The ethics and politics of cyborg embodiment: citizenship as a hypervalue'. *Cultural Values* 1:2 (1997): 252–8.

Gray, Chris Hables, Steven Mentor and Heidi J. Figueroa-Sarriera. 'Cyborgology: constructing the knowledge of cybernetic organisms'. In *The Cyborg Handbook*. Ed. Chris Hables Gray. London: Routledge, 1995. 1–16.

Harvey, David. 'The time and space of the Enlightenment project'. *The Condition of Postmodernity*. Oxford: Blackwell, 1989.

Kolb, David. *The Critique of Pure Modernity*. Chicago: University of Chicago Press, 1998.

Luke, Timothy W. 'Cyborg enchantments: commodity fetishism and human/machine interactions'. *Strategies: Journal of Theory, Culture and Politics* 13:1 (2000): 39–62.

McLuhan, Marshall. *Understanding Media: The Extensions of Man*. London: Abacus, 1973 (1964).

Menzel, Peter and Faith D'Aluisio. *Robo sapiens: Evolution of a New Species*. Cambridge, MA: MIT Press, 2000.

Weber, Samuel. *Mass Mediauras: Form, Technics, Media*. Ed. Alan Cholodenko. Stanford, CA: Stanford University Press, 1996.

PART 1

The Cyborg Links

CHAPTER 1

High-Tech Frankenstein, or Heidegger Meets Stelarc

MARK POSTER

'We human beings have bodies' are the first words of Mark Johnson's deservedly acclaimed philosophical study of the relation of cognition to imagination, *The Body in the Mind*. This flat assertion may not be easily disputed. One might protest that bodies are located in one place or another, that they have sexual traits, that they have various characteristics of height/weight, illness/health, markings/scars, hair and skin colour, age, and so forth. One might also protest that their significance varies a great deal in different societies and eras. Each of these objections might be shunted off with a flail of the arm. After all, 'We human beings have bodies.' Yet today the assertion, along with the objections, is in doubt. What it means for a human being to have a body is now altered by medical transplants, various technologies of reproduction, and by bio-engineering. Human clones, like sheep, are technically possible. For a human clone, 'We human beings have bodies' is a troubling sentence. Prosthetic limbs and animal organs are, if not commonplace, certainly no longer extraordinary. Robots, androids and artificial life forms now inhabit the planet with us and also 'have bodies'. Many assumptions stuffed like sardines into the phrase 'we human beings have bodies' are today in doubt. In this chapter I shall examine one such premise: that a human body is different from a machine. I shall inquire about the body by asking what happens to the concept of technology when mechanical and information machines are combined with the human body.

One difficulty that must be faced is that machines are changing. For instance, new technologies such as the Internet are objects like none before them. Whereas mechanical machines are inserted into hierarchically organized social systems, obeying and enhancing this type of structure, the Internet is ruled by no one and is open to expansion or addition at anyone's whim as long as its communication protocols are followed. In 2000, for instance, a 19-year-old college student, Shawn Fanning, wrote a program for sharing files called Napster. The program is designed to allow user-to-user exchanges of compressed music files that are very close to CD quality. When a person logs on to Napster it reads the computer's hard disk for music files, adding them to its database. The user can search the database for artists or songs and, with a click, download them. Within months the music industry was up in arms, claiming the program placed it in dire straits. Or, again in 2000, some disgruntled employee in the Philippines wrote a virus program that disrupted governments and economies across the globe. With the Internet, Goliath is having fits with David.

This contrast between old and new technologies was anticipated theoretically by Gilles Deleuze and Félix Guattari, especially in *A Thousand Plateaus* (1987), where they distinguished between arboreal and rhizomic cultural forms. The former is stable, centred, hierarchical; the latter is nomadic, multiple, decentred – a fitting depiction of the difference between a hydroelectric plant and the Internet. In *Chaosmosis* (1992), Guattari, in a critique of Heidegger's machinic synecdoche of the hydroelectric plant in 'The Question Concerning Technology' (1955), elaborated this opposition into an ontology of the 'heterogenesis' of machines, the most rigorous effort thus far to comprehend the being of machines beyond a humanist framework. Guattari attempts an ontology of machines outside all subject-based perspectives such as psychoanalysis. He develops a category of the assemblage to suggest combinations of machines and humans in surprising and unanticipated configurations (*Chaosmosis*). The question concerning technology, then, is no mere exercise about the destruction of nature by the irresponsible deployment of machines, or the loss of human reality into machines, or even the cultural 'misshaping' of the human by its descent into the instrumental, the bringing forth or challenging or enframing, as Heidegger would say, of the human by the technological. Instead, the conservative, 'sensible' question of technology is now one of the nature of the cyborg, of the new order of humachines. And the rigorous or outrageous question of technology must include the possible inheritance of the globe by a species we call 'machines' but whose nature we can barely foresee. We must therefore rethink the question of technology in the context of bioengineering, globally networked computing and, above all, in relation to the figure of the post-human body or cyborg. To further this thinking I stage a meeting of Heidegger and Stelarc, a confrontation or exchange between the most brilliant philosopher of technology and the most daring explorer of the humachine. I shall first examine Heidegger's concept of technology to determine what is at stake in the question of the humachine.

THE QUESTION CONCERNING HEIDEGGER

Technology poses profound, even overwhelming, questions, and no one has confronted them more acutely and suggestively than Heidegger. At first glance, a resort to Heidegger may seem inappropriate in this context since he is known for attributing to modern technology 'the spiritual decline of the earth'. Yet his antipathy to technology is matched by his sensitivity to its importance, as in the following:

> At a time when the farthermost corner of the globe has been conquered by technology and opened to economic exploitation; when any incident whatever, regardless of where or when it occurs, can be communicated to the rest of the world at any desired speed; when the assassination of a king in France and a symphony concert in Tokyo can be 'experienced' simultaneously; when time has ceased to be anything other than velocity, instantaneousness, and simultaneity, and time as history has vanished from the lives of all peoples; when a boxer is regarded as a nation's great man; when mass meetings attended by millions are looked on as a triumph – then, yes then, through all this turmoil a question still haunts us like a specter: What for? – Whither? – And what then? (*An Introduction to Metaphysics*, 31)

So Heidegger is no simple technophobe.

To the end of carrying forward and clarifying further the theoretical issues of the matter of technology, a scrupulous re-examination of his position is required. I undertake such an interrogation with no interest in an overall evaluation of Heidegger's work and certainly not of his life or his lamentable political commitments.[1] I wish to hold in suspense or, better, to bypass the effects of 'the author function' as Foucault calls it, whereby evaluations of discourse are placed in reference to a name, an author's name, as the final level of consideration (Foucault, 101–20). I turn to Heidegger's essay 'The question concerning technology' with the single concern of delimiting its discursive accomplishments and confusions and with the hope, still flickering in its Enlightenment lamp, that this will contribute to allaying some anxiety in those who so greet the topic. I pose the following question to the text: to what extent can Heidegger's discussion be applied to information technologies? And I reply: not very much.[2]

Heidegger's argument may be summarized, however inadequately, as follows. The question of technology is not about technology *per se* but about modern humanity's way of being. Technology is fundamental to modern 'culture,' a term I will use for Heidegger's *Dasein*. This relation of technology to culture is always important since humanity brings itself forth in part through its way of using things, its arts and crafts. The peculiar aspect about humanity is that it brings itself forth in order to be and must recognize this process as it is happening in order to have a free relation to itself. But modern technology is a way of using things and bringing humanity into appearance that conceals this process, does violence to nature ('challenges' it) and finally ends in treating humanity with the same violence that it treats nature. Heidegger calls this way of being or culture of technology 'enframing'. If humankind can recognize the process of enframing for what it is, joggle its consciousness to understand the grave stakes in its deployment of technology, then it may establish a different relation to itself and to technology, one that is free in the sense that it recognizes and accepts its own cultural form, its own being. Heidegger's solution is not to abandon technology in some return to nature but to offer a spiritual shift in which technology would become entirely different from what it is.

One may approach 'The question concerning technology' from a rhetorical point of view. In this case, Heidegger tells the reader a story: there is 'an extreme danger' facing humanity. His tale, he says somewhat coyly, is 'almost harmless' (*The Question*, 20), but as a result of listening to the tale we may be saved and be free. Within this charming and alarming tale there is an argument. And within this argument Heidegger reflects on his own writing and is surprised to discover that the topic, technology, is actually important, if not apocalyptic (30). In narrative form we have an American Gothic tale or horror movie with a possible happy ending. As a consequence of hearing the story one must be frightened by the imminent and horrible danger facing us all; yet thanks to Heidegger, there is a way out. The escape is not high-tech, as in James Bond movies, but is achieved through thinking, through becoming a philosopher (what else would one expect a philosopher to propose?). The narrative also partakes of the suspense genre. The danger to the characters ('man') is hidden from them, though the narrator, an omniscient voice if ever there was one, lets the audience know about it. The narrator himself is in a dangerous position: he is revealing a danger to the reader but one that might backfire. If the story is not effective, the audience might feel manipulated and get angry at the narrator, not believing there is any danger at all. So Heidegger protects himself by insinuating that what he has to say is after all harmless. If one does not become exhilarated at the prospect of being saved, one may still forget the harmless story and go on with one's life.

The effectiveness of the horror story depends on convincing the audience that there is a terrible danger. The audience must be scared. This is particularly difficult since Heidegger thinks that the danger is dangerous because it is concealed and hidden. If it is concealed, the audience cannot know about it beforehand but must learn of it from Heidegger's tale. Heidegger must somehow present technology as a danger, reveal it, bring it out into openness in such a way that everyone will come to see the horror of it. Since everyone is already quite familiar with technology, Heidegger is confronted by a difficult rhetorical task. To accomplish it, he turns to a tried and true method, the flashback. The flashback is able to shake up the audience, take it out of its normal consciousness, like a Brechtian alienation effect, by moving to another point in time. Heidegger moves to ancient Greece, a time, he thinks, when the danger did not exist. In Greece, technology was different, was not hidden but part of the openness to Being of that culture. After glimpsing a different imbrication of technology in culture through the flashback, the reader can appreciate the horror of his or her own circumstances.

I shall present my evaluation of 'The question concerning technology' in terms of five theses. The first thesis is that culture is invisible to its members or, in relation to technology, that the instrumental attitude which is commonly attributed to technology obscures its cultural aspect. Outside the academic disciplines of the humanities, technology is treated as a neutral tool for the accomplishment of pre-given ends and is judged by an economic criterion of efficiency. This understanding of technology places it within a social world composed of rational, autonomous agents and passive objects. Heidegger brilliantly and convincingly shows how one must step back from such a social world and see how technology is no mere object or set of objects within it but rather is the way this world is set up or brought forth. The set-up includes human beings within it so that the traits one normally ascribes to technologies also apply to human beings.

The essence of technology is, then, a way of being in the world, a manner of appearing to oneself and others such that everything emerges as ready at hand for use or as a 'standing reserve', or as prefigured for instrumental action. Such 'making things ready for use' involves a drastic reduction of other possible ways of being in the world, so drastic that Heidegger terms it a 'challenging'. To transform the Rhine into an energy source by means of the technology of the hydroelectric plant is for Heidegger a severe, unlikely form of acting upon things. And yet modern humans are within this frame in such a manner that they are unaware of its cultural form. As a result of the unconscious quality of modern humans' relation to their framing of things, they do not perceive the setting up of the scene in which they act and take their own cultural shapes. The problem Heidegger raises concerning technology is not simply that it rudely transforms nature and our relation to others but that our own being in the world is invisible to us.

The second thesis is that one can dispel this invisibility by studying ancient Greek philosophy. Heidegger goes back to another culture (the Greek) as a point of difference, in order to distance himself from today's culture and thereby to see it from outside. As a result, he is able to depict it, to define its limits, to critique it. Greek artisanal culture is a different framing, a different set-up, one that in qualitative terms is just as much a determining of being, just as serious a form of bringing forth both objects and subjects. But it is so in a manner, he thinks, that draws attention to the process itself, letting it emerge as a realization of Being. Precisely because humans are not prefigured as agents counterposed to an object world that is other to them, they paradoxically are able to perceive their agency within Being. The modern, privileged agent is for him less of an agent, a diminished agent, because it is cut off from its relation to Being. It conceives itself as transcendent to objects rather than existing within Being, and as a being whose being can exist only as a bringing forth or an appearing.

The third thesis is that the return to Greece is taken as a discovery of 'the truth'. The Greek way of bringing forth is at some level *the* way. It establishes human beings in a relation to Being that Heidegger once termed 'authentic' and continues in 'The question concerning technology' to treat them in a similar fashion. From the Greeks, Heidegger learns that bringing forth entails revealing, for example. From this he concludes that the main understanding of technology in the modern West – as a tool – is simply wrong. In no uncertain terms, he pronounces 'Technology is therefore no mere means. Technology is a way of revealing' (*The Question*, 12). Heidegger is aware that he may be accused of universalizing the local conditions of Greek technology, that technology may have been a revealing for the Greek but remains a means for 'modern machine-powered technology'. Heidegger insists that modern technology is a revealing but agrees that it differs from the Greek in that the latter was a revealing as *poiesis* (i.e. bringing out, or bringing forth) whereas the former is a revealing as 'a challenging, which puts to nature the unreasonable demand that it supply energy that can be extracted and stored as such' (13–14). As a result, modern revealing is a concealing that blocks human beings from entering into a free relation to technology. In italics Heidegger states flatly: '*In truth . . . precisely nowhere does man today any longer encounter himself, i.e., in his essence*' (27). The important words here are 'any longer', as if man once did so encounter himself (*sic*). It was of course in the time of the ancient Greeks that this encountering occurred.[3] The Greek way of revealing in technology provides Heidegger with a basis to critique the modern but in a manner that places the Greeks as the limit case. Heidegger frames his departure to the Greeks as 'the truth', elevating his critique into universality and losing its specificity and power to the disciplined gesture of the philosopher – as in *the* human essence.[4]

The fourth thesis is that the philosopher's transcendentalism still affords an understanding of technology as culture. He does give us a beginning point in the theorization of the relation of technology to culture by allowing us to see technology *as a culture*, what he calls a revealing. In the current conjuncture it is essential to insist upon this point and to underline it.

The fifth thesis is that this understanding is flawed by its inability to discern different technologies, different technocultures, different modes of revealing.[5] In his Greek-dominated insistence on the question of the essence, Heidegger underplays the search for difference. All technologies are, in essence, modes of revealing, but all modern technology reveals as enframing. The limits of this position are that it captures the revealing of modern technology only, not postmodern technology, of technology in its debt to physics and in its 'unreasonable' action upon nature, not technology as information processing, storage and dissemination. Heidegger considers the question of the multiplicity of technologies: 'Is then the essence of technology, Enframing, the common genus for everything technological? If that were the case then the steam turbine, the radio transmitter, and the cyclotron would each be an Enframing' (*The Question*, 29). He complains that he does not mean essence as a genus, a category that includes like singulars. Instead of being a 'revealing', the essence of technology is its inner cultural form ('challenging forth') in which both the turbine and the transmitter are included. I contend that some information technologies, in their complex assemblages, do not partake only of enframing but also partake of forms of revealing that do not conceal but solicit participants to a relation to Being as freedom.[6] And these do so not as a return to the Greeks but as a departure, as a new imbricated configuration of human and machine, ensconced with a new space–time continuum eliciting new combinations of body and mind, object and subject.

The very strength of Heidegger's treatment of technology as culture is also its weakness. Technology is one thing for him, a unified field, a homogeneous domain that he connects so brilliantly to the deepest issues of human life. To the extent that technology is not so unified, his analysis loses its force, or so I will argue below.

Technology is often treated as unitary both from the favourable perspective of toolmaking and progress and from the negative stand-point of degradation and loss. Heidegger has no sympathy for the former position, but in many places he betrays an affinity with the critics of technology. In these places he presents the commonplace jeremiad of technology as the loss of high culture, the descent into mass society. In *An Introduction to Metaphysics*, from 1953, he writes, 'From a metaphysical point of view [one which is not necessarily his own], Russia and America are the same; the same dreary technological frenzy, the same unrestricted organization of the average man' (31). In nationalist terms, Germany may provide the antidote to the twin superpowers surrounding it to the extent that it resists technology. But Heidegger also goes beyond this critique of technology as mass culture when he perceives this critique as itself part of the phenomenon it depicts. In 'The Turning' (1949) he warns, 'All attempts to reckon existing reality morphologically, psychologically, in terms of decline and loss, in terms of fate, catastrophe, and destruction, are merely technological behavior' (*The Question*, 48). Although there are many traces in Heidegger of a disdain for mass society and a Black Forest peasant's distrust of modern society, Hubert Dreyfus is surely correct when he dismisses these misunderstandings of Heidegger as a simple technophobe (97–107).

The homogeneity of technology in Heidegger is the key to the limits of his critique. He is able to recognize and mention some different forms of technology: ancient Greek artisanal culture, medieval Euro-pean windmills, industrial hydroelectric plants, tourism, mass media.

The chief question is this: what does the understanding of tech-nology as enframing enable in the study of information machines? One may argue that information technologies are no different from other modern technologies with respect to enframing.[7] Computerization transforms analogue text, images and sound into a digital code that may be considered a bringing forth which is a challenging, an enframing. Here the sequence of bits of 1s and 0s does violence to the alphabet, the visual play of light or the aural movement of air in waves. Once in its digital form, information may be stored, transmitted, edited and reproduced in ways that are at best much more difficult and often impossible in analogue form. In this way, computer processing of information might be regarded as enframing. And Heidegger says as much: 'Today, the computer calculates thousands of relationships in one second. Despite their technical uses they are inessential' (*Identity*, 41).

But the question of the appropriateness of the category of enframing for information technologies is not rightly posed at this level. Heidegger does not coherently raise the issue of enframing by an analysis of technologies. Quite the contrary: he argues that enframing is not a property of technology but of the manner in which humans bring forth technology and themselves. It is a relation of being, not of the object *per se*. What makes the hydroelectric dam different from a Roman aqueduct is not any quality of the technologies but of the 'set-up', the way the technique is placed in the world and the related meaning it has for those who encounter it. It might appear otherwise, that Heidegger is speaking about qualities of machines. He complains, for instance, that the hydroelectric plant is 'monstrous' since it dams up the river for the sake of a power plant (*Identity*, 16). What renders the machine 'challenging' is not so much the mechanical engineering of the dam but the instrumental stance that places nature as object; that is where the 'set-up' resides. Only because the set-up is crucial can Heidegger claim that a free relation to technology is possible, that we may be saved from it without literally destroying it.

I want to argue the opposite: that there is a being of technology and that it varies depending upon the material constraints of the technology. Surely the engineering of information technologies may partake of enframing, but originate in the same 'set-up' as the hydroelectric plant. If Norbert Wiener is our guide to information technologies, they are indeed framed in the physicist's standpoint of a ratio of signal to noise (*The Human Use*, for example). Who is to deny the advantages in efficiency gained by the use of computerized word processing over the typewriter or the pen? Yet careful attention to the way some information technologies position their human agents – or, better, an analysis of the assemblages of humans and information machines – suggests a different possible interpretation.

An alternative understanding of information technologies may be approached through raising the question of technological determinism and doing so in relation to Heidegger's concept of destining, of sending, of starting upon a path. The enframing of technology starts humanity upon a path of concealment, of the hiding of our relation to being. But for Heidegger, destining is not technological determinism: 'Always the destining of revealing holds complete sway over man. But that destining is never a fate that compels' (*Identity*, 25). We are under the influence of technology as enframing only in so far as it is concealed from us. The notion of technological determinism on the contrary is itself part of enframing, part of the culture of technology. Thus for Heidegger, enframing sets up humankind as determined by technology in the mode of a 'standing reserve'. While Heidegger counters the problem of technological determinism, his notion of destining also sidesteps the role of the specificity of technology. He avoids the trap of technological determinism by lifting the question of technology so far from the technological that he loses the capacity to make distinctions among technologies. The windmill no less than the hydroelectric plant may fall within the enframing of technology. As paradoxical as this may sound, Heidegger remains within a humanist frame in so far as he does not allow the inscription of meaning through the machinic.

MACHINIC EPISTEMOLOGY

The materiality of technology may be recovered without returning to technological determinism by going farther than Heidegger away from the humanist position. Technological determinism is the mirror opposite of Heidegger's culturalist understanding of technology as bringing forth. His critique of the Cartesian dualism of subject–object, *res cogitans–res extensa*, as an unconscious articulation of enframing retains the privilege of the subject, but in a form different from that of Descartes. The other way around the problem of the essence of technology is through the specificity of the machinic. In this regard, Félix Guattari's *Chaosmosis* attempts to grasp the being of technologies not as an emanation of *Dasein*, but by a sort of phenomenology of technics, a very different project from Heidegger's. Guattari announces his aim: 'For each type of machine, we will pose a question . . . about its singular power of enunciation: what I call its specific enunciative consistency' (34). The machine itself inscribes meaning, enunciates, but it does so within its own register, not as a human subject would. It is a form of presencing, to use Heidegger's term, of the object.

To refute the Heideggerian position on technology, Guattari turns to the example of an aircraft on the runway. For Heidegger this is a pure case of a 'standing-reserve'. The being of the vehicle is contained by its enframing, its being set up as a useful object for travel. For Guattari, on the contrary, the realm of the machinic incorporates intersections of widely diverse domains, constituting an assemblage of enunciation in that 'the machine speaks to the machine before speaking to man' (47). Instead of the Heideggerian subject gazing at the aircraft on the runway, inscribing its meaning for the singular philosopher, Guattari proposes to delve beyond the appearance for the individual to the heterogeneous domains that interpellate the object. With this in mind we may grasp that the aircraft, a Concorde, say, may not be ready at hand at all. Guattari writes:

> The Concorde object moves effectively between Paris and New York but remains nailed to the economic ground. This lack of consistency of one of its components [the economic] has decisively fragilised its global ontological consistency. Concorde only exists within the limited reproducibility of twelve examples and at the root of a possibilist phylum of future supersonics. (48)

Economic constraints prevent the use of the aircraft, reconfiguring its significance from use for travel to economic waste, a reconfiguration that may be discerned only by examining the full array of heterogeneous machinic domains of the object.

These domains are not equally subject to the cultural logic of enframing. Information machines in particular resist instrumental enframing, especially those that are embedded within complex congeries of technologies, and they do so particularly in their interface with humans. Take, for example, the Internet. The telephone network was in part appropriated by the US Defense Department for advanced research projects by connecting computers to it with protocols that assured a decentralized structure. Any individual or group could communicate through text with any other individual or group. Individuals who happened to be graduate students reappropriated this apparatus adding Usenet and MUDs (multi-user dungeons, i.e. role-playing games). Physicists in Switzerland added graphics and, later, sound and moving images. These enhancements enabled the further dimensions of hypertext, hypermedia and virtual reality. In addition, real-time audio and video exchanges became possible. The network has become more and more complex as dimension has been overlaid upon dimension, progressing to the point where Cartesian configurations of space/time, body/mind, subject/object – patterns that are essential components of enframing – are each reconstituted in new, even unrepresentable forms. What began as a Cold War effort to speed up communications has become cyberspace, an electronic geography that reterritorializes pre-existing geographies, opening new social and cultural worlds that are only beginning to be explored but that quite probably are already redefining what it means to be human.

To bring forth in an electronic café is a presencing that returns to the individual an insistence upon his or her absence and concealment. *Dasein* emerges or appears as an opening/concealing in which neither term cancels the other. Ancient Greek *alethea* (truth) becomes not a lever of critique of a modern falling away from being but just one possibility, somewhat quaint perhaps and certainly no Archimedean point of reference for humanity. In electronic cafés one cannot be authentic or be present in full presence since one's body is not there and one's identity is fabricated by design. Individuals may 'feel' more real in cyberspace, or more artificial, alienated, disjointed. Yet the machinic solicitation is to reveal to oneself that one is never oneself and that this is legitimate, a condition of the new human–machine interface, the being of technology that has seduced humanity into its own heterogenesis. And what is more, things have only begun to get interesting because the current state of the Internet is clearly a bare beginning of things to come.

The Gothic tale of technology as the being from the dark lagoon is perhaps, then, narrativized otherwise as a romance with an alien cyborg, a monster who is always already none other than ourselves.

INTERNET MAN

There are two sides to Stelarc's work. One is a series of performances that integrate technology and the body in ways sometimes provocative, sometimes disturbing and sometimes banal; the other is a set of essays that speculate on the nature of the human body in the context of contemporary technology. In these efforts, Stelarc puts into motion Heidegger's pronouncement that technology brings into question the human essence.

Since the 1960s, Stelarc has been testing the limits of the human body by deploying new technologies in inventive constructions. His home page lists performances of the past decade and provides graphic illustrations that capture these events. Two in particular illustrate, for my purpose, Stelarc's peculiar exploration of the humachine: 'Fractal Flesh – Internet Body Upload Event' of 1995 and 'Parasite: Involuntary Body and Internet Upload' of 1998. In these performances Stelarc attached to his body a robotic third arm and then wired his body to computers connected to the Internet. Inputs were sent to his body and his extra arm from remote computers, in one case deliberately, in the second as randomly monitored activity on the Net. These performances were on display worldwide through the Web. One may easily dismiss Stelarc's performances as scientifically off-base, morally repugnant, politically naive and psychologically disturbed (Dery, 151–69). Yet they dramatically draw our attention to the fate of the body under the conditions of global connectivity.

Stelarc's Internet performances depict and literalize the relation of the body to the global communications system. Internet activity, whether as deliberate computer commands or as generalized signals relayed to Stelarc's body and attached to a machinic extremity, present for all those online to see the extended sensorium that is our current, embodied condition. Our skins no longer demarcate a line between inner and outer except in the limited sense of the body's endurance. What is generated within the body as information is hooked into global networks. Even the voice and the image of the body are no longer limited to displacing air in territorial space. What began with the simplest information machine – carved rock or smoke-signal – now is amplified beyond imagination through the facility of the Internet.

Phenomenologically, our bodies are out there extended through the infinite wires and radio waves that criss-cross the planet continuously and in ever-increasing density. Our being-in-the-world, to echo Heidegger's term, is now as a body draped over the globe.

Stelarc's discourse is far less interesting than his performances. In his writing, Stelarc bemoans the limits of the body, declares the body outmoded, and proclaims the new day of machine-upgraded soma. The skin is the first organ to go: 'Invading technology eliminates skin as a significant site, an adequate interface, or a barrier between public space and physiological tracts' (116). Next to be eliminated is ageing: 'Extending life no longer means "existing" but rather being "operational". Bodies need not age or deteriorate; they would not run down nor even fatigue' (120). Then nanotechnology improves upon nature: 'It is time to recolonize the body with MICRO-MINIATURIZED ROBOTS to augment our bacterial population, to assist our immunological system and to monitor the capillary and internal tracts of the body' (121). In the end the refurbished body is ready for space travel: 'it is now time to REDESIGN HUMANS, TO MAKE THEM MORE COMPATIBLE WITH THEIR MACHINES' (121). Stelarc's fanciful, reckless and, to some, noxious speculations do little to further the inventions of many of his performances.

What those performances suggest is a technological culture that bridges the human and the machine, a new bringing forth, in Heidegger's sense, of the human and of being that renders obsolete not so much the body but the culture of instrumental technology, the Cartesian positioning of the human body as the ruling force, deploying nature and machines at will. The technoculture suggested in Stelarc's performances is a radical departure from modern understandings of the body. It foreshadows a fundamental reconfiguration of the relation of human to nature, body to mind, individual to society, man to machine. A politics of this mind-boggling technoculture would have to formulate its projects along lines not envisioned by earlier social theory. The new Gothic tale ends not with Heidegger's narrative closure but with a much broader question about human essence: what place will the human have in a world of bio-engineered nature and information machines?

High-tech Frankenstein, as a figure for the relation of humans online to machines, also intervenes in the discussion of the subject. Internet communication restructures the relation to the body (Stone), configuring the desiring body through the wires and interfaces that set aside the recognized body as a base of fixed identity and substitute a deterritorialized or unmarked body in relation to a composed identity, inscribed in conversations in chat rooms. The body online and wired unsettles pre-existing identity formations: national, gendered, ethnic, racialist, and so forth. None of these can be effectively reproduced in cyberspace because its media conditions are of a heterogeneous space–time order. One cannot be a white, male American in cyberspace even if everyone online is predisposed to think so and even if one performs one's identity as one. This is so simply because the conditions of being recognized as a white, male American are territorial, are of a space–time dimension that is impossible in cyberspace. One may find examples, say, of sexism in cyberspace that are word-for-word repetitions of those uttered in the street by construction workers at passer-by women. The person who typed them might have the same stupid intentions as the man on the street. But as traces on the screen these same words only mimic street sexism; they cannot be sutured to the street identity. Hence the words float in a new machinic dimension in what I would call a performative excess and deficit that opens them to entirely different constructions. To be sure, high-tech Frankenstein might find new hierarchies and new subalterns, but they will be those peculiar to the global machinic apparatus and will, of necessity, put into question territorial identities, identities constructed through earlier media, and all previous configurations of identity. High-tech Frankenstein therefore functions as an opening to globalized, machinic post-humanity, one who will stare backwards at us, his/her historical ancestors, like Benjamin's angel, as if observing a monster.

NOTES

1. For a discussion of Heidegger's politics in relation to the issue of technology (and modernity more generally), see Michael Zimmerman, *Heidegger's Confrontation with Modernity*.
2. This criticism is also raised by Coyne (98).
3. Here is an example of Heidegger's extravagant evaluation of the Greeks: 'In Greece, at the outset of the destining of the West, the arts soared to the

supreme height of the revealing granted them. They brought the presence of the gods, brought the dialogue of divine and human destinings, to radiance' (*Identity*, 34).

4. See the critique by Jacques Derrida in 'Geschlecht II: Heidegger's hand' (161–96).

5. This argument is also made by Simon Cooper (23–56), but he does not explore the difference between mechanical and information technologies. The literature on Heidegger's view of technology is enormous and I cannot review it in the context of this chapter.

6. For an opposite view, see Chesher, who writes, 'Computers store up the real in digital domains as symbolic standing reserve' (88), thereby equating information and industrial technology as enframing.

7. Samuel Weber has made this argument to me. See his important treatment of Heidegger on technology in *Mass Mediauras*.

WORKS CITED

Chesher, Chris. 'The ontology of digital domains'. In *Virtual Politics: Identity and Community in Cyberspace*. Ed. David Holmes. London: Sage, 1997.

Cooper, Simon. 'Heidegger and a further question concerning technology'. *Arena* 9 (1997): 23–56.

Coyne, Richard. *Designing Information Technology in the Postmodern Age: From Method to Metaphor*. Cambridge, MA: MIT Press, 1995.

Deleuze, Gilles and Félix Guattari. *A Thousand Plateaus: Capitalism and Schizophrenia*. Trans. Brian Massumi. Minneapolis: University of Minnesota Press, 1987.

Derrida, Jacques. 'Geschlecht II: Heidegger's hand'. Trans. John Leavey. In *Deconstruction and Philosophy*. Ed. John Sallis. Chicago: University of Chicago Press, 1987. 161–96.

Dery, Mark. *Escape Velocity: Cyberculture at the End of the Century*. London: Hodder & Stoughton, 1996.

Dreyfus, Hubert. 'Heidegger on gaining a free relation to technology'. In *Technology and the Politics of Knowledge*. Ed. Andrew Feenberg and Alastair Hannay. Bloomington: Indiana University Press, 1995. 97–107.

Foucault, Michel. 'What is an author?' Trans. Josue Harari. In *The Foucault Reader*. Ed. Paul Rabinow. New York: Pantheon, 1984.

Guattari, Félix. *Chaosmosis: An Ethico-aesthetic Paradigm*. Trans. Paul Bains and Julian Pefanis. Bloomington: Indiana University Press, 1995.

Heidegger, Martin. *Identity and Difference*. Trans. Joan Stambaugh. New York: Harper & Row, 1969.

Heidegger, Martin. *An Introduction to Metaphysics*. Trans. Ralph Manheim. New York: Anchor, 1959 (1953).

Heidegger, Martin. *The Question Concerning Technology and Other Essays.* Trans. William Lovitt. New York: Harper & Row, 1977.

Johnson, Mark. *The Body in the Mind: The Bodily Basis of Meaning, Imagination, and Reason.* Chicago: University of Chicago Press, 1987.

Stelarc. 'From psycho-body to cyber-systems: images as post-human entities'. In *Virtual Futures: Cyberotics, Technology and Post-human Pragmatism.* Eds Joan Broadhurst Dixon and Eric J. Cassidy. London: Routledge, 1998.

Stone, Allucquere Rosanne. *The War of Desire and Technology at the Close of the Mechanical Age.* Cambridge, MA: MIT Press, 1995.

Weber, Samuel. *Mass Mediauras: Essays on Form, Technics and Media.* Stanford, CA: Stanford University Press, 1995.

Wiener, Norbert. *The Human Use of Human Beings: Cybernetics and Society.* New York: Doubleday, 1950.

Zimmerman, Michael. *Heidegger's Confrontation with Modernity: Technology, Politics, and Art.* Bloomington: Indiana University Press, 1990.

CHAPTER 2

The Human / Not Human in the Work
of Orlan and Stelarc

JULIE CLARKE

This chapter attempts to trace the human/not human in particular
aspects of the work of the performance artists Orlan and Stelarc.
I will refer to Dr Frankenstein's monster, plastinated bodies, prosthetics and insects as examples of a transitional state of being that
currently marks the human body. In this way, I will investigate
the relationship between liminality and pollution, often represented
through the notion of the uncanny which surrounds animate and
inanimate beings alike.

THE *POST*-HUMAN?

Genetic engineering (transgenics and xenotransplantation)[1] is creating
an identitarian category that Kelly Hurley calls 'a human/not human'
(220), something Louise Chapman regards as having the potential to
'introduce new infections of public health importance into the human
community'.[2] Significantly, bodies that have been modified are often
described as *polluted* by technology. These transformations have given
rise to the emergence of the notion of the post-human, describing the
state of being simultaneously one thing and another. Positioned in a
liminal zone, the post-human is neither male nor female, neither
human nor machine, neither dead nor alive. Indeed, mutation is central
to the notion of the post-human, describing a human identity which is
caught between the idea that the self is becoming 'other' than itself,
and the image of that self which is being mediated by the very
technology that determines it.

Technologies such as television, film and the Internet, which impact on the human body, are also the vehicle for portraying that impact. The post-human body is therefore a body authored by its technologies, which is also retelling and reconfiguring what it means to be human. Consequently, the supposition and visual image of the post-human is both a fact and fiction in that it is constructed as real by its representation and its theorization, while simultaneously being the product of the imaginary.

The term 'post-human', however, can appear to be an endpoint in which the human body is discarded as no longer a viable species, as compared to organisms that have overcome their biological limitations through advanced technologies. It seems to me that the term 'trans-human', describing a transitional state in which the becomings are multiple, engages with the notion of liminal personas in a more complex way. As Donna Haraway suggests, the prefix 'trans-' cuts a line between nature and artifice, and nature and culture (56). Meaning 'across' or 'beyond', it implies a process and evidence of a connection. The notion of the trans-human points to a gentle transition, or even a subtle interaction between two objects, neither of which is made obsolete in the process.

An example of the fusion of the organic and the inorganic was presented in an exhibition of plastinated bodies, entitled 'Anatomy Art: Fascination beneath the Surface', which was held in Vienna in 1999.[3] The plastinations, which are technological constructs, have come to represent in my mind the most distinct example of post-human bodies. Although they retain human morphology, they have been transformed into a mere representation of the human. Plastinated cadavers are thus rendered dry and clean, and are devoid of infection or disease. In this way, they can easily be handled by the general public. In the exhibition catalogue, plastinations are described as follows:

> Invented and developed by Gunther von Hagens, the water and fat of human tissue is replaced with special plastics. The cells and the natural surface relief permanently retain their original form down to the microscopic level. The plastinations are dry and odourless and have a rigidity that allows completely new types of artistic display. (Von Hagens, non-pag.)

Although the abject body is made clean and proper, in its transformation it also becomes 'not human'. The abject object, the corpse, is
thus erased – that is, it becomes absent – by the overwhelming
presence of the plastination. Interestingly, Georges Bataille has
described the corpse in the following terms: 'The object, then, is less
than nothing and worse than nothing', concluding further that 'The
horror we feel at the thought of a corpse is akin to the feeling we have
at human excreta' (57). Both the cadaver and excrement remind us of
death: no longer needed, they are dispelled and pushed out of sight.
This exhibition, however, brings to the surface that which is usually
kept secret. It also suggests that in a cybernetic future the post-human
body will be a simulacrum, a representation of the wounded body
which has been displaced by an artificial construct.

LIMINALITY

The notion of liminal existence is important to the understanding of
the terms 'trans-human' and 'post-human'. In his discussion of the
rites of passage between various states of being of an individual or a
group, Victor Turner speaks of the liminal states of a person, in which
'the state of the ritual subject (the passenger) is ambiguous; he passes
through a realm that has few or none of the attributes of the past or
coming state' (94). Drawing on Arnold van Gennep's *Les Rites de
passage*, published in 1909, in which he (van Gennep) has shown that
'all rites of transition are marked by three phases: separation, margin
(or limen), and aggregation' (30), Turner observes that liminal perso-
nae 'are at once no longer classified and not yet classified, the symbols
that represent them are, in many societies, drawn from the biology of
death, decompositions, catabolism, and other physical processes that
have a negative tinge, such as menstruation' (96). He also tells of
instances wherein a neophyte is 'structurally "dead"', and 'may be
buried, forced to lie motionless in the posture and direction of
customary burial' (96). Liminal beings are thus perceived as polluting,
since they are neither one thing nor the other, and are more often
than not characterized as monstrous, diseased, queer, marginal, black,
insane or female. The alchemist Paracelsus believed that monstrous
states of being, such as hermaphroditism and androgyny, were the sign

of 'secret sins in the parents' (Paracelsus, 173), but there were other factors, such as the imagination of the mother, that contributed to monstrous births. He wrote, 'Hence, through fear or fright on the part of those who are pregnant many monsters are born, or children signed with the marks of monstrosity in the womb of their mother' (173).

In the current milieu, to be perceived as monstrous, or consciously to construct oneself as monstrous, is to have an affinity with disorder, chaos, mutation and transformation, in an attempt to work against logic, rationality, normality, purity and science. It can often be seen as a way of both undoing and resurrecting the past and its fictions: in order to create some new forms, connections, leakages and abstractions. As Mary Wollstonecraft Shelley, the creator of Frankenstein, said, 'Invention, it must be humbly admitted, does not consist in creating out of void, but out of chaos; it can give form to dark, shapeless, substance but cannot bring into being the substance itself' (8).

Cyborgs and transgenders are two of the most potent metaphors in the theorization of the trans-human condition, for both can be described as liminal creatures. In contemporary science fiction films such as *The Terminator*, *Tetsuo*, *Hardware*, *Westworld* and the *Star Trek* series, the imaginary fusion of the human being with cybernetics has been represented by the image of the cyborg. The cyborg body, as part human, part machine, exhibits both fragility and strength. The monstrous prosthetic attachments that characterize the cyborg are often conflated with the rather benign prosthetic limbs allocated to amputees; and the presence of the prosthetic as a distinctly different material to the human body represents the loss not only of the body but also of the self, while simultaneously marking the site of the absent wound. Moreover, the fusion of the organic and the synthetic portrays the cyborg as a metaphor for pollution.

Computer technologies as non-organic, clean and functioning prostheses are transformed by their coupling with the human body. Likewise, the human body is perceived as augmented and enhanced by its attachment to technology. Prosthetic body parts herald loss and expose the human body as a structure that may be disassembled. The abject, which may be associated with the amputated body through the prosthetic attachment, is thus assimilated. As feminist film theorist Barbara Creed reminds us, 'Although the subject must exclude the abject, the abject must, nevertheless, be tolerated for that which threatens to destroy life, also helps to define life' (9). In the case of a prosthetic limb, its addition highlights the importance of maintaining self-image and bodily unity. The integration of the human body with its technologies has thus become a benchmark for redefining the traditional humanist ideas of the human.

The Third Hand which the Australian performance artist Stelarc wears in his performances mimics this substitution of the body by a technological construct. Although Stelarc maintains that the prosthetic attachment represents excess, demonstrating body extension through technology, this kind of excess is always accompanied by loss. Stelarc's projects of the prosthetic Third Hand, Extended Arm and proposed Extra Ear may in fact represent psychic extensions of the abject, in that technology – in its historical connections with the fear of the other, of difference and pollution – may symbolize the object that needs to be expelled. The partial coupling of the mechanical with the organic might be read as Stelarc's attempt to integrate and interiorize the unnameable and therefore to come to terms with mortality and separation. As Stelarc himself says, 'We've created the potential of life without humanity' ('An interview with Stelarc', 17). Given that the abject is defined as ambiguous and liminal, and is usually associated with the female gender, technology and its apparent integration into both the interior and the exterior of the body represent the assimilation of the other.

This assimilation may be read in a number of ways. Either Stelarc is consciously attempting to nullify sexual difference by alluding to a hybrid connection between the masculine and the feminine enabled by computer technologies, or he intends to create isomorphism between his body and that of a machine to emphasize the symbiotic and parasitic relationship between humans and technology. He explains, 'Extending life no longer means "existing" but rather being "operational". Bodies need not age or deteriorate; they would not run down or even fatigue: they would stall then start' ('Prosthetics', 595). Stelarc's language is infected with machinic metaphors, describing a human self that is also inherently cybernetic. This kind of self is fashioned from, and is inherently linked to, technology. As such, it is therefore not separate from culture. By introducing technology into the inside of his body and onto its surface, Stelarc stresses our reliance on technology for the construction of our internal and external self-identity.

Stelarc's prosthetic attachments cause some concern for his audience because they portray the collapse of the organic body into the synthetic realm of the cyborg. He states:

> The body may have been demystified and passified, but it has not yet been deactivated. It is obsolete in form, but still capable of instigating an evolutionary dialectic – a synthesis of organic and synthetic to create a new hybrid human. ('Triggering an evolutionary dialectic', 52)

This 'demystified and passified' body is the body that has been thoroughly interrogated, dissected and displayed by technological means.

Stelarc and Orlan are described by McKenzie Wark, Mark Dery, Paul Virilio and Arthur Kroker as exemplifying the posthuman condition. Both artists have, in distinctly different ways, referred to the Frankenstein monster as a way of describing our historical and hysterical responses to body fragmentation and the impact of medical technologies on the body. The monster without a name is the chimera that haunts their performances. The work of Stelarc and Orlan echoes the societal fear of technology as depriving us of our (imaginary) control over the world. Both artists interact with communication and medical technologies, which enable body modification and extension. In her operation/performances, Orlan engages with the rhetoric of cyberspace and the seduction of multiple personas. By redesigning her face to mirror more closely that of her imaginary self-image, Orlan reveals that the self, like knowledge, is a shifting construct. Stelarc's self-image of his physical body as 'data contained in cyberspace' allows him, in turn, to become part of a feedback loop with other bodies and minds, which coagulate into hybrid states of activity.

MONSTROUS BECOMINGS

The monster of Mary Shelley's *Frankenstein, or The Modern Prometheus* (1816) is an abomination, an unholy patchwork of severed organs and limbs secreted from both male and female cadavers. As such, it is humanity's refuse, disposable, abject. When Dr Frankenstein brings together what he considers the most perfect parts of each of the bodies, he unwittingly constructs a body of scar tissue and deformity. He says, 'I collected bones from charnel-houses and disturbed with profane fingers, the tremendous secrets of the human frame' (Shelley, 52), and describes the reanimated monster as a 'demoniacal corpse to which I had so miserably given life' (56).

What is terrifying to the reader of Mary Shelley's work, or the viewer of the numerous films made about Frankenstein, is not only that the monster is piecemeal, stitched together, highlighting the capacity for the human body to be carved up into independent fragments, but that the body as we know it is the sum total of all its separate parts. This revelation emphasizes the machine-like function and structure of the body. The monster represents a human/not human being that is both 'like us' and 'not like us', and it is precisely this recognition that elicits our sympathy and repulsion. Death, which has already overtaken and inhabited the corpse, creates an aura even after the monster has been reanimated, thus rendering the object both dead and undead.

Both Frankenstein's monster and the cyborg solicit the uncanniness associated with body mutation and fragmentation. As Sigmund Freud has explained, 'the "uncanny" is that class of the terrifying which leads back to something long known to us, once very familiar' (370). Freud also speaks of the uncanniness associated with the movement of artificial dolls and automata. Drawing on the writings of E. Jentsch, he concludes that 'A particularly favourable condition for awakening uncanny sensations is created when there is intellectual uncertainty whether an object is alive or not, and when an inanimate object becomes too much like an animate one' (385). Our basic understanding of the process of life is that the dead do not return to the living. However, the Frankenstein myth challenges what we believe to be true, for corpses do not remain silent or intact in it. Interestingly,

39

Freud states that our fear 'still contains the old belief that the deceased becomes the enemy of his survivor and wants to carry him off' (396). This is the reason for the taboos that surround the corpse, for to touch death means to be partially inhabited by it.

Although the Frankenstein monster was imagined at the beginning of the nineteenth century, it remains a potent metaphor for the collapse of the biological and the technological. In the present milieu, human bodies are being carved up, fragmented and reassembled in seemingly less sinister ways through medical CAT scans, DNA splicing, genetic engineering, organ transplants, cosmetic surgery and prosthetic implants; or through media interventions in which body images are digitally manipulated.

The French performance artist Orlan has made direct visual reference to the monster and the monstrous by being photographed in 1990 in a *Bride of Frankenstein* wig.[4] Represented for the male gaze, her image is cropped just above her breast to reveal only the artist's head and naked shoulders. With her newly constructed chin leaning provocatively on her gloved hands, Orlan's pose draws our attention to contemporary constructions of the ideal and admired woman through the technologies of photography and film.[5] However, the photograph's function is not only aesthetic; it points directly to the cosmetic industry and the role that medical technologies, particularly prosthetic implants, play in the construction of artificial selves and bodies.

Orlan's project speaks of the unwanted and excessive female body, which is continually represented as controlled and modified through medical and media technologies. She presents the excess of female bodies, already perceived as overflowing by menstruation, childbirth and lactation. Exposed more so by its association with body modification through technology, it is the female body that has been the subject of plastic surgery, liposuction, breast augmentation and reduction, stomach stapling, IVF, superovulation and foetal scanning. Through various technologies, it has been fragmented, carved up and reconstructed to form an ideal woman.

In the original *Bride of Frankenstein* film, the Bride is an artificial woman created for the monster, who desires a friend of his own species – that is, a technological construct like himself. The Bride, who is fabricated by Victor Frankenstein and Dr Praetorius, is, like the monster, a patchwork of limbs and organs with an 'artificially developed, human brain' inserted into her cranium. Grown from what Praetorius has called 'seed', the Bride's brain as a scientific development is different from the brain of the Monster, which is considered more 'natural'.[6] This 'brain grown from seed' may be contrasted with recent investigations into primordial stem cell technology for the growth of organs for transplant.

> Primordial stem cells are relatively undifferentiated stem cells that possess the power to differentiate into many different types of cells of incalculable value to medicine. Unfortunately, until recently human primordial stem cells have proven impossible to grow in the laboratory leaving medicine with no choice but to seek transplantable cells from aborted fetuses, cadavers, and so on. (Advanced Cell Technology Web site, non-pag.)

Orlan's reference to advanced medical technologies alerts us to the various ways in which the human body may be reanimated and transformed by technology. So, just as Victor Frankenstein selected beautiful features for his monstrous creation, Orlan constructs her new self-identity by combining the ideal features of women depicted in various paintings throughout art history. In doing so she not only draws attention to genetic engineering, but, through the Frankenstein myth, introduces us to the science of physiognomy, in which the face features as a site of either terror or admiration. For it was not the body of the monster that instilled dread into Victor, but rather its face which filled his heart with 'breathless horror and disgust' (Shelley, 55). Orlan establishes that those who are physically or socially different are often depicted as outcasts, like the monster and Mary herself, who was 'cast out by her father' (Bronfen, 34). Elizabeth Bronfen points out that 'Mary Shelley offers an analogy between herself and Victor Frankenstein, for, given that she called her novel her "hideous progeny", she too obliquely articulates an "anxiety of authorship"' (35). Orlan's monstrous birth produces a new self that she has fashioned from reconstructed flesh. Outcast as the performance artist who is only trying to make herself beautiful, by inserting two horn-like 'bumps' into her forehead Orlan in fact turns herself into a monstrous 'other'.

In her photograph *Imaginary Generic No. 31: Successful Operation(s), 1990*,[7] Orlan is standing in front of a large canvas that portrays a black-and-white reproduction of the faces of selected women. The features chosen for the redesign of her face have been framed with red transparent rectangles, with the completed composite face placed in the centre, and with red arrows denoting the position of her new characteristics. The title of the photograph, with the emphasis on the word *generic* (which has associations with the term 'eugenic', i.e. 'good stock'), points to Orlan's concern with genetic engineering, while the blatant depiction and selection of ideal features alludes to the idea that desirable characteristics can be achieved by technological intervention. Orlan has also been photographed in a *Bride of Frankenstein* wig, and presented as a Siamese twin.[8] The artist's depiction of herself as an individual with two distinct selves raises ethical questions regarding cloning and 'designer bodies'.

Fashioned from death and reconstructed flesh, Frankenstein and his Bride return to haunt us in the figure of Buffalo Bill, the transsexual in *Silence of the Lambs*, who is making a 'girl suit' from the murderous skin of his victims (Harris, 157). Judith Halberstam points out that 'always behind the making of gender is a bloodied female body cut and measured to the right proportions' (*Skin Shows*, 169). Through her gory surgeries Orlan unmasks the tension that gender identities are fraught with in our culture and highlights the role that media and medical technologies play in their construction. She resurrects the image of the monster as a defence strategy against the rational quantifiable body, for Frankenstein does not have one single identifiable DNA, history or language: it is multiple and fragmented.

Orlan's invocation of the *Bride of Frankenstein* enables us to conflate Orlan's wrapped and bandaged face, after her operations/perform-ances, with that of the newly constructed Bride, who appears fully draped and presented to the monster as a gift. The blue Gothic lightning marks on the wig are a reminder of the role that electricity and technology played in both the reanimation of the Bride and the construction of the new self-image that Orlan has created. Describing the influence of the theories of evolution and galvanism on her book, Mary Shelley explains, 'Perhaps a corpse would be reanimated; galvanism had given token of such things: perhaps the component parts of a creature might be manufactured, brought together, and endued with vital warmth' (9). David Ketterer maintains that 'the most vital spirit in *Frankenstein* – at all stages of its textural history – is the natural spirit of magnetism/electricity' (69), which was then perceived as a powerful, unseen energy. Similar language is often used to describe the nature of twenty-first-century technology.

In her performances Orlan is virtually a cadaver, as, in creating a wound, she brings her body into continuity with all bodies that have experienced pain or death. The wound is a violent portal between life and death, interior and exterior, victim and slayer, controller and controlled, nature and artifice. In a strange circumcision of images the wound draws us back again to the Bride, who is also the dead/undead. Orlan thus embraces humanity's relationship with death that is always played out in a celebration of life, thus embracing the Bataillian logic of ecstasy and continuity (Bataille, 24). According to Bataille, 'A violent death disrupts the creature's discontinuity; what remains, what the tense onlookers experience in the succeeding silence, is the continuity of all existence with which the victim is now one' (22). Orlan's action of instigating pain (albeit psychological) in members of the audience is conducted in a celebration and continuity with other bodies. The 'continuity' and space of non-existence that Bataille speaks of, and the 'infinity' that Emmanuel Levinas discusses in his writings, represents the other to which we have no access. As Levinas has put it, 'So little does the Other deliver him or herself over time that he does not fit into the adequate idea of being but only in the inadequation par excellence of the idea of the Infinite' (12).

In contrast to Orlan's celebration of life in metaphors of body resurrection, Stelarc, who declares and denounces the body as a 'death machine', adds non-human attachments to his body in a cyborg fantasy that delimits continuity (*Monograph*, 150). While Stelarc's cybernetics portrays Western society's love affair with a technological apparatus, depicting a desire for the transcendence of the body and escape from death, Orlan's performances/operations display a transcendence of life and its pain. In terms of her relationship with the technological body,

Orlan evokes artificial life through the imagery of Frankenstein's Bride, the artificiality of images and their link to history and mythology. This evocation of artificial life may be contrasted with Stelarc's most recent performance with an artificial life form, an on-screen Avatar, which generates various movements through his body. The Avatar may also be perceived as a phantom electric body, similar to the deathly moving screen shadows that Orlan refers to.

HIVE MIND

Stelarc's two most recent projects are Exoskeleton and Movatar/Avatar.[9] In each he augments his body with exoskeletal attachments. Movatar/Avatar involves an upper body motion prosthesis, while Exoskeleton includes a six-legged, pneumatically driven locomoter and extended arm. He performs in Exoskeleton by being connected into the middle of the apparatus while operating its forward and sideways motion. Attached to the contraption is an extended arm of primate proportions, which Stelarc protrudes, antenna-like, into the performance arena. While the total unit metaphorically presents a taxonomy of viruses, insects, primates, humans and technology, it is the machine's massive insect morphology that suggests that this performance may be a referent to the collective or hive activity of social insects. The idea that humans may be moving towards a collective consciousness through the use of the Internet and the development of Borg-like characteristics is displayed in the uneasy and tentative steps of the Hexapod's pneumatic legs. Stelarc's performance intimates that this stage of human/machine hybridity is still in its infancy, or even that it is just one possible evolutionary path for humanity.

Whereas insects shed their rigid exoskeletons in order to grow and adapt to new environments, Stelarc has constructed an exoskeleton to explore the parameters of human/machine movement and cybernetic interaction. He has been saying for some time that human beings need to develop new perceptions and to shed their skin in order to adapt to this new electronic and technological terrain ('Towards the post-human', 20). In many of his performances, Stelarc amplifies the unseen and unheard bodily functions of brain waves, heartbeat and blood flow as a way to extend the interior of his body into the exterior

Plate 1 EXOSKELETON, Cyborg Frictions, Berne 1999. Photo: D. Landwehr, © Stelarc

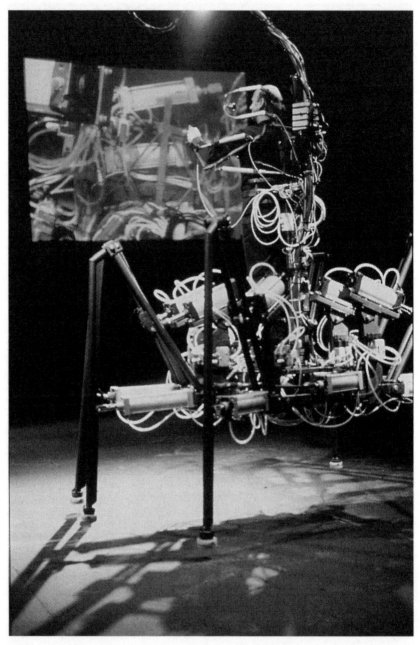

Plate 2 EXOSKELETON, Cyborg Frictions, Berne 1999. Photo: D. Landwehr, © Stelarc

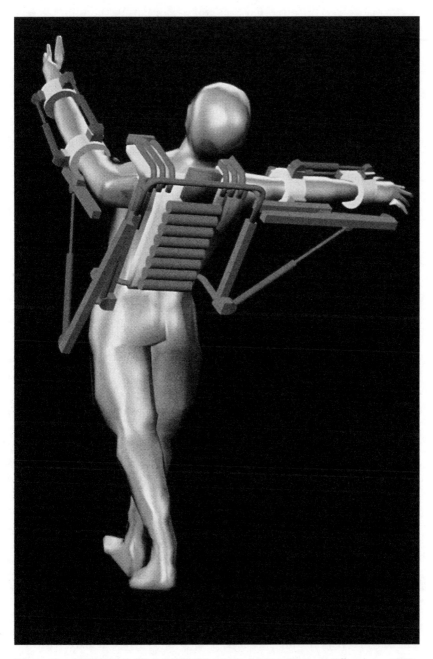

Plate 3 MOTION PROSTHESIS FOR MOVATAR, Melbourne 1999.
Image: S. Middleton, © Stelarc

performance space. In the Exoskeleton performance, the multiple legs and extended arm draw attention to the significance of the insect–human coupling. Often preceded by alien sounds, insects are uncanny reminders of unseen things that suddenly come into view. The excessive hissing sounds and lurching movements of Stelarc's Hexapod depict a clumsy counterpoint to fluid and elegant insect forms. But the pneumatic sounds emitted from this mimetic apparatus herald the birth of a living, breathing hybrid, with the exoskeleton functioning as conduit and bridge, relayer and receiver of messages from the world of computer data.

The six-legged Hexapod is a legacy of NASA's robots, designed to navigate the uneven terrain of the moon. Stelarc's interest in them developed from his association in the 1980s with Shigeo Hirose at the Tokyo Institute of Technology, who was interested in developing an alternative robotic mechanism and who constructed insect-like loco-moters. Prior to this, in the 1960s the US Army together with General Electric was developing 'pedipulators' to be controlled by infantry-men. These six-legged giant walking machines were to be used for 'carrying supplies, fighting fires, effecting rescues and carrying litters of injured' (Halacy, 145). It is worth noting that the American military have been interested in developing the idea of the cyborg as presented in science fiction to eliminate the time lag between the instructions and the execution of a command. As Haraway states in the 'Cyborg manifesto', 'Our machines are disturbingly lively, and we ourselves frighteningly inert' (152). Stelarc's Movatar/Avatar performances lead the way towards eliminating the interface to form a discrete union between humans and cybernetics. In his performance, Stelarc draws us away from science fiction portrayals of the cyborg into more intimate relationships with virtual body images. However, the question of autonomy or the absence of it still hangs over his performance.

THE BORG

The science fiction film *Star Trek: First Contact* deals in part with the question of defining humanity. It depicts the Borg, an organic artificial life form that assimilates other species into its own by augmenting and connecting them into one consciousness, and thus diametrically opposing the individual and particular consciousness of the human species. The Borg are not interested in power or politics, only in consuming information.[10]

To be human within the context of the film is to be an individual. However, members of the crew who are assimilated by the Borg are considered by non-assimilated crew members to be less than human or to be polluted by technology. The assimilated lose their identity and are absorbed into a hive colony, following orders and working for the good of the collective Borg. It is not surprising, then, that the Borg in *First Contact* are represented as female. When they first appear in the film, a Borg's upper torso, decidedly alien and cybernetic, is gently lowered into a dress. Species superiority is claimed by the Borg, who perceive 'three-dimensional thought' and fragility as inferior 'human' characteristics, while simultaneously admiring altruism, which they lack. Humans tolerate species other than the Borg because their difference is biological; however, the Borg are different because they are human–cybernetic hybrids. The contrast between the crew of the *Enterprise* and the Borg is that humans perceive themselves as operating with autonomy, as opposed to the loss of personal freedom recognized in the collective Borg. Also, humans are shown to be active participants in the decision-making process, whereas the decision-making of the Borg is seamless and integrated.

Stelarc's Movatar/Avatar performance interrogates the intricate divisions between controlled and controller. Remotely activated by a constructed virtual entity, his body is moved not by an inward desire or automatic response, but by artificial external stimulus. Stelarc is interested in the unconscious and mechanical aspects of the human body and often seeks to separate the informational from the material, focusing on the intrinsic similarities between body data and information generated by computer technologies. He is primarily interested in the way in which humans operate within the world, and the varying positions they occupy in relation to others. His performances interrogate the symbiotic relationship between humans and technology, in which neither one is either controller or controlled. Consider the Stimbod, a touch-screen muscle stimulation system conceived by Stelarc so that his body may be moved from a remote source. It is a

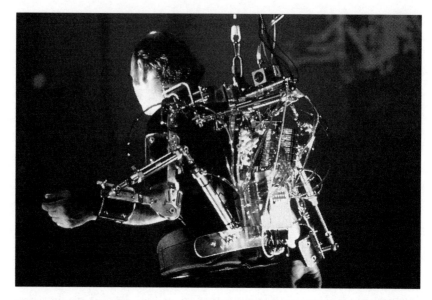

Plate 4   MOVATAR, Cybercultures. Casula Powerhouse 2000. © Stelarc

system that would 'create a possessed and possessing body – a split physiology to collaborate and perform tasks remotely initiated and locally completed – at the same time in the one physiology' (Stelarc, 'Parasite visions', 121).

If Stelarc can be seen to be highlighting internal body information, its circuitry, neural connections and feedback loops – particularly in human–computer symbiosis – then Orlan has been working against the notion of the body as coded information. 'My work is a struggle against the innate, the inexorable, the programmed. Nature, DNA . . . and God' (91), she said, referring to the paradigms of religion and science, which have historically sought to fragment the human body and separate it from its lived experience. By denying the reduction of the human body to code and therefore its biology, Orlan seeks to undermine the order and rationality imposed on the female body. However, by changing her visage she establishes that identity, particularly linked to facial features, is a new site of contestation since the development of advanced surveillance technologies, and a return to physiognomy earlier utilized in the eugenics movement to mark people as different, alien or 'other'.

In his Movatar/Avatar performance, Stelarc empties his body of its own desire and fills it instead with the desire of an autonomous Alife entity, literally acting out the human characteristic of reacting/moving/desiring the desire of another. The Movatar is the total operational system – with the human body as prosthetic to the on-screen Avatar – which makes the body move through its connection with the motion prosthesis. The nexus between Stelarc's body and the Avatar is a pneumatic exoskeleton that Stelarc has connected to his arms and upper torso. It is a jointed structure that restrains and contains his body, leaving only his legs and feet to operate indepen-dently. The Avatar as a viral entity prompts his body to move. His body as host to the data affects and alters the responses of the Avatar. Stelarc's body and the strings of information generated from the Avatar create an exchange between two distinctly different species. Wet life and digital life coalesce here. While in the six-legged walking robot the exoskeleton on Stelarc's upper torso enables him to prompt the robot to walk, in the Movatar/Avatar project it is the Avatar which moves Stelarc's body through the motion prosthesis. In Exoskeleton he operates as master to the slave machine, whereas in the Movatar/Avatar performance he occupies the dual positions of master and slave. Although the Avatar moves Stelarc's body (which he refers to as 'the body'), he has the ability to control the performance aspects by accessing floor switches with his feet, which can determine the sound generated and possible mutant by-products of the Avatar's behaviour. In this way both the human body and the virtual body have input into the operational behaviour of one another.

Human and machine evolution are particular concerns in Stelarc's work and are explored in the Exoskeleton performance, in which primate, human, insect and technological tropes form a monstrous unit from discrete and different parts. The reference to insect life and the extended arm of primate proportions cross-fertilize with the genetic algorithms used in the Movatar/Avatar performance, in which strings of data are generated producing an evolution of the computer program and possible emergent behaviour from the Avatar. There is a difference between predictable behaviour and emergent behaviour in that no one ultimately knows what movements will be generated into Stelarc's body. This is typical of Stelarc's performance, which should be seen as an investigation, rather than explanation, of the body and its interactions with new technologies. Stelarc remains interested in the unexpected outcomes of his performances. In Movatar/Avatar he demonstrates that subjectivity is dispersed among objects in the world, and not contained solely within an individual. Perhaps we could even conclude that both subject and object have been erased in the performance. As Stelarc explains,

> If the avatar is imbued with an artificial intelligence, becoming increasingly autonomous and unpredictable, then it would be an AL (Artificial Life) entity performing with a human body in physical space. With an appropriate visual software interface and muscle stimulation system this would be possible. The avatar would become a Movatar. ('Parasite visions', 125)

Attached to this Alife entity, Stelarc would in fact become a prosthesis of the Avatar, operating without his own desire and without autonomy. Is Stelarc proposing that in the future we may merely serve as the flesh of superior machines? He has said on many occasions that he is not sure whether we have in fact ever had a mind of our own, and that we may rather be like the Frankenstein monster, who is not controlled by our will any more. Significantly, when Victor refuses to make him a companion of the same species, the monster declares: 'You are my creator, but I am your master' (Shelley, 168).

Hiro Protagonist, the main character in Neal Stephenson's novel *Snow Crash*, constitutes an interesting reference point here. Hiro lives most of his life in the Metaverse as an avatar 'in a computer generated universe that his computer is drawing onto his goggles and pumping into his earphones' (22). He inhabits the avatar while being simultaneously inhabited by it, and is caught somewhere between his physical self and his virtual self in a continuous feedback loop between the material plane and the virtual body of desire. Perhaps the state of being 'human/not human' is akin to Ira Livingston's speculation about how things unseen and unknown may act upon us. Livingston maintains that 'Reconfiguring humanity as posthumanity means recognising the priority of betweenness, of a continuous fractal relation with otherness that necessitates and equates both care and perversity' (20). He uses the example of a crossed line during a telephone conversation. What he uniquely points out is that noise, silence, half-sentences, people, objects and events are continuously intersecting with the human body, creating unusual juxtapositions and hybrid couplings. This 'between-ness' that Livingston speaks about seems to sum up what it means to be human. The liminal state of being 'betwixt and between' is the uncanny penumbra that haunts the performances of Orlan and Stelarc, and perhaps also describes the state of humanity at the beginning of the twenty-first century.

NOTES

1. A xenograft is the grafting of tissue from one species to another, and currently includes experimentation with rats, pigs and non-human primates as possible tissue donors for human beings. There are an estimated 3400 Web sites devoted to xenogenics. Transgenic organisms are those that have been modified to carry a gene from a different species (*Encarta Encyclopedia*, <www.encarta.msn.com>).

2. Louise Chapman, paper presented to the 4th National Symposium on Bio-safety: <http//hivinsite.ucsf.edu/topics/xenotransplantation/2098.389c>.

3. The flyer was given to me by Stelarc, who was quite intrigued and perplexed by his reaction to the plastinated organs (conversation between myself and Stelarc in July 1999). Stelarc also spoke about his experience of the plastinated bodies in 'The Augmented Body', *Masters of New Media Lecture Series*, 12 August 1999, Radio Theatre, RMIT, Melbourne, Australia.

4. Official portrait with *Bride of Frankenstein* wig, 1990, photograph F. Leveque, *Art in America* February 1992: 96.

5. Orlan's prosthetic chin operation was carried out on 27 July 1990.

6. This reference is to the germ/seed theory of species reproduction in eighteenth-century mechanical philosophy, which maintained that the seed was carried from each generation via the female of the species. See Peter J. Bowler, *Evolution: The History of an Idea*.

7. Photograph by Alain Dbome, *MONDO 2000*, Fun City MegaMedia, Berke-ley, CA, 13 (1995): 106–11.

8. Orlan, untitled photograph by F. Leveque, photoshop manipulation by Di De Pholi, *MONDO 2000*, p. 108.

9. *Movatar/Avatar* performance, *Cybercultures, Post Human*, Casula Powerhouse, Sydney, Australia, 19 August 2000.

10. The information was gleaned from *Star Trek: The Next Generation*, 'Q-Who', Paramount Pictures, 1989.

WORKS CITED

Advanced Cell Technology Web site <www.advancedcell.com/StemCell Research.html>.

Bataille, Georges. *Eroticism: Death and Sensuality*. Trans. Mary Dalwood. London and New York: Marion Boyars, 1987 (1962).

Bowler, Peter J. *Evolution: The History of an Idea*. Berkeley and Los Angeles: University of California Press, 1984.

Bronfen, Elizabeth. 'Revisiting the family: Mary Shelley's *Frankenstein* in its biographical/textual context'. In *Frankenstein Creation and Monstrosity*. Ed. Stephen Bann. London: Reaktion Books, 1994.

Creed, Barbara. *The Monstrous-Feminine: Film, Feminism and Psychoanalysis*. London: Routledge, 1993.

Freud, Sigmund. 'The uncanny'. *Collected Papers*, vol. 4. Authorized translation by Joan Riviere. London: The Hogarth Press and the Institute of Psycho-Analysis, 1971 (1919).

Halacy, D.S. Jr. *Cyborgs: Evolution of the Superman*. New York: Harper & Row, 1965.

Halberstam, Judith. *Skin Shows: Gothic Horror and the Technology of Monsters*. Durham, NC: Duke University Press, 1995.

Haraway, Donna. *Simians, Cyborgs and Women: The Reinvention of Nature*. London: Fab, 1991.

Harris, Thomas. *The Silence of the Lambs*. London: Heinemann, 1988.

Hurley, Kelly. 'Reading like an alien: posthuman identity in Ridley Scott's "Alien" and David Cronenberg's "Rabid"'. In *Posthuman Bodies*. Ed. J. Halberstam and I. Livingston. Bloomington and Indianapolis: Indiana University Press, 1995.

Ketterer, David. 'Frankenstein's "conversion" from natural magic to modern science – and a shifted (and converted) last draft insert'. *Science-Fiction Studies* 23 (1996): 57–78.

Levinas, Emmanuel. 'Transcendence and height'. In *Basic Philosophical Writings*. Ed. A.T. Peperzak, S. Critchley and R. Bernasconi. Bloomington and Indianapolis: Indiana University Press, 1996.

Livingston, Ira. Introduction, 'Arrow of chaos: romanticism and postmodernity'. In *Theory out of Bounds*, vol. 9. Minneapolis, London: University of Minnesota Press, 1997.

Orlan. 'Conference'. In *This Is My Body . . . This Is My Software*. Ed. Duncan McCorquodale. London: Black Dog Publishing, 1996.

Paracelsus. 'Concerning the nature of things'. *Book The Ninth, Alchemical Writings of Paracelsus the Great*. Ed. Arthur Edward Waite. Temple Chambers, Fleet Street, London: James Elliott & Co., 1894.

Shelley, Mary Wollstonecraft. *Frankenstein, or The Modern Prometheus*. London: Arrow Books, 1973 (1816).

Stelarc. *Monograph*. Norwood, South Australia: Ganesh Publishing, 1976.

— 'Triggering an evolutionary dialectic'. In *Obsolete Body Suspensions*. Compiled and edited by James D. Paffrath with Stelarc. Davis, CA: JP Publications, 1984.

— 'An interview with Stelarc'. In *Obsolete Body Suspensions*. Compiled and edited by James D. Paffrath with Stelarc. Davis, CA: JP Publications, 1984.

— 'Prosthetics, robotics and remote existence: postevolutionary strategies'. SISEA, Groningen, the Netherlands, *Leonardo* 24:5 (1991): 591–5.

— 'Towards the post-human (from absent to phantom bodies)'. In *25 Years of Performance Art in Australia: Performance Arts, Performance and Events*. N. Waterlow (curator). Ivan Dougherty Gallery, Marrickville, NSW. R.F. Jones, 1994.

— 'Parasite visions: alternate, intimate and involuntary experiences'. *Body and Society* 5:2/3 (1999): 117–28.

Stephenson, Neal. *Snow Crash*, Harmondsworth: Penguin, 1992.

Turner, Victor. 'Betwixt and between: the liminal period in *Rites de passage*'. In *The Forest of Symbols: Aspects of Ndembu Ritual*. Ithaca, NY: Cornell University Press, 1967.

van Gennep, Arnold. *The Rites of Passage*. Trans. Monika B. Vizedom and Gabrielle L. Caffee. Introduction by Solon T. Kimball. Chicago: University of Chicago Press, 1960; London: Routledge & Kegan Paul, 1977.

Von Hagens, Gunther. *Anatomy Art: Fascination beneath the Surface*. Exhibition Flier. Vienna: Korperwelten, 1999.

FILMOGRAPHY

Bride of Frankenstein. Dir. James Whale, 1935.

Hardware. Dir. Richard Stanley, 1990.

Star Trek: First Contact. Dir. Jonathan Frakes, 1996.

Star Trek: The Next Generation 'Q-Who?'. Dir. Robert Bowman, 1989.

Star Trek: The Next Generation 'I Borg'. Dir. Robert Lederman, 1992.

The Terminator. Dir. James Cameron, 1984.

Tetsuo: The Iron Man. Dir. Shinya Tsukamoto, 1989.

Westworld. Dir. and writer Michael Crichton, 1973.

CHAPTER 3

Stelarc and Orlan in the Middle Ages

MEREDITH JONES AND ZOË SOFIA

> As individuals, we eat into culture, continually oscillating
> between primary, natural and necessary acts, as, simul-
> taneously we consume and ingest our identities. (Elspeth
> Probyn, *Carnal Appetites*)

As performers of body-based art in the context of (predominantly
Western) *fin de siècle* postmodern culture, Orlan and Stelarc have all
of the past and future of body transformation techniques potentially
available for reinscription and reconfiguration. Perhaps this is what
engages so many of us: the simultaneous working through of several
layers of historical and cultural meanings about the body and its limits.
Interwoven with contemporary media and postmodern themes are
statements that come from an earlier, Cartesian, modernity, while the
performances themselves, we will argue, bear distinctly medieval
characteristics.

In her excellent essay on these artists of 'un-natural selection', Jane
Goodall likens them to researchers in long-term projects who carefully
plan and endure experiments in body transformation, exploring the
limits of agency and identity. While the provocative *rhetorics* of Stelarc
and Orlan may contribute to 'overheated imaginings' (150) about
progress, evolution, technology and bodies, Goodall makes the important point that their *performances* may have the opposite effect, cooling
down cybercultural fantasies, demonstrating how difficult and painful
it is to embody them in practice (167). Goodall's essay helped define
our interest in those dimensions of performance which exceed rhetoric,
especially the element of pain. Both artists deny the importance of
pain, but what about those who witness (or simply hear tell) of their
sufferings? Each claims not to be religious – Orlan is specifically

blasphemous, Stelarc rigorously atheist – yet by placing themselves as the ones prepared to suffer bodily in their critiques of collective secular ideals (whether of art, beauty or techno-evolution), they can be positioned alongside mystics of the Middle Ages who voluntarily suffered for the sake of holiness.

In the following consideration of the postmodern, modern and especially medieval elements of Orlan's and Stelarc's words and per-formances we take our general bearings from Philip Mellor and Chris Shilling, who in *Re-forming the Body: Religion, Community and Modernity* trace the varied ways in which people of European cultures have *inhabited* and *owned* bodies from medieval times through the Enlighten-ment, modernity and postmodernity. In their broad overview, they focus on what ideal bodies have incorporated into themselves and what they have excluded or expelled. They argue that neither the 'embodied identity-construction' characteristic of modernity, nor the Enlighten-ment priority of mind over flesh, was available to people in medieval times. While medieval attitudes towards the body mostly categorized flesh as sinful, this did not impel abandonment of the body, but rather prompted a 'flight into physicality' (Mellor and Shilling, 37; see also Bynum) that offered carnal forms of knowing through immersion in direct physical experience (Mellor and Shilling 55–8). Instead of annihilating or ignoring a sinful body of flesh, attempts were made to bring it into line via various 'body regimes', including – for an extremist minority – fervent religious acts such as self-flagellation and starvation (37). For the populace, carnivalesque imagery and behaviour broke body regimes in their celebration of a grotesque laughing body 'marked by open orifices which facilitated a merging with other people and with the wider environments and resisted categorisation' (41). In the formation of 'Protestant modern bodies', previous sensual and inspirational experiences of the natural or supernatural became suspect. The emphasis shifted to cognitive, verbal and textually mediated forms of knowledge, and an individualistic self-identity shaped around linguis-tic symbols and narratives in which one's mind sought but never managed to sustain control of one's body and passions: bodies, and now especially women's (and witches') bodies, troubled the categorical order (41–7). In what Mellor and Shilling call the 'baroque modern' body of the late modern or postmodern cultural epoch, the shift of emphasis to visually mediated sensual experiences helps restore some degree of corporeal knowledge and emotion but also brings about 'somatic anxieties' about the instabilities of body-identity, and the relation between self and body-image. The body re-emerges from the Cartesian split as 'a semi-autonomous zone' — for example, the disciplined 'hard body' worked upon in gym culture (48) — and can be transformed by 'an unprecedented range of body options' (49) to embody the image of a different identity. From Mellor and Shilling's framework, we identify Orlan and Stelarc as staging 'baroque modern' forms of embodiment involving interchange between image and flesh: Orlan remakes her face according to a computerized plan; Stelarc declares, 'The body now performs best as its image.' However, we will argue that the extreme physicality of the performances opens these bodies to the social world in ways legible in terms of medieval body regimes.

MY MIND, THE BODY: A (NOT VERY) *POST*MODERNITY

The most readily available interpretations of the works of Orlan and Stelarc are as postmodern, cyborgian and posthuman forays at the limits of identity and corporeality. (See Clarke, Chapter 2 in this volume; also Dery, 156–9.) Statements like Orlan's 'This is my body, this is my software' (Orlan, Web site) or Stelarc's 'the self is no longer meaningfully located in the biological body' do much to encourage these interpretations. Both artists have been exploring limits of the contemporary 'body options', which Mellor and Shilling define as 'technologically informed methods of radically restructuring human embodiment which extend the possibilities associated with having a body, by a direct assault on the limitations connected to being a body' (49). When Stelarc insists that 'the body is obsolete', we understand him to mean that we have technologies and imaginations to put it into situations for which it is not engineered, thereby potentially assaulting it. In agreement with Stelarc on this point (Orlan quoted in Goodall, 151), Orlan has taken to extremes the postmodern 'body option' of cosmetic surgery, exploring what Jane Goodall aptly specifies as 'the invention of an "I" that refuses to take its identity from its corporeal form', so making explicit '[t]he lack of fit between body and self'

(Goodall, 187), a typical anxiety of discontinuity associated with contemporary body options (Mellor and Shilling, 50).

A key dimension of the works of both artists is the question of agency. In what Goodall describes as 'action experiments which problematise the idea of the individualised body as agent' (151), Stelarc has explored dispersing agency over his body through a network of human and non-human interactants. When developing his Ping performances, he imagined exchanging agency with other bodies:

> I'll be able to borrow a part of your body and perform a physical action through your body in another space – [this] means that I can in fact move your body. But it's not the notion of remote-controlling you – rather I want to use a part of your body to perform a motion or an action in another space. This means that my physical action is transduced into another body that performs it. And of course it can be a two-way thing.

Stelarc's imaginings illustrate Mellor and Shilling's point that postmodern and cybercultural body options 'promise us the potential of exploring and even occupying bodies which differ in time and space' (49). Orlan by contrast does not yield her agency but enlarges it in a carnivalesque inversion of the 'passive patient–active doctor' relationship.

These explorers of postmodern body options also reveal certain early modern or Cartesian tendencies, especially on the split between mind and body. Stelarc famously never refers to 'my body' but only to 'the body', something for which feminists have criticized him (Marsh, 107–8), though perhaps not fairly (Goodall, 162). Neuropsychiatrist Richard Retsack has diagnosed Stelarc's objectification of the body as expressing a kind of self-hatred and 'a distorted Cartesianism . . . that we're a mind and the body is an it and we treat it as an it' (quoted in Dery, 164). Stelarc himself denies that he holds Cartesian or Platonic views of the mind–body split:

> I'm not talking about that Cartesian split between body and mind but rather that total physiological, phenomenological, cerebral package that operates in the world. The Body for me is an all-inclusive

word – not a word that splits from the realm of mind or that should be distinguished from the realm of the mind.

Despite this denial, in Stelarc's descriptions of staged losses of agency, it is not just the mind split from the body but the body from itself:

[A]t a performance I was able to choreograph all the movements of the body. The body was split in two: on the left side it was voltage in, the muscle stimulators producing involuntary movement, and on the other side of the body it was voltage out, electrodes picking up internal electrical signals [that] controlled external devices like the third hand. So the body was conceptually split into voltage-in and voltage-out. That performance surprised me. I was watching my limbs moving in space. I've neither willed that action nor am I contracting my muscles to perform that action. That action is occurring beside, before, it predates myself as a free agent. In other words, half of my body has nothing to do with my free agency . . . I was looking in sort of wonderment.

Stelarc's is a perverse Cartesianism in which mind and cognitive knowledges are deployed (behind the scenes and on stage) so as to give away control of the body. This redistribution of agency paradoxically leads to a heightened experience of the separation between the observing mind and the semi-autonomous body, upon which the artist's consciousness gazes 'in sort of wonderment'.

The mind–body split is also expressed by Orlan, for whom the body is an 'envelope', a covering that can be decorated and transformed at will, a container that can be opened and closed and into which things can be inserted (such as her forehead lumps) and removed (such as fat from her thighs). The artist declares that a revelation came at puberty, when she grew breasts and pubic hair: 'I couldn't stop it, it was against my will' (Brand, 301). And later, when she became pregnant, the shock of the uncontrollable body was profound: 'It was so unbelievable at first that I thought that my will alone would cause me to abort; but it didn't, nature kept it going' (Brand, 301). Instead of a postmodern celebration of the sensual body, or a post-human interest in its automatism,[1] Orlan narrates a horror at the body's uncontrollability that recalls earlier modern anxieties about the need, yet the impossibility, for the will to be in complete control of a body from which it is separated.[2] In a plea strongly evocative of Platonic and Cartestian dualisms valuing intelligible (cognitive) forms of knowing over the sensible (sensuous), Orlan asks those revulsed by the sight of her being operated upon to 'not be fooled by the images but keep on thinking about what is behind them' (Orlan, 'I Do Not Want to Look Like . . .', non-pag.).

PAINFUL REALITIES

Certainly there are cognitive meanings behind these artists' operations, but they remain carnal practices with meanings and effects difficult for audiences to ignore. Neither the 'overheated imaginings' of the post-human nor the cooler cognitive knowledges of modern Enlightenment adequately address the question of pain: 'Despite the artist's [Stelarc's] futuristic vision, his body is in the here and now; it bleeds and pulsates, experiencing the reality of pain' (Marsh, 111). The witnessing of pain is an important part of the performance of both artists, and one that not all can endure, especially when surgery is performed:

> Soon, the surgeon is sawing away, methodically scraping out flesh from below the hairline. The gallery empties of a third of its audience. After forty-five minutes, the monitor is finally turned off – that's all for now, announces gallery owner Gering, smiling, to the few hardy souls who remain. (Lovelace, 13)

Orlan insists that her 'Carnal Art does not conceive of pain as redemptive or as a source of purification' (Brand, 311). Similarly, Stelarc asserts that the intrusions he makes on his body are a means to an end and are only coincidentally painful: 'It's [considered] natural to experience pain during childbirth, but you can't [are not supposed to] experience pain doing other creative things. You don't get pregnant to experience pain; I don't do my artwork to experience pain either.'

During her operations Orlan tries to show no distress, but this doesn't mean that the pain disappears, or that we don't see in her the marks of a suffering (even dying) patient.[3] The pain does not become impotent, but is displaced onto the audience via kinaesthetic identification, something she acknowledges:

> I am sorry to make you suffer, but remember, I am not suffering, except like you, when I look at the images. Only a few kinds of images force you to shut your eyes: death, suffering, the opening of the body . . . (Orlan, 'I Do Not Want to Look Like . . .', non-pag.)

While Orlan shows a process of suffering that is usually hidden, Stelarc demonstrates how 'impossible' imaginary feats can be achieved. He is intent on bursting the bubble of 'easy science fiction' where future bodily transformations are imagined but never attempted, and is more interested in 'how we manifest these ideas'. In showing how science fictional techno–body fusions can happen in real time and space, Stelarc reveals that to be post-human involves much physical trauma to a body that is not equal to the technology it faces:

> In some ways I saw the actual suspension event as a kind of authentication of the idea [of flying or floating]. The notion of flying, as a fantasy, can easily be expressed by drawing or by the illusion of theatre. But the experience of suspending the body, it was something brutal. The body [in suspension] is under a lot of trauma.

Stelarc's suspensions show that the difficulties in freeing the body in space, in visually separating it from the gravitational force, paradoxically involve a huge emphasis on physicality. The enactment of imagined events to surpass the body contains a referent to limited body capabilities that cannot be ignored.

Stelarc vigorously defends himself against those who interpret his practices as masochistic, narcissistic or shamanistic; he denies getting any kind of masochistic sexual pleasure or spiritual experience from suspensions and other body traumas. Our contemporary understanding of masochism is limited to notions of sexual perversion, and pain leading to pleasure. We no longer appreciate, as did the medievals, that some kinds of extreme carnal experiences can be associated with quests to embody higher values and achieve integration into a collective, whether holy or secular. From the *audience's* point of view those suffering bodies occupy a religious structure where the higher values at stake are not Christian ones of holiness but secular ideals about beauty, agency, technology, progress and evolution.

THE COMMUNION OF SUFFERING

In the medieval Church, bodies performed physical rituals that furnished their religiosity and sense of God: baptism, marriage, funerals, mass, confession and communion were all more lengthy and intense physical acts than they are today, and carried with them both real and symbolic connections with God. Christians transported this corporeal–supernatural link beyond the church and into their working and social worlds with rituals such as fasting, celibacy, prayer and pilgrimage. An intense somatic quality pervaded spirituality in medieval times, and people were seen as psychosomatic unities: '[f]ar from being caught up in a human culture of ideas and objects, medieval bodies maintained a sensual relationship with the sacred' (Mellor and Shilling, 39). Resurrection applied solidly to body as well as soul (Bynum, 183). In addition to the everyday practices of normal Christians, medieval society supported mystics, visionaries and flagellants who occupied sites where corporeal and sacred merged and fed off one another. Ecstatic states, miraculous anorexia, levitation and stigmata were body effects that showed and facilitated a connection with Christ.

Like the medieval society surrounding a suffering mystic or visionary, the audiences of Stelarc and Orlan become part of a communion of suffering. The penitence of the artist is refracted into members of the 'congregation', allowing them to experience higher ways of being/seeing – to go beyond images that 'fool' and delve into what is deeper or 'behind'. Like watching medieval saints hang themselves 'in elaborate pantomimes of Christ's Crucifixion' (Bynum, 184), there is a redemptive dimension to witnessing the pains of Orlan and Stelarc. Their bodies become conduits or nodes through which pain can be gathered, redistributed, made visible and expressible.

Fervent religious practices such as self-flagellation, starvation and 'walking around with pins stuck in the flesh' achieved a living death (Mellor and Shilling, 37). Comparing these acts with modern body disciplines, Piero Camporesi suggests that 'No one, in these days of mass beauty culture and subliminated corporeality, would be prepared voluntarily to transform his or her body into a gruesome dummy of dead and larval matter' (*The Incorruptibility of the Flesh*, 43, quoted in Mellor and Shilling, 37). Yet these two high art practitioners do precisely that: they transform their flesh and turn the body inside out – physically, visually and aurally – in spectacular ways that are arguably as medieval as they are modern or postmodern.

While great physical suffering in life was a mark of high religiosity and even sainthood in the Middle Ages, it was paradoxically coupled with the oft-reported occurrence of holy cadavers that spontaneously rejuvenated, did not decay, and discharged sweet-smelling oils.

> [W]e can sometimes, in hagiographical accounts, see a woman turning into a relic even before her own death. Moreover, incorruptibility, either of the whole cadaver or of a part, seems a virtual requirement for female sanctity by the early modern period. (Bynum, 187)

The catatonic trances, miraculous anorexia, cessation of menstruation and visions of heavenly bodies experienced by holy women were recognized as an earthly achievement of the incorruptibility of the resurrected body in Heaven. In our times, cosmetic surgery is about staving off decay, delaying or halting the ageing process and rendering bodies forever youthfully 'pure'. Showing the actual process of transformation, which is usually obscured in the gap between the 'before' and 'after' images of cosmetic surgery, Orlan takes the position of the willing martyr. Her consciousness during surgery is akin to a living death: a motionless body with metaphorically closed, unworking orifices that nevertheless breathes is not very different from a cadaver that doesn't rot. Post-recovery, Orlan's highly groomed, artificial-looking face invokes saintly corpse referents, and relics of her body are rendered incorruptible by being sealed into Perspex boxes, to be sold in a kitsch combination of aesthetic, religious and consumer experience.

Orlan's revelation of what is between the before/after of cosmetic surgery is a 'letting', a purging, that presents us with bizarre, bloody and dramatic images of what is usually hidden and 'behind the scenes'.

This spectacle is reminiscent of medieval carnival[4] celebrations of bodies in grotesque forms, including the spectacle of public anatomy, where

> skinning flesh, cutting up organs and reassembling the stripped bones into a skeleton (the image of 'dried death') all belonged to a liturgy of corruption and regeneration, decay and rebirth, and the journey from and to the land of death through the territories of life. (Camporesi, *Anatomy of the Senses*, 138)

The official purpose of carnival was to reveal, expunge and purge sin. Sexuality and consumption were literally 'acted out' so people could enter Lent purged of carnal indulgences. But celebrating the grotesque also meant a secular overturning of hierarchies, a rebellion against body regimes and a transcendence of bodily inhibitions: 'Instead of purging the body in preparation for a regime of denial during Lent, these carnivals were associated with an intensification of the body's loss in both itself and in the fleshy bodies that were other people' (Mellor and Shilling, 41).

Stelarc's performances can be read in terms of both pagan and spiritual medieval practices. They are carnivalesque in disrupting conventional categories and hierarchies, upsetting systems of agency and visibility, and confusing inside/outside, mind/body and human/machine. He makes a spectacle of the body, performing grotesque feats that stretch our understandings of what the body is and what its capabilities are. He externalizes the internal by amplifying sounds from within the body; his mechanical arm and third ear make distinctions between human and machine difficult and his forfeit of agency makes the idea of a mind 'owning' a body questionable.

Stelarc is an atheist, but for him – and many of his contemporaries – technology holds an almost divine status. Not only do we glorify its powers, and turn to it for the future salvation of the planet, we increasingly seek cyborg union with it (Haraway, 152). Stelarc embraces and magnifies machinic intimacy in projects exploring the body's interface with technologies, seeking out experiences of in-betweenness that evoke the medieval intertwining of the sensual and the sacred. Between human and machine, spanning both technology and flesh, the performer surrenders his ego in order to become a bridge between categories usually kept separate:

> In most of my performances there is a willingness to submit to machinic experiences. . . . The reason I do this is not so much because of a feeble mind [laughter], this submission is the desire to experience the alternate, to experience what it means to be neither human nor machine but something in between.

Although bodiliness was important spiritually in the Middle Ages and could even be salvific, body was still inferior to soul, and was presented in twelfth- and thirteenth-century literature 'not merely as dust but as rottenness, a garment masking the food of worms' (Bynum, 202). The body could help create a pathway to heaven but was also the locus of lust and decay. Whereas the soul is immortal, whether in hell, purgatory or heaven, the body is corruptible and must die and decay before being summoned up at the Resurrection: this was the basic philosophical reason given by medieval theologians for the inferiority of the body (Bynum, 236). Punishment of the flesh was an integral part of religiosity. Spirit and flesh were said to war with one another, and flesh was often described as a black mantle that needed to be overcome using pain, thirst and hunger. Christina Mirabilis, a thirteenth-century Flemish saint, wrote, 'O miserable and wretched body! How long will you torment me? Why do you delay me from seeing the face of Christ? When will you abandon me so that my soul can return freely to its Creator?' (quoted in Bynum, 236). This inferiority of the body is reiterated in Stelarc's declaration that 'the body is obsolete', expressing deep dissatisfaction with the body's inability to keep pace with either the imagination or technology. His performances stage a tension between the limits of tolerance of the body and the will of the imagination, which can result in a punishment of the body because of its inadequacy. 'The self is no longer meaning-fully located within the biological body' is a statement about postmodern embodiment but also a wail of entrapment. The self (or soul) is utterly bound with the body, which therefore must be subjected to happenings invented by the self that it may not be designed to withstand.

Medieval body regimes and contemporary body preoccupations each offer some sort of redemption to be gained on earth by way of acts upon the body, its theological or technological inferiority notwithstanding. In medieval times, some holy individuals (particularly women) were able to refashion their identities in dramatic ways via body modifications and disciplines, making the body into a sensual symbol of the truth and piety they had attained. Through extreme fasting, ecstatic states, catatonic trances and visions, women were able to bypass the more prosaic roles traditionally assigned to them from the formal hierarchy and gain a (small) degree of charismatic authority. '[W]omen *had* to stress the experience of Christ and manifest it outwardly in their flesh, because they did not have clerical office as an authorisation for speaking' (Bynum, 195). The similarities can be taken further: just as the ecstatic, visionary medieval woman risked being disbelieved by the Church and burned as a heretic, her modern-day equivalent, the anorexic, treads a fine line between congratulations and condemnations on her control over her eating habits. Modern manifestations of the ideal body – thoroughly worked, disciplined, pumped and smoothed – are not symbolic of their owner's relationship with a higher being but rather signal that this person occupies a privileged position of beauty gained through acts of self-management.

EATING – BEING EATEN INTO

In the field of moral meditations and edifying sermons, human dissection became *an anatomy of our emptiness*, executed by 'the knife of the divine word' which enters man 'to discover the very last fibre of our emptiness'. (Luigi Giuglaris, *Avvento et altre prediche insigni*, quoted in Camporesi, *The Anatomy of the Senses*, 141; emphasis in the original)

I feel that the body is hollow. [My sense of a hollow body came about] initially, subjectively, when I amplified body signals and sounds. Here [were] all these internal operations being externalised. You had this acoustical aura but the functions were displaced from the inner to the outer. There was this sense that it was no longer happening *in* [the body] – the body was hollow. (Stelarc)

Mellor and Shilling describe the medieval Church as seeking to *manage* the immersion of individuals and bodies within the natural and supernatural world. They describe a 'collective effervescence' gained through very physical participation in religious rituals, and a desirable state where sacred experience was utterly bound with feelings created in flesh. The Church saw itself as the body of Christ, and the main cultic act was the Eucharistic eating of Christ's body. But as these authors point out, rituals of transubstantiation had a reverse effect: through them the Church sought to 'eat into' the identity of its adherents (39). By being a physical part of the Church, which is itself symbolically the body of Christ, and by taking in his flesh and blood, the bodies of individuals were 'eaten into': enveloped and appropriated as part of a larger unity. When a body is affected this way it is both opened and hollow – undone, it can be simultaneously cavernous and indefinitely extended.

These notions of an unlimited, unsealed body are explored in the works of Orlan and Stelarc. Stelarc amplifies internal body sounds to the outside, making it 'hollow'. He opens his body to machinic and distant human agencies in his Ping and more recent Movatar perform-ances, which display him as a body and a will that can be 'eaten into' by a dispersed collective. Orlan enacts literal, structured openings of her body, and plans to make this aspect central in a future project, *An Operation of Opening and Closing of the Body* (as discussed in interview with Peggy Zeglin Brand, 312). She plans to have her underarm sliced open, as deeply as possible. The gap will be held open while she smiles, laughs and reads, before being sutured closed. Unlike her cosmetic surgery operations, where the body was opened as part of a process towards the desired result, this operation has no goal other than creation of the temporary wound. The operation would show that a body need not be opened for reasons of war, torture, or sickness – an open body need not be one that is suffering. Orlan exhorts her audience to dispense with 'old' ways of seeing, to join with her seeing her 'own body cut open without suffering! All the way to the viscera, a new stage of the gaze' (Orlan, 'Carnal Art Manifest', unpublished, quoted in Brand, 31). But rather than enacting a new stage of the gaze, the operation harks back to medieval openings of the body in public:

[A] certain Piron da Bazzano was cut with pincers as he went to the scaffold to be quartered alive . . . the said Piron looked at himself every time the executioner stuck his knife into his chest, until he could see all his chest was open, even his heart and his other organs. (Camporesi, *The Anatomy of the Senses*, 139)

While poor Piron's cuts were part of his capital punishment, the public display of anatomy was not uncommon. Anatomy lessons were open to the public and were carried out by people as diverse as medics, priests, barbers and artists. The insides of the body were seen as uncharted, fascinating territory ripe for exploration and interpretation. Like unclaimed land, the anatomical body was owned in a visual and interpretative sense by the body politic:

It should be placed on a bench which can be surrounded, and the barbers, surgeons and assistants should stand in the middle of the room with lancets, needles, hooks, scalpels other irons and sponges. When each is in his appointed position, let the anatomical operations commence in the name of the Lord. (Camporesi, *The Anatomy of the Senses*, 132)

Camporesi describes a 'certain rhythm' and 'liturgy' present in the rituals surrounding the dissection of a corpse: the similarities between the sacred and the corporeal are outstanding.

In a sacred context, transparent or open bodies were often seen by medieval women visionaries: 'the immaculate womb of the glorious Virgin, as transparent as the purest crystal, through which her internal organs, penetrated and filled with divinity, shone brightly' (Bynum, 198, quoting Gertrude of Helfta). So Orlan's 'new stage of the gaze' is not new at all, but a complex referent to old ways of seeing spliced with contemporary values. Twenty-first-century 'new' ways of seeing into the body are based on *not* cutting through the skin: X-rays, ultrasound, computerized tomography scans, magnetic resonance imaging and various endoscopes work by translating and transforming the corporeality of the body into visual and audio data. In fact, it is the least invasive biomedical procedures that result in what is currently understood to be the most comprehensive picture of the human body:

DNA mapping requires only the tiniest swab of tissue from the body's exterior.

Caroline Walker Bynum has stated that '[t]here is something profoundly alien to modern sensibilities about the role of body in medieval piety' (182). But when we look carefully at the bodies of Stelarc and Orlan — extremist visionaries of our own time, the high priest and priestess of 'post-human' body art and technology — we discover that the medieval is not as alien as we might think. Like medieval mystics whose views of the body as deficient led them towards, not away from, corporeal experiences of holiness, these contemporary artists demonstrate a willingness to subject the body to suffering for not meeting imagined ideals of beauty and technology. Whereas medieval mystics suffered to enact a relationship between their bodies and the Church, these artists allow themselves to be 'eaten into' by medicine and technoscience. Orlan and Stelarc disavow any redemptive meaning of pain, but their suffering nevertheless means something for those who witness it. For we audiences too have already been psychically eaten into, cut up and hollowed out by secular ideals of beauty and technological progress. Contemplating the artists' traumas, we are further eaten into as we become implicated in a collective communion of suffering. The redemptive value from the audience's viewpoint is that their bodily suffering spares us the greater agony of having to find out more directly what is entailed in transforming ideals into flesh.

NOTES

Unless otherwise indicated, all quotations of Stelarc's speech are from the interview he did with Zoë Sofia in Helsinki, at the International Symposium on Electronic Arts, August 1994.

1. Compare with Sadie Plant's cyberfeminist conjecture that the automatism of the female body permits cooperative affiliation with other rebellious smart machines of the computer age.
2. Although this insistence on mind over body can be critiqued from a certain feminist perspective as a repetition of the old masculinist Enlightenment project, Jane Goodall suggests that Orlan's work might also be interpreted as a feminist deviation from it: 'If women are trained to see themselves as

totally identified with and determined by their embodiment, perhaps the principle that the body is obsolete has much a [*sic*] more trenchant edge when it is a woman who proposed to act on it' (152).

3. Orlan's action against the docility of the contemporary body which undergoes surgery harks back to a raging debate that occurred when anaesthetics came into widespread use. The ethics of operating upon a body while it was unconscious were much discussed. It was believed that the experience and expression of pain by the patient was part of the healing process: 'The notion that a sensation should be expressed by cries and moans followed in the same model as that governing unwholesome humours and tainted, retained blood: it involved the same logic that led to excising a wound, to encouraging suppuration and giving vent to pain' (Rey, 93). Another concern was around the ethics of making a body unconscious and operating upon it without the supervision of the patient. Before general anaesthetics, patients would suffer surgery while conscious, but at the same time they were able to monitor the 'quality' of a surgeon's work. 'In a state of wakefulness, the patient was still able to judge the heavy-handedness of a surgeon, how little attention he paid, or what mistakes he made, thus, in the conscious presence of the person being operated on, there was a source of constraint or at least a contract of obligation on the part of the surgeon while, in contrast, the etherised patient was delivered defenceless at his mercy' (Rey, 163–4).

4. For an extended discussion of carnival in postmodern culture, see John Docker's 'Carnival and Contemporary Popular Culture' in his *Postmodernism and Popular Culture: A Cultural History*. Also see Umberto Eco's chapter 'Living in the New Middle Ages' in his *Faith in Fakes: Travels in Hyperreality*.

WORKS CITED

Brand, Peggy Zeglin. 'Bound to beauty: an interview with Orlan'. In *Beauty Matters*. Ed. Peggy Zeglin Brand. Bloomington: Indiana University Press, 2000: 289–313.

Bynum, Caroline Walker. *Fragmentation and Redemption: Essays on Gender and the Human Body in Medieval Religion*. New York: Zone Books, 1991.

Camporesi, Piero. *The Incorruptibility of the Flesh: Bodily Mutilation and Mortification in Religion and Folklore*. Trans. Tania Croft-Murray. New York: Cambridge University Press, 1988.

— *The Anatomy of the Senses: Natural Symbols in Medieval and Early Modern Italy*. Trans. Allan Cameron. Cambridge: Polity Press, 1994.

De Groen, Geoffrey. 'Barriers beyond the body: Stelarc'. In *Some Other Dream: the Artist, the Artworld and the Expatriate*. Sydney: Hale & Iremonger, 1984: 79–117.

Dery, Mark. *Escape Velocity: Cyberculture at the End of the Century.* London: Hodder & Stoughton, 1996.

Docker, John. 'Carnival and contemporary popular culture'. *Postmodernism and Popular Culture: A Cultural History.* Melbourne: Cambridge University Press, 1994. 273–84.

Eco, Umberto. 'Living in the new Middle Ages'. *Faith in Fakes: Travels in Hyperreality.* Trans. William Weaver. London: Minerva, 1986. 73–85.

Goodall, Jane. 'An order of pure decision: un-natural selection in the work of Stelarc and Orlan'. *Body and Society* 3:2/3 (1999): 149–70.

Haraway, Donna. 'A cyborg manifesto: science, technology and socialist-feminism in the late twentieth century'. *Simians, Cyborgs and Women: the Reinvention of Nature.* London: Routledge, 1991. 149–81.

Lovelace, Carey. 'Orlan: offensive acts'. *Performing Arts Journal* 17:1 (1995): 13–25.

Marsh, Anne. *Body and Self: Performance Art in Australia, 1969–92.* Melbourne: Oxford University Press, 1993.

Mellor, Philip A. and Shilling, Chris. 'Re-formed bodies'. *Re-forming the Body: Religion, Community and Modernity.* London: Sage Publications, 1997. 35–63.

Orlan. 'I do not want to look like . . . Orlan on becoming-Orlan'. *Make: the Magazine of Women's Art* no. 72, London, October/November 1996. <www.cicv.fr/creation_artistique/online/orlan/women/women.html>.

— Web site: <www.orlan.net/index.html>.

Plant, Sadie. 'The future looms: weaving women and cybernetics'. In *Cyberspace/Cyberbodies/Cyberpunk: Cultures of Technological Embodiment.* Ed. Mike Featherstone and Roger Burrows. London: Sage/Theory, Culture and Society, 1995. 45–64.

Probyn, Elspeth. *Carnal Appetites: Food, Sex, Identities.* London: Routledge, 2000.

Rey, Roselyn. *The History of Pain.* Cambridge, MA: Harvard University Press, 1995.

Stelarc. Web site: <www.stelarc.va.com.au/>.

CHAPTER 4

Towards a Compliant Coupling:
Pneumatic Projects, 1998–2001

STELARC

In the recent pneumatically powered projects, there is an attempt to construct extended and interactive operational systems. EXOSKELETON is an insect-like six-legged walking robot. The EXTENDED ARM lengthens the right arm to primate proportions with an eleven-degree-of-freedom manipulator. MOVATAR is an inverse motion capture system that allows an avatar to access a body and activate it using a six-degree-of-freedom motion prosthesis. In each of these projects the body becomes a split body. It is sometimes automated, sometimes involuntary, sometimes improvising and always experiencing the alternative and the alien. As well as extended human–machine systems, actual–virtual interactions and the mapping of sounds to movements are attempted. A new walking robot, HEXAPOD, will be a more compliant coupling with the human body. In this novel design, the intrinsic dynamics of the machine are exploited, with only a tripod gait allowed. The propulsive force comes from the natural dynamics of the leg suspension design. The walking mechanism converts potential to kinetic energy. In this chapter, the mechanical systems and the performances with these machines will be described, while the new project will be introduced.

EXOSKELETON is a jerky and powerful 600-kg machine. It is stiff-jointed, requiring eighteen pneumatic actuators to drive the three-degree-of-freedom legs. The robot walks forwards and backwards with a kind of ripple gait, and sideways left and right with a tripod gait. It can turn on the spot, squat and stand as well as sway from side to side. Positioned on a turntable, the body can rotate on its axis, adding another motion in the choreography of the machine. The body is not merely a passenger. With an exoskeleton wrapped around its upper torso and magnetic sensors on each jointed segment, arm gestures can be recognized, enabling the selection of the mode and direction of locomotion. The body becomes integrated into the operation of the machine and becomes visually connected to it. The performance is essentially a walking performance. There are no other pyrotechnics. In Berne at Dampfzentrale, as part of Cyborg Frictions, the performance lasted 45 minutes. The performance was largely improvised, within the dimensions of the space and the confines of the lighting. The overhead grid of lights meant the machine was either walking out of the light into darkness or emerging into the light from the darkness. As well as being attentive to the mode and direction of the locomotion, the artist is listening to resultant sounds. Composing the sounds means choreographing the movements of the machine. The compressed air sounds, relay switch clicks and the impact of the legs hitting the concrete are acoustically amplified. These sounds are augmented by the clicking and rotating actions of the large manipulator that extends the exoskeleton. Rhythmic loops of sounds can be generated by the repetitive finger movements of the manipulator. The switch signals are used to generate synthesized sounds to create a counterpoint to the industrial, mechanical sounds of the robot. There is a video surveillance system that monitors the moving parts of the robot and its position in the performance space, producing images that are mixed live and projected onto a large screen. There is a camera mounted on one leg (looking at the torso of the body and producing a close-up image of the manipulator) and a camera mounted on the back of the exoskeleton (looking down at the turntable and pneumatic cylinders). The exoskeleton, mounted on the turntable, rotates, producing a dynamic image. There is also a ceiling camera mapping the choreography from above, a side camera, and a hand-held camera that provides slow-motion and close-up shots to counterpoint the static images of the other cameras. Although the robot may be seen as clunky and clumsy, it is a large walking machine that can support a human body with an arm gesture control system. This is a human-user interface that makes its operation a much more hybrid one . . .

The EXTENDED ARM is constructed using materials such as stainless steel, aluminium and acrylic in a similar aesthetic to that of the THIRD HAND. The manipulator functions are activated by small pneumatic cylinders and rotary actuators. It is a five-finger human-like hand with novel capabilities. Its functions include wrist rotation, thumb rotation and individual finger flexion. The fingers also split open, allowing each finger to be a gripper in itself. The EXTENDED ARM acrylic sleeve fits over the right arm, whose fingers rest on an array of four switches, allowing the actuation of pre-programmed sequences of manipulator motion. The right arm becomes primate in proportion. The first performance was in Avignon as part of a programme called Mutalogues, organized by AVIGNONumérique. It was a continuous four-hour event (a kind of performance/installation) that allowed people to circulate and come and go in the small gallery space. While the right arm was extended and automated, the left arm was moving involuntarily to eight channels of muscle stimulation, not only allowing bending of the arm and wrist with deltoid, biceps, flexor and extender muscles but also activating some individual finger flexion: a split body performing both automated and involuntary motions. Again, the sounds and finger clicks were amplified acoustically and the switch signals were used to trigger synthesized sounds. The performance rhythms were largely orchestrated not only by the visual choreography, but also by the sound composition. On the far wall was cast a large shadow of the body and its extended arm. On the right-hand wall was projected the live video mix of four camera views – including a camera positioned above the body and a hand-held camera for improvised, close-up and slow-motion shots. On the left-hand wall was projected a VRML model of the manipulator, which was looping a sequence of movements, sometimes mimicking the physical device . . .

MOVATAR is an inverse motion capture system. Instead of a body animating a computer entity, it allows an avatar to perform in the real world by possessing a physical body. The Motion Prosthesis interface which wraps around the upper torso has only three degrees of freedom for each arm, but this allows for 64 possible combinations. The body is split not from left to right but, rather, from torso and legs. The arms are actuated by the avatar's code, but the legs are free to move, turn and press floor sensors that in turn can prompt and modulate the avatar's behaviour. Changes in rhythm, mutation rate and the complexity of posture strings, for example, can be effected. The Motion Prosthesis can be seen as the physical muscles of the avatar. The floor sensors can be considered the avatar's organs in the real world. This is a virtual–actual interface where a dialogue is generated. The issue thus is not of control, but of interactivity, of a gesture dialogue between physical bodies and virtual entities, of an extended operational system. Whereas in FRACTAL FLESH the body becomes a host for a remote and alien agent (another person who is in another place), here the body shares its agency (or doubles its agency) with an artificial entity: a virtual body that is capable of evolving its behaviour within the duration of the performance. The avatar can be seen as a kind of viral life form. It is benign and passive as a computer entity, but when connected to a host body it can affect physical behaviour – producing giff-like animation of the arms. The body becomes simultaneously a possessed and a performing body. And if the avatar is a VRML entity on the World Wide Web, then anyone, anywhere can connect, enabling it to perform with a body sequentially, or with clusters of bodies simultaneously. Movatar has been implemented as a full system only for the Cybercultures programme at the Casula Powerhouse Arts Centre. The avatar was visualized as a doppelgänger – human in form and limb movements. It was projected onto a large screen behind the body, superimposed on its shadow. At times the video projection was mapped precisely onto the shadow form as the body was activated and as it turned and performed with its images . . .

HEXAPOD is a novel walking machine, with a leg-spread of 5 metres. Although it looks like an insect, it will walk more like a dog, with dynamic locomotion. The legs are a pantograph structure, suspended from the body chassis and sprung to swing forward when pneumatically released. So the pneumatics are not so much to drive the robot as to allow the switching from one set of legs to the other. Effectively, it walks with two sets of three legs, with a tripod gait. The intrinsic dynamics of the robot's architecture are exploited for more efficient motion. EXO-SKELETON is stiff-jointed; each degree of freedom has to be actuated with a pneumatic piston. This is not the case with HEXAPOD. Instead of being tethered to a compressor, it requires only a tank of compressed air fixed on the machine. A car battery operates the cable and winch system that lifts the robot from its sitting position to the walking height. The body is positioned on a turntable, and by shifting its body weight and turning on its axis, it can activate the leg movements and point the robot in different directions. The robot moves in the direction in which the body is facing. Also, by timing its stepping, the body can vary the speed

Plate 5   HEXAPOD, Stelarc. 3D image: Steve Middleton

of walking. When the body sits, the robot lowers; when the body stands, the robot lifts. The experience will be a more intuitive and interactive human–machine hybrid. The propulsive force comes from the natural dynamics of the leg suspension design. Its flexibility and compliance make the robot more an extension of the body. And the body becomes more than a brain for the machine. Instead of the powerful stiff and jerky locomotion of EXOSKELETON, HEXAPOD will glide more smoothly over the ground. Future performances will explore alternative forms of choreography and navigation with this hybrid body–machine system. The intelligence of the system, which results in its effective operation in the world, is the result of its architecture – not simply being agency driven by the human body. Sensors will be attached to the robot to make it more responsive to its environment and sounds will be mapped to its motions . . .

CREDITS

EXOSKELETON:

MACHINE CONSTRUCTION: Stefan Doepner, Gwendolin Taube and Tom Diekmann

MACHINE ELECTRONICS AND PROGRAMMING: Lars Vaupel

COMPUTER SIMULATION: Steve Middleton

MANIPULATOR CONSTRUCTION: Jan Cummerow

MANIPULATOR INTERFACE AND PROGRAMMING: Ulf Freyhoff

This project was sponsored by SMC Pneumatics Germany and coordinated by Eva Diegritz as a co-production of Kampnagel Hamburg, F18 and Diekmann Enterprises. It was first performed at Kampnagel Hamburg on 5, 6, 7 and 12, 13, 14 November 1998.

EXTENDED ARM:

MANIPULATOR CONSTRUCTION: Jason Patterson

PNEUMATIC SYSTEM: Jan Cummerow

CONTROLLER AND PROGRAMMING: Lars Vaupel

This project was first researched during an Australia Council Visual Art/Crafts Board Fellowship. Funding to complete the pneumatics system and controller was provided by AVIGNONumérique for the programme Mutalogues. It was first performed in Avignon on 5 May 2000. This project was sponsored by SMC Pneumatics Australia.

MOVATAR:

CONSTRUCTION OF MOTION PROSTHESIS: Stefan Doepner, Gwendolin Taube and Jan Cummerow

CONTROLLER AND PROGRAMMING: Lars Vaupel

VRML AND DIRECTOR PROGRAMMING: Gary Zebington

JAVA PROGRAMMING: Damien Everett

SOUND AND SYSTEM DESIGN: Rainer Linz

The first performance was for Cybercultures at the Casula Powerhouse Arts Centre on 19 September 2000.

HEXAPOD:

MACHINE DESIGN: Inman Harvey

RESEARCH AND SIMULATION: Neil Pattinson

PROJECT COORDINATOR: Barry Smith

CHOREOGRAPHY: Sophia Lycouris

ENGINEERS: John Luxton and William Bigge

This project is a collaboration between the Digital Research Unit at Nottingham Trent University and the Evolutionary and Adaptive Systems Group COGS at the University of Sussex, with funding from the Wellcome Trust.

PART 2

The Obsolete Body?

CHAPTER 5

What Does an Avatar Want? Stelarc's E-motions

Edward Scheer

'Can I get disconnected?' (Stelarc, 25 August 2000, 7.05 p.m.)

> Defined emotions are like a substance with outstretched
> arms. . . . They pass from object to object, from desti-
> nation to destination, without power to stop. (Massimo
> Cacciari, *Posthumous People*)

MOVATAR: WORLD PREMIERE PERFORMANCE, SATURDAY 19 AUGUST 2000[1]

In an old power station at Casula in Sydney's western suburbs there is
a huge room in the middle of which one can see a shiny metal jacket
suspended from a cable. It looks startling, like a techno toreador's coat
of light. Or is it a backpack for the travelling cyborg? As with all
Stelarc's contraptions,[2] it is an elegantly and exactly finished piece of
techno sculpture, which he calls a 'Motion Prosthesis' (MP). (He
trained as a sculptor, after all, and not, or not only, as a prophet of
the post-human.) The MP has the aura of an art object. The audience
stands back from it.

The system boots up and the avatar begins its clumsy choreography.
We watch it on the screen, waving its extended arms like a B-grade
sci-fi bot from *Forbidden Planet* or *Lost in Space*. But then on the stage
Stelarc's upper body begins to follow suit. The arm movements are
sudden, giff-like, as he puts it, none too subtle. They are a product of
the pneumatic actuators, which provide for obvious movement but are
not able to evoke gradual or subtle gestures. Subtlety in this context is
expensive, as Stelarc is acutely aware.

The system is a servo-mechanism, a machine for staging feedback loops, in this case from the avatar to the body and back. Stelarc likens the MP to the 'muscles of the avatar' and the six foot pedals (i.e. midi pedals) on the floor of the stage to the avatar's remote organs in the physical world. He explains the use of these organs as follows:

> The mutation mode is one pedal. If I like what the avatar is doing to me, I might allow it to persist or I might wait to see what happens, as there is a completely unpredictable change of posture strings occurring. But if I hit the 'mutate' switch, I can then choose one of the six other switches to select rates of mutation, thus feeding back into the avatar's code and prompting changes in its behaviour. (Stelarc, Interview)

In this way Stelarc is able to 'contribute to a change of choreography'.[3]

Stelarc's body seems much livelier than the avatar's, which is stiff and wooden in its movements. But there is life in the old Movatar yet. . . . The image changes from live action to animation. There is also a menu listing features of the system, such as posture strings and mutation values. The menu display is a familiar feature of Stelarc's recent cyber work and assists in orienting the viewer. The sonic barrage that accompanies the piece is also a familiar aspect of the recent work. It keeps the audience well back. However, at one point a child runs across the stage. This Disney effect strikes me as one of the most artificial features of the event, though it is probably purely accidental. I later see the child playing a puppet game with his father's arm, making the arm move in different and not entirely comfortable ways. The loop of interactions is always broader than Stelarc can foresee.

VIRTUAL PERFORMANCE, OR WHAT DOES AN AVATAR WANT?

But in what exactly does this performance consist?[4] One basic way of understanding performance art (we will return to this topic later) is in the sense of a demonstration and testing of a concept involving the active presence of the artist's body. In the Movatar, we can see Stelarc standing, often with his back to the bulk of the audience. He is wearing an impressive pair of black, shock-absorbing boots. He can move the lower half of his body, while his upper body is strapped into the MP (which is suspended using a tensioner so the weight is not carried by the body of the performer). As in all Stelarc's work, the body here is liminal; it functions as an interface between technologies. Its movements consist of swinging arm gestures produced by the avatar's code. These minimal gestures are non-expressive and, as in all dance performance, useless. It is precisely the uselessness and purpose-lessness of a gesture that illustrates not an artist's design but rather a virtual entity's desired movement, something Stelarc refers to as the 'whims of the avatar'[5] (Stelarc, Interview). Significantly, 'gestures' do not stand for 'expressions' here. It is the latter that Stelarc is particularly interested in exploring in his work.

Perhaps the quality of the gestures is beside the point. After all, it is not the dance itself but rather the choreographic origin, the determinant of the gesture, the source for the motivation to move, that here constitutes the performative nucleus of the event. Given that the origin of the impulse to move is in the code of a digital entity, this approach to choreography is entirely new. The lines of code constitute the avatar and its movements, which are then moving Stelarc. Stelarc can modulate the moves of the avatar, thus creating a loop. This is a performance of a cybernetic prototype, the first time that the software has been tested against the 'real-world object' of the MP in a multimedia performance event (Stelarc, Interview).

Stelarc's use of the notion of the 'inverse motion capture system' suggests another productive mode of interpreting the event as perform-ance art. He says that the Movatar is 'not a normal motion capture system in that it's not simply a physical body mapping its movements onto a computer model. Instead, you have feedback loops that are constantly modifying and modulating the relationship between the two' (Stelarc, Interview). In the Movatar, the computer model maps its motion onto the physical body and so has to tread carefully. In theory, it could swivel its head through 360 degrees of rotation or bend its arms backwards, which is why due caution was exercised in the programming phase of the project. This caution partly accounts for the severely limited range of movements exhibited by the avatar in its first performance. As Stelarc explains, this is also a function of the engineering of the MP in relation to the available bending motions of the human arms. 'Ideally,' he says,

> as the avatar becomes more autonomous (i.e. develops more artificial intelligence), the relationship will become more complex. I looked at the avatar as a kind of viral life form, dormant in its computer state but able to generate an effect once it is connected to a host body. (Stelarc, Interview)

As a virus, the avatar infects the body in barely visible ways. This bare visibility is one of the difficulties with the Movatar performance, as so many of the interesting interrelations are not communicable to the audience without the testimony of the artist. For the record, Stelarc says that 'It was exciting to feel the modifying effects of the code and of the feedback from the real world' (Stelarc, Interview). While motion capture subtracts the body's appearance and leaves a record of its motion, inverse motion capture subtracts the body's motions, making it hostage to a (hopefully) benign virtual entity that just wants you for your body.

RHETORICAL SCULPTURE v. PERFORMANCE

We are used to seeing much more of Stelarc's body in performance. He explains:

> Since the walking machine (Exoskeleton, 1999), in which I was clothed, owing to the fact that I needed to wear shockproof boots, I have decided to remain clothed in these new pieces, as there is really no reason for the nudity any more. The magnetic sensors are attached to the exoskeleton of the MP, whereas with the Third Hand there were electrodes placed all over the body. As the sensors taped to the skin were really delicate, the wearing of clothing would have interfered with them. In Movatar there are no sensors or electrodes required at all. So nothing needs to be stuck to the skin. (Stelarc, Interview)

The body that has experienced so much stress and conducted so much electricity is now a prosthetic device for a semi-autonomous virtual being. Despite the rude instrumentality of its new role, the body of Stelarc is still clearly a soft machine: there is a reassuring curve to his belly, the comforting expanse of his baldness.

The basic contradiction of all Stelarc's actions consists in their return to the image of the artist's body in a way that reinforces the effect of its presence and its adaptive capacities. This is not to say that this body is not problematic; it is not a self-evident body. It remains open in its connections with the world and its agencies are disturbingly dispersed. But if we ignore the performances and focus on his rhetorical productions, presence becomes only a detour for Stelarc. He recedes from us into the hollow body, emptied of qualities associated with personality and affect.

Jane Goodall has emphasized the importance of maintaining a critical differentiation between the rhetorical provocations of artists such as Stelarc and Orlan and their performances. While this is an important point, it is not to say that the rhetorical devices are separable from the actions, but rather perhaps that they constitute different registers of the work. In this case, the Movatar work-in-progress necessitates a consideration of Stelarc's plans for the extension of the project. For the sake of clarity, I will refer to his provocations as 'rhetorical sculptures' – works in themselves that accompany the performances. Goodall argues that the performances need more attention and 'may actually have a cooling effect on the overheated fantasy life of those who just can't wait to be post-human'[6] (167). Stelarc's statements, seen as separate from his actions, seem to generate a proliferation of disembodied fantasies, as if we could leap from the body into virtual reality and never return.

INTIMACY WITHOUT PROXIMITY

Stelarc insists on the value of cybernetic connections. His actions show the adaptability of the body in dealing with new contexts and prostheses. The challenge he poses is to think about the relationship between body and technology in terms of connections and not in terms of a logical separation of bodies from the world. For example, he wonders if we may be able to extend our abilities to satisfy our wants in cybersexual encounters. With the right sensors and web interfaces, Stelarc suggests that it might be possible to stroke a loved one's nipple on the other side of the world. This 'intimacy without proximity' (Stelarc, Performative Sites) may not add up to a 'want' yet, but, at the same time, this form of tele-erotics might be a solution to the very loss of interpersonal intimacy that some argue is a feature of the information age.

Intimacy, the closeness of emotional connection, still constitutes a limit for cybernetics which the contemporary avant-garde edge of the industry is exploring. John Canny and Eric Paulos have argued, for example, as a result of their Prop experiments (Personal Roving Presence, 1996–9), that 'without intimacy and trust, our existence in cyberspace will remain an impoverished substitute' (Canny and Paulos, 279). Their work in building 'human proxies in the physical world' (280) attempts to realize the complexity of human behaviour in social environments through telerobots. The robots, moving as blimps or on wheels (Props), do not look like humans but instead approach what they call an 'anthropomorphism of function' that mirrors behaviours rather than forms (278). Canny and Paulos point out that while we can build telerobots to target, arm and deliver live explosive ordnance, we cannot yet conceive of a way to build a robot to hug people.[7] This argument suggests that the military genealogy of cybernetics may yet determine and delimit the future of its applications. At least we can still hug Stelarc. He seems to realize this, which is why he is using the Movatar-based interface, the MP and his own body, rather than telerobots.

This form of intimacy and the emotions it generates and protects are more than a kind of 'last hurrah for humanism'. Even in post-human performance, embodiment is still necessary, something of which Stelarc, as a performer, is acutely aware: 'These ideas emanate from the performances. Anyone can come up with the ideas, but unless you physically realise them and go through those experiences of new interfaces and new symbioses with technology and information, then it's not interesting for me' (Stelarc, 'Extra Ear/Exoskeleton/Avatars'). For Stelarc, ideas are authenticated through physical actions. Perform-ance is central to his aesthetic concerns, with art perceived as having an operational role – that is, testing design concepts and aesthetic imaginings in actual environments. This aesthetic is concerned with the activation of sense perceptions rather than the construction of beautiful objects. But the perceptions do not arise independently of the production of the objects. They occur, as it were, inbetween the objects and the viewer in the moment of performance.

CYBORG ANGER/ZOMBIE ANXIETIES

Stelarc depersonalizes the experience of his body, a position which, one might think, would be difficult to sustain given his distinctive, mad scientist's laugh. He always refers to his body as 'the body', defining it as an organization of structural components infused with intelligence – that is, a smart machine. But what separates his thesis from, say, the rhetoric of VW Kombi owners is the idea that the body is not simply a vehicle to transport a disembodied consciousness through space/ time. As Stelarc has repeatedly said, 'We've always been zombies behaving involuntarily' and 'we don't have a mind of our own' (Stelarc, Interview). His discourse of the body exposes the primal fear of the zombie – that is, of our bodies being animated by a distant alien intelligence – in our imagining of the body and its functions. On the other hand, he provokes in his audiences the anxiety of the cyborg in arguing that 'we've always been hooked up to technologies and have always been prosthetic bodies, augmented and extended' (Stelarc, Interview). He knows that when he says this, part of his audience imagines that he is describing an unfeeling, dehumanized droid self.

At the first public demonstration of the Movatar animation at the Museum of Sydney on 20 February 1999, one of the topics raised in the panel discussion following Stelarc's presentation centred on the anxiety his work seems to provoke in his audiences. Both the figure of the zombie and that of the cyborg can seem disturbing in so far as they displace our sense of the humanistic self, a self that is separate from others and from the world, that is present to itself, and that remains in charge of its intentions and agency and located within its own affective field.

So perhaps it is not surprising that people get upset by Stelarc's statements. I have seen it time and again in public situations. There is a degree of outrage at what he says about the obsolete body: 'So you think humans are finished and that's OK?!' [8] It's as if he were attacking our bodies. Attacking us! Some of us don't like being described as zombies and cyborgs (see Dery, Marsh).[9] However, this form of anger seems misdirected as Stelarc is referring not to the idea of subjectivity in his work but rather to a model of the body as 'an evolutionary architecture for operation and awareness in the world' or, in other words, 'an engineering entity, always modifiable, and never defined essentially' (Galison, 259, reading Haraway). So we're only shadow boxing! Infuriatingly, Stelarc also points out that anger is learned behaviour and can be chemically monitored and controlled. Stelarc himself seems more fascinated by 'bodies acting without expectation, producing movements without memory'. He asks, tellingly, irritatingly, 'Can a body act without emotion?' (Stelarc, Parasite Visions). The question posits a link between motion and e-motion, while opening a gap in our thinking about this relationship, a gap that is not ready to be closed by thought alone. It is in the space of this question that his work takes place.

Although emotion represents a limit for the type of performance Stelarc engages in, he never shows much emotion in his performances; he just gets on with the job of inserting shark hooks, attaching electrodes, swallowing sculptures and dodging killer industrial robots. Yet his work inspires much emotion in response. Not only does it radically question our physical being in the world (are we zombies and cyborgs?), but it also continually reminds us that the loop of our sensory apparatus always takes us back into the world. As Susan Buck-Morss notes, 'The circuit from sense perception to motor response begins and ends in the world.' So the concept of the cybernetic connection should not trouble us if we reflect on how the world is now. But Stelarc also wants us to reflect on how the changes in the world feed back into the human system. He emphasizes that we need to interact more effectively with the increasingly denaturalized environment this system finds itself in. Accordingly, his performances imagine the extension of the body's capacities for useful (and useless) action.

ELECTRONIC EMOTIONS: THE LIMITS
OF THE CYBERNETIC

But are these interactions reducible to the locomotive? As the lingering emotive residue haunts Stelarc's opus, his question about the nexus joining action and emotion could be rephrased as 'What moves us?' But such rephrasing may cause us to stray from electricity and pneumatic motion prostheses, and approach the problem from the angle of affect and energy. Stelarc has not thus far directly addressed such topics, yet he has suggested that it is one of the areas he would like to explore in the development of the project – that is, to 'develop Movatar using a muscle stimulation system on the facial muscles to express the avatar's emotion' (Stelarc, Parasite Visions). How is this development thinkable? The emotions surely lie beyond the scope of digital technologies. Are electronic emotions anything other than techno-fantasy? No avatar can by definition experience emotion, as the avatar's condition is disembodiment. Is this another case of the attraction of the rhetorical sculpture winning out over the extant work? The question of emotion seems to be so central to Stelarc's approach that it deserves to be explored further.

It is significant that, in relation to the Movatar, Stelarc addresses the question of emotion directly, in a manner that reveals the extent to which his views are informed by a pragmatic reading of phenomeno-logical and behavourist explanations of the topic. More importantly, his response suggests that, as he understands it, emotion is not situated beyond the scope of cybernetic experiment at all:

> The word 'emotion' needs to be clarified. What do we mean when we refer to someone as an emotional person? What it means in the world is that the emotional person responds rather abruptly and displays abrupt behaviour in visible ways: a red face, a loud voice, etc. And, of course, the body is constantly being influenced by electrical signals within the neural and synaptic structures of the brain and the peripheral nerve endings of its locomotors and manipulators, the ebb and flow of adrenaline levels, hormonal levels, etc. So if you try to say that emotion is somehow largely hormonal or adrenal or chemical and that it represents another kind

of inner quality, I'd say it's not the whole picture. One can also argue that emotional displays are learned behaviour. There are significant cultural differences between, say, Mexican, Greek or Italian cultures and English or Japanese cultures regarding the display of emotion and the use of gesture to express feelings in conversation. So the term itself is very obscure and fuzzy. In the end, you are determining your emotional levels simply through the way you express yourself and your mode of behaviour. Now I'm not simply a behaviourist but it's undeniable that subjective experience is a part of a living creature's operation in the world. (Stelarc, Interview)

This account risks reductionism through its avoidance of any discussion of internal states, simply reading actions in the place of emotions, divorced from the complex affective field (which must include psychological processes and intentions, as well as physiological and neurological processes, chemical flows and social contexts).[10] But it is not surprising or even radical that Stelarc should renounce any internalized reading of the event of emotionality. He is, after all, in good company. Maurice Merleau-Ponty, for example, in his 1945 essay 'The film and the new psychology', argues that emotions 'are not psychic facts hidden at the bottom of another's consciousness: they are types of behaviour or styles of conduct which are visible from the outside. They exist on this face or in those gestures, not hidden behind them' (338). He also asserts the primacy of a functionalist reading of the signs of emotion:

> To create a psychology of anger is to try to ascertain the meaning of anger, to ask oneself how it functions in human life and what purpose it serves. So we find that emotion is, as Janet said, a disorganizing reaction which comes into play whenever we are stuck. On a deeper level, as Sartre has shown, we find that anger is a magical way of acting by which we afford ourselves a completely symbolic satisfaction in the imagination after renouncing effective action in the world. (Merleau-Ponty, 338)

This may go some way towards explaining road rage – surely one of the dominant cyborg emotions of our time.

The application of a phenomenological perspective to the issues of cyberspace allows for the possibility of scanning emotional behaviour which can be then interpreted and reproduced by a telerobot or an avatar. For instance, Australian cybernetic experimenter and artist Simon Penny has developed a 'mood analysis engine' which, rather than relying exclusively on position detection technology, enables the camera to pick up rates and patterns of movement in people visiting the cave site of his installation. These vectors form the basis of what the software treats as a given 'mood'. This concept has been actualized in two recent cybernetic works, *Fugitive* (1997) and *Traces* (1999), both cave-based interactive multi-camera and multi-projection environments drawing on the kinetic input of individual users. In these environments, users' movements (audience does not seem the right word here) are picked up on camera and employed to trigger images and sounds in the space (Penny, Performative Sites). Perhaps the existence of an emotional avatar using filters to determine its own or others' behaviours in terms of moods presents itself in this sense as a distinct possibility. Stelarc, however, is cautious about this, regarding the mood analysis engine as 'an arbitrary way of observing and attributing certain movements to certain emotions'. After all, as he does not fail to note, 'one can be angry and agitated or one can be angry but constrained' (Stelarc, Interview).

EMOTION AS DEEP AFFECT

Of course, there exist some other interpretations of emotion, warning us not to confuse motor coordinations, the 'signs of emotion', with the emotion itself. One ethologist arguing against the conflation of expression and emotion uses the example of the politician on the hustings: 'when a human [sic] politician kisses babies, we don't expect that he feels the same paternal emotions as a father kissing his own infant' (Masters, 274). But then one might argue that the 'human politician' and the avatar have a similarly evolved emotional repertoire. Stelarc defends the avatar in pointing out that its 'failure to express emotion is because of its rather simple and unsophisticated behaviour. It does not possess or express enough micro-motions to appear in any other state than a kinematic one' (Stelarc, Interview).

Emotion is an enabling tool for anyone involved in symbolic work. What, after all, drives these creative behaviours, these experiments in problem-solving technologies? In *Gilles Deleuze and the Ruin of Representation*, Dorothea Olkowski argues, through Deleuze and Bergson, that '[w]hat forces us to think is a particular encounter that deranges our ordered schemas and produces a profound affectivity: terror, rage, wonder, hatred, suffering, awe' (231). This is the originary moment of creativity, 'when emotion itself produces and drives intelligence from its affective stirrings', and it explains why Deleuze links 'emotion with intuition' (Olkowski, 234). Here emotion appears to be considered as 'profound affectivity' rather than simply corporeal patterning. While this is argued from a perspective of a 'creative evolution' and not a post-evolutionary discourse, it is worth noting that the intimacy between intuition and emotion is, according to Olkowski's thesis, the very origin and product of Stelarc's work as an artist. It is also the very thing he seems to deny most forcefully. The disconnection between emotion and intellection does not stop Stelarc from being a source of inspiration for other people, nor does it seem to prevent him from developing his projects in new and creative ways.

ACTIONS, ABREACTIONS AND DEEP MIMETIC OPERATIONS

The discharge of affect is a dominant feature of much performance art. Performance art is usually abreactive, as the artist purges him- or herself of a trauma by re-enacting it or re-inscribing it into a ritual gesture, which often involves a threat of damage, or actual damage, to the body. The trauma is neither actual nor fictive but present; that is, it is not a genuinely or personally felt trauma, nor a purely characterized or represented one, as in conventional drama, but one that is carried into the present moment with a genuine force. McKenzie Wark argues in a discussion of the importance of Stelarc's cyber-actions that this abreactive approach to performance is based on an outdated experience of the body. He gives the example of the American performance artist Karen Finley, whose performances often feature violent language and aggressive gestures, striptease, smearing the body with food (famously chocolate, more recently honey) and monologues, delivered as if in a trance, on topics such as incest and abuse or, in her most recent piece, *Shut Up and Love Me* (PS 122, New York, 6, 7, 13, 14 October 2000), on other forms of botched intimacy and frustrated desire. Wark argues that 'the limitations of an artist like Karen Finlay [*sic*] lie here: in a defiant and ultimately nostalgic assertion of a body's right to itself' (non-pag.). This, for him, is a kind of 'retro humanism', not post-humanism. Wark adds:

> a rage against the machine, an oedipal shriek against daddy is not the same thing as a figuring and a figuring out of the patriarchal structures of second nature. It is, once again, a self ghettoisation within art as a romantic refuge. The refuge late 19th century romantics sought in framing landscape on the wall, late 20th century romantics seek in performing the body in the gallery. (non-pag.)

But 'performing the body in the gallery' is precisely what Stelarc has been doing for the last quarter century.

Stelarc, of course, deploys an extended concept of the corporeal, but always in relation to a very present physicality that does not repudiate the body, as Wark seems to want. This is perhaps an example of a reading that buys into Stelarc's rhetoric without due attention to his performances. On the other hand, Finley's work performs the body in a way that underscores its linkages to psycho-social processes and systems and is concerned with narratives of ecstatic emotion such as anger, lust and loathing which animate a different perception of the body as visceral and interiorized. This is not quite the kind of dead-end narcissism to which Wark alludes either.

Finley's work also exhibits emotion as a site of transduction, developing an energy in one symbolic system for use in another, from body to language, from artistic corpus to social body, etc., to generate a shift in potential and a symbolic transformation. Put simply, Finley's work is intended to allow more freedom for the body, however it is conceived. Her anger is hilarious, hysteric and performative, but also designed to shift the parameters of permissible behaviour by staging the unspeakable and the unthinkable. It operates on and in the world, though it is not framed in the same way as Stelarc's detached approach to emotion.[11] Hers is a visceral experience, invading every aspect of her work, which, in some ways, is only a transcription of an enduring experience of anger.

Performance art develops what Victor Turner calls 'life crisis rituals' in response to drastically changing social and personal conditions. It is the sense of a loss of capacity for affect, tantamount to a loss of humanity, that Finley's work seeks to dramatize. In Stelarc, it is the life crisis of an obsolete body finding itself without sympathetic environments in an age of technological innovation that is accelerating beyond the capacities of the organism to adapt. For him, it is a life crisis of the species.

Finley and Stelarc are driven to imagine and perform rituals that can also transcribe the crisis of the time, embody it and make it liveable. This, I would suggest, is the function of performance for both of them. I am not persuaded that one approach negates the other. They simply represent divergent approaches to the performance of the emotions and the use of physicality. Finley discharges affect into social space, while Stelarc does not perform this discharge but rather enacts a redistribution of energies and emotions throughout the cybernetic system. In any case, emotion in performance art is neither true nor false; instead, it constitutes a kind of deep mimetic operation, neither essentially locomotive nor purely internalized. In other words, even if emotion is virtual, it can perhaps be described as grounded virtuality, linked to the substantial if not the essential.

EVISCERATED PERFORMANCE/TWENTY-FIRST-CENTURY GOTHIC

Ultimately, the cyborg body produced in Stelarc's Movatar action is a passionless body, a body without depth and without viscera. The prominence of the 'hollow body' in Stelarc's 'rhetorical sculptures' may explain the diminished role that emotion plays in his work. Noting the significance of the etymological connection between motion and emotion, Drew Leder has argued in *The Absent Body* that 'emotion inaugurates our motor projects, propelling us toward desired goals. . . . Yet while guiding our sensorimotor engagements, emotionality is also rooted in the visceral' (136). He points out that emotions are registered in the secretion of hormones, which effects a 'realignment of visceral processes' (136). Anger, he argues, 'relies on a glandular flood of adrenaline and the increased sympathetic tone of the autonomic nervous system, transforming patterns of blood flow, body temperature, cardiac and respiratory function' (138). For Leder, the self recedes as this visceral depth surfaces in anger or fear and becomes a passive accompaniment to the passionate episode. 'The visceral exhibits an "I must" and "I cannot".' The self is compelled to follow behind the emotions, which sometimes get away: 'the emotions, at least for most of us, escape to a degree from our wilful command' (Leder, 136).[12]

Leder notes that this imperiousness of the emotions sometimes interferes with our intended projects, as powerful emotions can lead us away from our usual lack of awareness of the body. As a result, the body reappears in focus but as if estranged from us. We are outside ourselves to an extent, aware of our thumping heart, our sweating hands or tensed muscles. The body now appears as an 'alien or threatening thing', a state Leder refers to as 'dys-appearance'. It is perhaps not incidental that Stelarc has described his Stomach Sculpture (16 November 1993), which consisted of the insertion of an object into his stomach and the filming of its passage, as his most difficult performance. The visceral inversion, turning the stomach inside out with the aid of a camera, stages a form of the dys-appearance that Leder describes: the 'self' receding, leaving a gasping organism in its wake.

In the eviscerated world of the avatar, emotion prosthesis is as necessary as motion prosthesis if the cybernetic interaction is to produce a more fully experienced relation to the world and a more complex engagement with the human. After all, the cybernetics of movement as locomotion is as old as the bicycle. What looms as the next frontier for the field is this subtle pedagogical interchange between emotive behaviours of actual and virtual persons. Yet an exchange of gestures readable as emotions may also take us back to the future in the various nineteenth-century experiments in synthesizing emotions, attempting to capture and define emotions as gestures or expressions.

For example, in the late nineteenth century François Delsarte devised a system for use in actor training which sought to synthesize the expression of specific emotions in particular physical postures and gestures. Such a method could be adapted for the Movatar project in developing posture strings for the avatar which embody, after Delsarte, particular emotions. For example, the back of the hand against the forehead could express anguish.[13] More important for the Movatar's future as Stelarc envisages it could be the work done by Duchenne de Boulogne in his study *Mécanisme de la physiognomie humaine* of 1862. Duchenne sought to capture in image and text the nexus between facial muscular configurations and the emotions which Stelarc is also interested in examining. The photographs he took of his experiments show electronic muscle stimulation used on the facial muscles to reproduce emotions. With Stelarc's own history of employing electronic muscle stimulation systems and his plans to apply them on his face, Duchenne is clearly a fellow traveller.

These photographs used in Duchenne's text would themselves become influential a decade later for Charles Darwin in his proto-ethological treatise *The Expression of the Emotions in Man and Animals*. In this book, Darwin refers to the technique of muscle stimulation as 'galvanism' (25), a method of which he clearly approves, but – beware, Stelarc – the art critic in Darwin warns that 'in works of art, beauty is the chief object; and strongly contracted face muscles destroy beauty' (22). Darwin includes a number of these images in his text, along with some others by the photographer O.G. Rejlander. Perhaps the most famous of these images is the shot called Ginx's baby (149) showing the detailed features of a baby in the action of crying. It has recently emerged that this is not actually a photograph at all but a 'photographic copy of a drawing after an original photograph' (Darwin, 147). This image was said to have 'scattered to the winds' previous representations of the emotions. What it actually shows is that the emotions are always partly a matter of the imagination and the intentions (creative or habitual) of individuals. Here it is the imagination of the eager Rejlander, keen to help Darwin establish a case for his reading of emotional expressions, whose intervention makes the image clearer but muddies its significance (Darwin, 147). His actions remind us that emotions are always part performances, not shallow brush strokes but deep mimetic operations. Their representation is never simply a matter of transcription but rather one of reinscription and invention.

If the Movatar system is to develop in accordance with Stelarc's vision, then he will have to emote a little more than he currently does in performances. (Or maybe Karen Finley could just be asked to collaborate?) But the real irony lies in the fact that the future of cybernetic interaction depends on more unambiguously readable displays of emotional behaviour in the style of the nineteenth-century image-makers and researchers such as Delsarte, Duchenne and Darwin, so that the entire system develops more characteristics and greater degrees of behavioural complexity. Just as virtual evolution may have something to learn from the studies of human evolution, the performance of post-humanism needs to look towards the emotions for its development. And this means that Stelarc is right to insist on using his body as the prosthesis for the virtual entity. For without the embodiment provided thus far by Stelarc's body, connected through the MP, Movatar is just an animation sequence with very limited behaviours. Disconnected but desiring intimacy, the Movatar animation literalizes our condition of being trapped, as Wittgenstein says, 'inside a picture' (quoted in Leder, 154). But to find connections with the physical body in the actual world is to problematize this entrapment, if not to find a way out of it.

NOTES

1. Graphics + Director/VRML Programming Gary Zebington; AI Director, Midi + Java Programming Damien Everett; Sound + Technical Design Rainer Linz; Web Site Movatar Animations Steve Middleton; Web Site Sound Andrew Garton. Thanks to SMC (Germany) and F18, respectively, for sponsoring and constructing Movatar's motion prosthesis. Stelarc's presence here was part of the Cyber Cultures: Sustained Release programme at Casula Powerhouse Arts centre, in particular the 'exhibition capsule' with the theme of 'Posthuman Bodies' curated by Kathy Cleland.
2. By now there are many: the Third Arm, which has recently been auctioned off after doing its duty these past fifteen years, the Extended Arm and the Exoskeleton walking machine are some of the more recently utilized objects.
3. The other modes used in this prototype performance were, first, synchro-nous mode, in which 'the avatar is performing graphically and making my arms move at the same time'; second, dialogue mode, which uses a delay mechanism and in which 'it might do something and get me to do it later'; and third, a kind of 'solo mode in which it does its thing and I do my thing, though there's a constant dialogue of physical gesture' (Stelarc, Interview).

4. Stelarc insists on its status as a work in progress, and that is how I will try to read it here: in terms of the event itself and the planned development of the system.

5. In Kant, that which determines the category of the beautiful in general is precisely this 'purposiveness without purpose' (*Zweckmassigkeit ohne Zweck*) or 'finality without an end' (Carroll, 139). This reading is significant, as it reminds us of Stelarc's primary business as an artist and returns his experiments at the borders of hard science to the aesthetic domain, or at least the para-aesthetic.

6. Jane Goodall has also raised the notion of motivation in relation to movement and suggested that Stelarc disconnects the links between them, so that motion becomes mechanical rather than psychological and does not reflect the motivation of the mover. It is a manifestation, she says, of the unravelling of evolutionary thinking.

7. Researchers at the Artificial Intelligence laboratory at MIT are working on a similar problem with their Cog robot, which is being trained in embodied sociality. They also have an 'emotional-social learning' experiment under way with a disembodied or less-embodied robot called Kismet, which is really just an inside-out electronic head but surprisingly cute. (Claudia Dreifus, 'Do androids dream? MIT working on it' in *New York Times* Science Times section, Tuesday 7 November 2000, p. F3.)

8. Audience member at premiere screening of the documentary film *Stelarc/Psycho/Cyber*, dir. Tim Gruchy at AGNSW, 1996.

9. In *Escape Velocity: Cyberculture at the End of the Twentieth Century*, Dery accuses Stelarc of 'narcissistic fantasies of complete isolation' (164). Anne Marsh's critique of the denial of gender in Stelarc's discourse of the body in *Body and Self* is similarly caustic. See Jane Goodall, 'An order of pure decision: un-natural selection in the work of Stelarc and Orlan', for an excellent discussion of this issue.

10. Do we detect shades of Taylor v. Wiener on the topic of teleology back at the dawn of the cyber age? This conflict occurred when the founder of cybernetics, Norbert Wiener, wanted to deal with behavioural data purely on the basis of what was observable. As a philosopher, Taylor found it objectionable in so far as the notion of the human as machine was not intended as a metaphor (it wasn't) (Galison, 251).

11. In a note on a draft of this paper, Stelarc argues that it is a case of being 'detached in that the art event is not meant as a cathartic experience. Because it is not about the individual's psycho-social concerns. The body is not seen as simply a site for the psyche. The body is not a Freudian construct' (Stelarc, email, 27 December 2000).

12. This does not mean, however, that involuntary emotion expresses the truth

of subjective experience. These intense affective states of rage or lust, however compelling, often represent humanity at its most machinic and habitual.

13. This notion of synthesis may seem clumsy now and redolent of the more labour-intensive practices of the industrial age when Taylorism promised increased productivity through increased efficiency of actions in the process of assembling parts in a factory. The age of the actor as a physical worker whose body needed to be trained to use a pick and a hammer has given way to the age of robots.

WORKS CITED

Buck-Morss, Susan. 'Aesthetics and anaesthetics: Walter Benjamin's essay reconsidered'. *October* 62 (Fall 1992): 3–42.

Cacciari, Massimo. *Posthumous People.* Trans. Roger Friedman. Stanford, CA: Stanford University Press, 1996.

Canny, John and Paulos, Eric. 'Tele-embodiment and shattered presence: reconstructing the body for online interaction'. In *The Robot in the Garden: Telerobotics and Telepistemology in the Age of the Internet.* Ed. Ken Goldberg. Cambridge, MA: MIT Press, 2000. 276–95.

Carroll, David. *Paraesthetics: Foucault Lyotard Derrida.* London: Methuen, 1987.

Darwin, Charles. *The Expression of the Emotions in Man and Animals.* 3rd edn. Oxford: Oxford University Press, 1998.

Dery, Mark. *Escape Velocity: Cyberculture at the End of the Twentieth Century.* London: Hodder & Stoughton, 1996.

Dreifus, Claudia. 'Do androids dream? MIT working on it'. *New York Times* Science Times section, Tuesday 7 November 2000, p. F3.

Duchenne de Boulogne, Guillaume-Benjamin. *Mécanisme de la physiognomie humaine.* Paris: Jules Renouard, 1862.

Galison, Peter. 'The ontology of the enemy: Norbert Wiener and the cybernetic vision'. *Critical Inquiry* 21 (Autumn 1994): 228–66.

Goodall, Jane. 'An order of pure decision: un-natural selection in the work of Stelarc and Orlan'. In *Body Modification.* Ed. Mike Featherstone. Sage: London, 2000. 149–84.

Leder, Drew. *The Absent Body.* Chicago: University of Chicago Press, 1990.

Marsh, Anne. *Body and Self.* Melbourne: Oxford University Press, 1993.

Masters, Roger D. 'Beyond reductionism: five basic concepts in human ethology'. In *Human Ethology: Claims and Limits of a New Discipline.* Ed. M. von Cranach, K. Foppa, W. Lepenies and D. Ploog. London: Cambridge University Press and Paris: Éditions de la Maison des Sciences de l'Homme, 1979. 265–84.

Merleau-Ponty, Maurice. 'The film and the new psychology' (1945). Trans. H.

and P. Dreyfus. In *The Robot in the Garden: Telerobotics and Telepistemology in the Age of the Internet*. Ed. Ken Goldberg. Cambridge, MA: MIT Press, 2000. 333–45.

Olkowski, Dorothea. *Gilles Deleuze and the Ruin of Representation*. Berkeley and Los Angeles: University of California Press, 1999.

Penny, Simon. Presentation at Performative Sites Symposium 'Intersecting Art, Technology, and the Body', 24–28 October 2000 at Penn State University. 26 October 2000.

Stelarc. 'Extra Ear/Exoskeleton/Avatars' presentation at the Museum of Sydney, 20 February 1999 (a dlux media/arts and Casula Powerhouse event).

— Interview, 26 August 2000 in Darlinghurst, Sydney.

— Parasite Visions Web site, <www.stelarc.va.com.au>, accessed 11 November 2000.

— Presentation at Performative Sites Symposium 'Intersecting Art, Technology, and the Body'. 24–28 October 2000 at Penn State University. 25 October 2000.

Turner, Victor. *The Anthropology of Performance*. New York: PAJ Publications, 1986.

Wark, McKenzie. 'Post human? All too human'. <www.mcs.mq.edu.au/staff/mwark/warchive/World-art/wart-posthuman.html>, accessed 9 November 2000.

CHAPTER 6

Planned Obsolescence:
Flying into the Future with Stelarc

JOHN APPLEBY

> It is time to question whether a bipedal, breathing body
> with binocular vision and a 1400cc brain is an adequate
> biological form. It cannot cope with the quantity, complex-
> ity and quality of information it has accumulated; it is
> intimidated by the precision, speed and power of tech-
> nology and it is biologically ill-equipped to cope with its
> new extra-terrestrial environment. (Stelarc, 'From psycho-
> body to cyber-systems')

> Make a rhizome. But you don't know which subterranean
> stem is effectively going to make a rhizome, or enter a
> becoming, people your desert. So experiment. (Gilles
> Deleuze and Félix Guattari, *A Thousand Plateaus*)

If there is one theoretical claim with which Stelarc is particularly
associated, it is that the body is obsolete. This chapter considers how
that statement can be interpreted, and investigates whether it holds up
in the light of the artist's performances. Stelarc says that his performances show the way forward to a post-human condition that represents
the move out of the 'standard' evolutionary system and prepares the
way for leaving the solar system. However, I argue that his pronouncements are not as radical as they might initially appear, in that they
constitute a straightforwardly teleological narrative and, as such,
partake of the humanist discourses arising out of the Cartesian dualism
that he claims to repudiate. I compare Stelarc's ideas to the concept of
cyborgian development first proposed by Manfred E. Clynes and

Nathan S. Kline in a paper they wrote for NASA.[1] Following on from this, I consider Stelarc's Internet-based performances in the light of Deleuze and Guattari's concepts of becoming and rhizomatics. I conclude that, while his performances neither demonstrate the obsolescence of the body, nor point towards the inevitability of interstellar migration, they do indeed create interesting possibilities for rethinking the way in which we interact with the world.

The first question that arises is what does Stelarc mean by the term 'body'? From the epigraph at the start of the chapter it seems fairly clear that he is talking about the human biological form, positing the surrounding skin as its limit.[2] In fact, his early suspension performances, deforming the body's boundaries by means of hooks that penetrate and stretch the artist's skin in the process of lifting him off the ground, could be said to demonstrate precisely these limits inherent in the skin. One might want to argue that this deformation is a problematization, rather than a breaking down, of the corporeal boundaries, which are only made more apparent in the process. However, in his own analyses of the suspensions, Stelarc actually goes beyond this interpretation to claim that they both open up the body's boundaries and point towards the desire to escape the Earth's gravity. As he explains in an interview with Atzori and Woolford,

> [T]he stretched skin was a kind of gravitational landscape. This is what it took for a body to be suspended in a 1-G gravitational field. The other context is the primal desire for floating and flying. A lot of primal rituals have to do with suspending the body, but in the 20th century we have the reality of astronauts floating in zero-G. So the suspension event is between those sort of primal yearnings, and the contemporary reality. (non-pag.)

This posited primal desire for flying is supposed to explain, at least in part, the inevitability of interstellar travel, driving humans outward from the planet. For Stelarc, this desire needs to be effectuated via strategies that focus upon redesigning the body in order to allow it to function optimally off-planet, preferably without the encumbrance of devices such as spacesuits that both separate the body from, and hinder its functioning within, extraterrestrial environments. This process is linked as much to the aesthetic appreciation of free movement as it is to the desire to carry out tasks with maximal efficiency. In coming to realize the necessity for such strategies, one arrives at a simultaneous appreciation of the obsolescence of the current human form because it cannot meet the criteria required to accord with them. Stelarc's contention is that such an appreciation will fuel a drive towards the development of post-humans.

The realization of the obsolescence of the body is accompanied by Stelarc's suspicion of the traditional Cartesian framework for modelling it: 'Can we re-evaluate the body without resorting to outmoded Platonic and Cartesian metaphysics?' (Stelarc, 560).[3] A re-evaluation of the body with a view to overcoming its supposed obsolescence leads him, in turn, to question the Cartesian model of the self as a fixed and stable entity and makes him contend that despite the use of prosthetic add-ons such as the Third Hand, his 'strategies towards the post-human are more about erasure than affirmation' (560). These strategies do not, however, lead to 'an erasure of agency, but rather to a complexity and multiplicity of operational spaces between bodies and within bodies' (Farnell, 135).[4] In other words, the process of adding to the body demonstrates the fluid nature of the boundaries of the self by raising, for example, the question of whether the Third Hand is or is not part of the body. One might perhaps want to argue that it is simply a tool, but given the fact that it is actually controlled via the artist's stomach muscles rather than his hands, as tools tend to be, the distinction becomes blurred here. This leads to a situation during performance where the artist's body is extended beyond its biological form, giving rise to a simultaneous perception of both complexification and erasure of that form.[5] Moreover, as will become clear below, the addition of multiple inputs to control bodily functions complicates the notion of agency further still.

Stelarc immediately contradicts himself by going on to claim that 'the fundamental freedom is for individuals to determine their own DNA destiny. Biological change becomes a matter of choice rather than chance' (561). Such a freedom does not appear to be consistent with a concept of erasure of the self, as it is difficult to conceive of a determining individual without a notion of self, particularly when linked to a term such as destiny (even a DNA one, whatever that could mean).[6] In fact, what one sees here is a strategic programme of individual adaptation for specific environments with a clear and distinct goal of improved functionality which is actively and knowingly striven towards. This is teleological in the strongest sense of the term, positing as it does a unidirectional 'ladder of progress' up which one is theoretically free to climb, but is in fact presented as an imperative for the species to cope with a future that has already been mapped out. So far from positing a complexity and multiplicity of potentialities, Stelarc provides a narrative that closes off futural divergence in favour of a universal goal. As such, it is strikingly similar to the humanist narratives which he claims to repudiate, and fails to move beyond that of Clynes and Kline.

Clynes coined the term 'cyborg' in a paper co-written with fellow NASA researcher Kline entitled 'Cyborgs and space'. Here they define the cyborg as a human who 'deliberately incorporates exogenous components extending the self-regulatory control function of the organism in order to adapt it to new environments' (31). The article proposes that in order to maximize their adaptation for space travel, humans should be adjusted so as to be able to exist in space without suits; this to be achieved 'by suitable biochemical, physiological, and electronic modifications' (Clynes and Kline, 29). For Clynes and Kline, these improvements were initially limited to the homeostatic systems of the body, hence cyborg – cybernetic organism.[7]

It is perhaps worth noting that, as engineers, Clynes and Kline are simply responding to the perceived problems of space travel for astronauts; they are not making any claims for the inevitability of space travel due to some instinct such as Stelarc's primal desire for flight.[8] In fact, this particular aspect of Stelarc's discourse is more akin to religious doctrines concerning the soul's transcendence, as humans escape the limitations of their bodies to freely soar among the heavens. This places it firmly within a Cartesian mind–body dualism, even if the obsolete body is discarded via piecemeal replacement rather than being cast off at the moment of death.[9]

Cyborgian improvement need not simply be a question of linking a human to technical, or inorganic, machines. As the above quotation implies, Clynes and Kline also advocate the use of psychopharmacology in order to enhance homeostatic function. This means, among other things, that any form of drug use that improves fitness for a chosen task makes the user a cyborg. The obvious (and oft-cited) example is the regimes to which athletes subject themselves in order to improve performance at their chosen sports, whether by means of illegal substances such as steroids, or simply through the use of isotonic drinks during sports events and vitamin drips afterwards. However, it should be noted that from a functional point of view, there is no real difference between athletes' regimes and people dosing themselves with stimulants in clubs so as to be able to dance all night. The fact that certain of these practices may have long-term deleterious effects is not germane, as it is improvement for a *given* function that is the issue in both. In the same way, even though some aspects of Stelarc's performances (such as the use of flesh-hooks) cannot be said to be particularly 'good' for his body, they allow him to do things with it that would not be possible otherwise and point to possibilities for expansion that are not immediately obvious.[10]

For Clynes and Kline, the concept of the cyborg is not linked to a notion of universality where all cyborgs would have a common programme, but rather to a question of organismic divergence.[11] The cyborg is not a stable creature; it adapts to specific tasks. Moreover, these tasks may be radically different depending upon the environment in which any given cyborg has to operate. Therefore, the development of cyborgs is initially posited as a form of specific technical perfectibility rather than a teleological move towards some ultimate goal (such as the achievement of the post-human form of life). Stelarc, on the other hand, has a general teleology, even if it is only the freedom to choose one's own destiny. For this reason, his post-human is actually more human than Clynes and Kline's cyborg, which may well have these alterations foisted upon it by engineers. This latter point can clearly be seen by the fact that, apart from the aforementioned technical implants and drug use, 'Cyborgs and Space' suggests such forms of 'enlargement of function' as hypnosis to combat disturbed vestibular function (i.e. problems with balance), and a remote triggering device to shut the astronaut down should he (*sic*) become psychotic (32–3). In these cases, control of the body is clearly being ceded to outside operators, leading to what Paul Virilio calls 'presence at a distance' – a process whereby an operator can cause affections via data transfer into remote units (16).[12]

Stelarc is, of course, well aware of such developments in external control of the body: 'Technology now allows you to be moved by another *mind*' (567, italics added). In fact, as alluded to above, several of the performances (such as Stimbod) have involved his movements being controlled via remote links. He has also reversed the process and controlled the movements of volunteers from the audience via such links. It is notable that in the above quotation, he again talks about a body being controlled by another mind. This might prompt one to conclude that despite his post-human rhetoric, Stelarc's strategies fall woefully short of the claims that he makes for them, inasmuch as they never escape from Cartesianism. However, with the advent of Ping Body and Parasite, a notable disjunction between theory and performance takes place.

For these performances, Stelarc was wired up to a muscle stimulation system but, rather than his simply being controlled by a remote operator as in the Stimbod performances, data were collected via the Internet from both remote human input, and also the traffic on the Internet itself.[13] In this way, his body was stimulated to move either via the collective inputs of multiple agents, or with no power of agency involved, as the determining flows of data could not be said to be under any particular form of control. Additionally, for Parasite, data from the movements of his body were 'uploaded to a website as potential and recursive source images for body reactivation' (Stelarc, 571). In such a performance there is no unified remote operator of the biological body, and, moreover, the two-way feedback between the biological body and the Internet leads to each having an effect upon the other.

Performances such as these can be made to open up all sorts of interesting questions about bodies and their interactions with their environments. Nonetheless, one has to wonder whether the theoretical narratives with which Stelarc accompanies them are at all convincing, given that, as we have seen, his theories actually partake of the discourses that they claim to repudiate. Is it sufficient to claim that what is happening is that the body moves from the human to the post-human as it comes under the sway of multiple operators of one kind or another? One alternative, non-teleological, conceptual framework by which to approach the performances would be a trans-human rather than post-human one, the distinction between the two being that while the post-human reifies the human as a fixed point that can be passed or overtaken, the trans-human problematizes any notion of a universal fixed human subject. In order to evaluate the performances as expositions of trans-human potential, they will now be considered in terms of Deleuze and Guattari's concept of becoming.[14]

For Deleuze and Guattari, the key point about becoming is that, in accordance with their constant objections to representationalist and teleological modes of thought, it does not proceed by resemblance. This is because such a process would be one of turning into something predetermined (which is teleological) by means of imitation (which is representational). To put this in terms of Stelarc: the post-human is a predetermined goal that is striven for by means of a moving away from a representation of a supposedly universal human condition. Therefore, to think his performances as processes of becoming in the Deleuzo-Guattarian sense is to think them outside a teleological framework, and so avoid the processes of closure identified with such a framework, reopening a space for multiplicity.

'Becoming is not to imitate or identify with something or someone' (Deleuze and Guattari, 272), as that would constitute a molar process, whereas 'all becomings are molecular' (275). This distinction between two types of processes is a compositional one, hinging upon the type of connection between flows with which each is associated.[15] Molecular connections are immanent and proximal, whereas molar connections are transcendent and can occur over distance. Another way of explaining this is to say that the molecular entails bottom-up organization, with any economies (or systems) created emerging from the flows being connected, whereas the molar enforces top-down economies upon the flows. For this reason, the molar level tends to be one of domination; a body may be controlled by forces outside itself.[16] This should not be taken as meaning that Deleuze and Guattari are claiming anything as simplistic as 'molecular – good, molar – bad'. They are not trying to set up a binary opposition, but are rather pointing to elements that combine in a multiplicity of ways. It is not possible to function continuously on a level that is either purely molecular or purely molar. What Deleuze and Guattari want to establish is a state of fluidity whereby the molar does not become rigidified in such a way that it completely dominates the molecular, which is to say that it becomes associated with the endpoint of a teleological narrative of some kind.

Intimately linked to the concept of becoming is that of the rhizome, which Deleuze and Guattari identify, in contradistinction to the tree, as the form of connectivity by which becomings are generated. Arborescent connections are molar, whereas rhizomatic connections are molecular, with each point, or node, of the rhizome having the capability of joining up with any other point in a heterogeneous fashion; 'any point of a rhizome can be connected to anything other, and must be' (Deleuze and Guattari, 7). This is not a question of joining up nodes in order to show how they relate to each other. What interests Deleuze and Guattari is not so much the connection of nodes (which is what an arborescent model does), as the movement between them: it is a linear as opposed to a punctual system.[17] This allows them to speak of lines and blocks of becoming that run in both directions simultaneously, as opposed to the unidirectionality of teleological narratives. Becoming is a process of continuous movement and experimentation, not something that arrives at a goal: 'To become is not to progress or regress along a series' (Deleuze and Guattari, 238). The lines of becoming that connect the nodes in a rhizome mutually deterritorialize the nodes in question, freeing them from notions of fixed identity. Molar connections, on the other hand, are always systems of territorialization or reterritorialization, pinning nodes back to fixed economies in which they are either static or simply move along a predetermined series. However, it is not really quite so clear-cut as this, because deterritorialization is always accompanied by reterritorialization:

> The fact that there is no deterritorialization without a special reterritorialization should prompt us to rethink the abiding correlation between the molar and the molecular: no flow, no becoming-molecular escapes from a molar formation without molar components accompanying it, forming passages or perceptible land-

marks for the imperceptible processes.[18] (Deleuze and Guattari, 303)

So the key point is that the molar can never deterritorialize; only molecular becomings can do this.

The nature of the rhizome is such that it allows one to map processes, unlike the tree, which can only provide a tracing. There are two major differences between these systems: first, maps have multiple points of entry, but tracings must always be followed along the same route; and second, maps are open systems that can be modified or added to, whereas tracings are closed systems that overcode that which they model. 'The map has to do with performance, whereas the tracing always involves an alleged "competence"' (Deleuze and Guattari, 12–13).

It should be readily apparent that owing to the lack of any single overall controller of his body, Stelarc's Internet performances are distinctly rhizomatic. Rather than being subject to straightforwardly external molar connections, the molecular proliferates, deterritorializing his body and reterritorializing it as an Internet node. Additionally, as the blocks of becoming move in both directions, Stelarc deterritorializes the sites on which information about his body movements is uploaded. Consequently, the multiplicitous nature of the body is made more apparent, as it is revealed as an economy of forces that may be both extended and folded back onto itself rather than a discretely bounded stable entity. This is not a case of making the body a multiplicity; it is that already. Rather, the connection of an increasing number of feedback loops serves to bring to the fore the fact that there is no overall controller with absolute power of agency over Stelarc's body: 'Puppet strings, as a rhizome or multiplicity, are tied not to the supposed will of an artist or puppeteer but to a multiplicity of nerve fibers, which form another puppet in other dimensions connected to the first' (Deleuze and Guattari, 8). This smearing of agency across the rhizome means that this is not so much a question of presence at a distance as of distributed presence.

Whereas Stelarc's suspensions can be said to involve a process of tracing, inasmuch as the forces that distort and penetrate the body are fixed via a set number of hooks which must be deployed in a specific order so as to avoid the risk of tearing the body, his Internet performances are true mappings that can be entered at any point. It might perhaps be argued that Stelarc's body is still the ultimate focus of the performance upon which all the nodes converge. That this is not the case, however, can be borne out by visiting his Web site, where one can access a simulation of the Ping Body which uses stored data collected during performance. This allows visitors to connect to, and thereby interact with, nodes of the initial rhizome even though the 'performer' himself is no longer present.[19]

In conclusion, Stelarc's explanations of his performances have serious shortcomings in that they fail to escape from the sort of discourse that they claim to repudiate. Additionally, appeals to such notions as a primal desire for flight make transcendent universalizing claims about what it is to be human, thereby instantiating any form of movement towards a supposedly post-human condition (even if that position is one of diversification) as strongly teleological. But, at the same time, at least some of his performances significantly problematize current dominant notions of subjectivity. In so doing, they can lead to an appreciation of how the human subject position may not be the fixed universal thing that it is often supposed to be.

Rather than exhibiting the obsolescence of the body, Stelarc's Internet performances demonstrate the importance of conceptualizing technological development in terms of bodily interaction, inasmuch as they open up new spaces for encounters between the human biological form and technology. Indeed, his work shows very effectively that it is not sufficient to define the human body as a 'bipedal, breathing body with binocular vision and a 1400cc brain', as it can be, and always has been, extended beyond these supposed constraints without any concurrent loss of humanity.[20] The body is a zone of organized forces rather than a discretely bounded entity. Thus the performances do not point towards a post-human condition; they open up the possibility of novel interactions and new forms of connectivity between bodies and their environments, leading one to wonder where the body ends and the environment begins. If Stelarc's work has any importance, it is tied not to the possibilities of interstellar migration, but rather to his problematization of our ideas about bodily limits and our definitions of the human.

NOTES

1. Republished as Manfred E. Clynes and Nathan S. Kline. 'Cyborgs and space'. In *The Cyborg Handbook*. Ed. Chris Hables Gray. London: Routledge, 1995. 29–33.

2. See also Farnell, where Stelarc discusses the human in terms of 'a biological body and a single "self" that we identify as being contained within the skin' (131).

3. The Cartesian mind–body distinction has been subject to refinement over the years. However, given that the majority of (and certainly the most popular) current theories of body and subjectivity derive from Kant and Freud, and that both these frameworks owe much to Descartes, it does not seem unfair to group them under the umbrella of Cartesianism.

4. The allusion to spaces within bodies refers to the series of performances such as Hollow Body, where various items, including sculptures and endoscopes, were inserted into Stelarc's stomach.

5. The idea of redrawing the body's boundaries via add-ons is not actually as novel as Stelarc might like to think; it was readily appreciated as early as the eighteenth century. Consider Immanuel Kant on the use of peripheral devices to upgrade and enhance data storage and retrieval: 'The pocket notebook is a great convenience in which to write everything stored in our head and to find it easily and exactly. The art of writing always remains a splendid art, because, even if it is not used to impart knowledge to others, it will still substitute for the most extensive and reliable memory, and can compensate for the lack of it' (76). Kant, of course, would claim that this is an extension rather than erasure of the self's boundaries, but one can see that the idea of technically enhancing the body in order to better suit it to particular tasks is not exactly new.

6. An alternative possibility would be that the erasure of self left one with a determining event, but then events are not *free* to choose, inasmuch as the concept of an event does not imply any notion of agency.

7. They later extended the definition to include systems other than the homeostatic; see Gray.

8. In fact, it is quite possible that the only reason they linked cyborgs to space travel at all is that they were being funded by NASA. Elsewhere, Clynes simply describes cyborgian development as 'a human enlargement of function' (Gray, 47).

9. Counter-arguments to this will undoubtedly point to Stelarc's mobilization of terminology derived from evolutionary theory ('DNA destiny', etc.). However, this is to read such theories as teleological, which is incorrect. Natural selection is not a question of a drive to improvement; it proceeds

via extermination. For a fairly straightforward exposition of this, see Gould (31–5).

10. The insertion of a stomach sculpture during Hollow Body, for example, though carried out mainly for aesthetic purposes, also demonstrates the ability of the biological body to carry functioning technological devices within it. In a way, it points on a large scale to the possibility of nanotech monitoring systems.

11. Cf. Stelarc: 'the body is redesigned – diversifying in form and functions' (560).

12. The example which Virilio provides is actually of a 'robotic double' (16). However, there seems to be no reason why it could not be extended to encompass remote-controlled humans.

13. Additionally, in some performances parts of his body remained under local control.

14. For a cogent exposition of Deleuze and Guattari as trans-human thinkers, see Ansell Pearson, esp. 123–50.

15. The term 'flow' is used to delineate the forces out of which the world is constituted.

16. Clynes and Kline's remote controlled cyborg and its operator constitute a molar assemblage, for example.

17. 'What constitutes arborescence is the submission of the line to the point' (Deleuze and Guattari, 293).

18. An example should help to clarify this: in its early stages, the Internet could be regarded as, for the most part, deterritorialized, in that molecular connections between ever-expanding nodes were occurring with very little in the way of control mechanisms. However, increased commercialization has brought reterritorialization by, among other mechanisms, content monitoring and preferred placements. Such features are molar in that rather than being immanent to the way the system functions, they are imposed upon it by external forces which then limit the potential of the system.

19. Underneath the simulation is the enticing message: 'Stelarc isn't currently attached but might be for future performances' (Zebington, non-pag.).

20. Additionally, there are large numbers of individuals in this world who do not fit this description, and would be very surprised, not to say distinctly unhappy, to discover that they are inhuman.

WORKS CITED

Ansell Pearson, Keith. *Viroid Life: Perspectives on Nietzsche and the Transhuman Condition*. London: Routledge, 1997.

Atzori, Paolo and Kirk Woolford. 'Extended-body: interview with Stelarc'. N.d. 28 September 2000. <www.ctheory.net/text_file.asp?pick=71>.

Clynes, Manfred E. and Nathan S. Kline. 'Cyborgs and space'. In *The Cyborg Handbook*. Ed. Chris Hables Gray. London: Routledge, 1995. 29–33.

Deleuze, Gilles and Félix Guattari. *A Thousand Plateaus: Capitalism and Schizophrenia*. Trans. Brian Massumi. London: Athlone, 1988.

Farnell, Ross. 'In dialogue with "posthuman" bodies: interview with Stelarc'. In *Body Modification*. Ed. Mike Featherstone. London: Sage, 2000. 129–47.

Gould, Stephen Jay. *Wonderful Life: The Burgess Shale and the Nature of History*. London: Penguin, 1991.

Gray, Chris Hables. 'An interview with Manfred Clynes'. In *The Cyborg Handbook*. Ed. Chris Hables Gray. London: Routledge, 1995. 43–53.

Kant, Immanuel. *Anthropology from a Pragmatic Point of View*. Trans. Victor Lyle Dowdell. Carbondale: Southern Illinois University Press, 1978.

Stelarc. 'From psycho-body to cyber-systems: images as post-human entities'. In *The Cybercultures Reader*. Ed. David Bell and Barbara M. Kennedy. London: Routledge, 2000. 560–76.

Virilio, Paul. *Open Sky*. Trans. Julie Rose. London: Verso, 1997.

Zebington, Gary, ed. *The Stelarc Site*. N.d. 28 September 2000. <www.stelarc.va.com.au/>.

CHAPTER 7

Probings: An Interview with Stelarc

JOANNA ZYLINSKA AND GARY HALL

Joanna Zylinska and Gary Hall: There have been a lot of scare stories recently concerning developments in technology. We wanted to start by asking you how you felt your work stood in relation to that. For example, to what extent can your art and performances be seen as part of, or as a reaction to, what is often described as a 'general crisis in the natural', revealed in debates over genetically modified food, cloning, prosthetics, cybernetics, globalization, surveillance, video games, technologies of war, etc.?

Stelarc: I started using technology when I was still at art school in the late sixties. I had constructed helmets and goggles that split your binocular perception, and sensory compartments that you plugged your whole body into. The body was immersed in a kinetic environment of images and electronic sounds. So I can't really say that any of the work is a counterpoint to, or a critique of, these recent issues. For me the body has always been a prosthetic body. Ever since we evolved as hominids and developed bipedal locomotion, two limbs became manipulators. We have become creatures that construct tools, artefacts and machines. We've always been augmented by our instruments, our technologies. Technology is what constructs our humanity; the trajectory of technology is what has propelled human developments. I've never seen the body as purely biological, so to consider technology as a kind of alien 'other' that happens upon us at the end of the millennium is rather simplistic. I don't see any of these recent controversies as a crisis of the natural, or if there has been a crisis, it's taken place over a much longer period of time due to all these cultural inscriptions, metaphysical assumptions and philosophies that we've been propagating.

J.Z. and G.H.: That's really interesting. It seems to clear up some of the questions that have been raised in relation to your work, particularly those concerning the idea that you're constructing some evolutionary narrative of development, from the human to what you call 'the post-human'. It's not that there was once a 'pure' body and that this has somehow been contaminated as we have entered the so-called 'technological age'. Rather, the human here seems to be born out of the relationship with technology.

Stelarc: Yes. I've done performances where my body becomes, or is partly, taken over by an external agency. I've become very intrigued about identity, the self, free will and agency in these performances. What happens when half of your body is being remotely prompted by a person in another place? It's strange when you find the other half can collaborate with local agency. From moment to moment your body is performing a movement that you neither have an immediate memory of nor a desire to perform. The more and more performances I do, the less and less I think I have a mind of my own – nor any mind at all in the traditional metaphysical sense. What you have here is an obsolete body that seems to have evolved as an absent body and has now been invaded by technology, a body that is hollow, that now performs involuntarily for remote people over the Internet. These alternative and involuntary experiences with technology allow you to question what a body is, what it means to be human. We have a fear of the zombie and an anxiety of the cyborg, but really it's a fear of what we've always been and what we have already become. I've always thought that we've been simultaneously zombies and cyborgs; we've never really had a mind of our own and we've never been purely biological entities.

J.Z. and G.H.: The 'zombies' and 'cyborgs' you are talking about are often associated with the sort of anxiety evoked by technology that we started by alluding to. However, your work also seems to create another sense of anxiety: that which is played out in critical responses to your art, and particularly your writing. We're thinking here especially of Keith Ansell Pearson's decision to turn away from what he regards as the 'banal' (231) interpretation that is put forward in your own commentaries on your work, towards your art practice, which Ansell Pearson sees as providing a more interesting and complicated reading of your art. Maybe it's this anxiety that is urging your interpreters and critics to pin you down and decide: you're either saying this or that?

Stelarc: I think it's also a result of my being found wanting between the realm of my production on the one hand and trying to articulate my ideas on the other. If you're doing performances simply to illustrate your ideas, that doesn't work! And if you're trying to justify your actions through a prosthesis of textual analysis, that doesn't work either. But there is sometimes an uncomfortable feedback loop when your performances start generating ideas, so it's not always easy to resolve or to evaluate what's affecting what. Unfortunately, what often happens is that people are critiquing your work more from what you've written than what you're doing. Often they haven't actually seen a performance. Then you've got other issues like 'art and the audience', and 'art and entertainment'. Doing the performance with three hands writing EVOLUTION at the Maki Gallery in 1982 was very tedious for the people who saw that, if we evaluate it as an entertaining action. The idea was that one can simultaneously write with three hands, each hand writing a separate letter at the same time. Not being ambidextrous, this was quite a feat for me. Sometimes one image can encapsulate a whole performance – and that's what happens with the EVOLUTION event. But that was probably not entertaining for the audience. On the other hand, there's EXOSKELETON, the six-legged walking machine. This is a 600-kilogram robot that walks on six legs. It walks backwards, forwards, sideways; it squats, it lifts, it turns. This performance can't be captured by one image alone. People are often unamazed because you can see much faster and fancier robots done with digital animation. But what's interesting for me is not simply going more and more virtual but rather exploring the interface between the actual and the virtual. I'm trying to investigate whether a physical body can function in a virtual immersive environment and whether an intelligent avatar might be able to perform in the real world by possessing a physical body. They are the sorts of issues that are more interesting – rather than moving increasingly into artificial intelligence and virtual reality.

J.Z. and G.H.: That seems to tie in with your description of the cyborg more in terms of a 'speculation' which we shouldn't see as 'a kind of either/or situation' or 'a dogmatic formulation of some utopian vision' (Stelarc, non-pag.). This element of hesitation, pointing to a process rather than a state of events, makes your perception of the cyborg quite different from some essentialist descriptions of cyborgs as people with artificial limbs, pacemakers or implanted corneal lenses.

Stelarc: I'm much more interested in what happens between states, between people – not so much at the boundary but *between* boundaries. And to question what constitutes boundaries, to undermine them altogether. I want to explore the slippage, the ambiguities, the ambivalences. I'm talking about redesigning the body because I see the body as an evolutionary architecture for operating an awareness in the world. Modify the biological apparatus and you modify its experience of the world.

J.Z. and G.H.: Virilio accused you of eugenics . . .

Stelarc: Well, speculating about the design of the body in this way does not sanction social engineering. It just confronts the problem of a body that could function in alternative ways. I like Virilio's writings, but I think his Catholic background allows him to accept the consequences of technologies and the accidents that emanate from them as long as they are seemingly external to the body. He sees the skin as a boundary. On the one side there is the bounded self and on the other there is the world. He found it very disconcerting when I started inserting electronic objects, like the STOMACH SCULPTURE, into the body. The point where technology invades the body is the point where hysteria is usually generated. In the early seventies I filmed 3 metres of internal space into the stomach, lungs and intestines, so right from the very beginning I was interested in these internal and external probes of the body. For me skin has never been a bounding interface. Of course, skin is the largest organ of our bodies and it contains heat sensors, touch sensors, pain sensors. It's also a very complex organ which allows us to perceive the world in all sorts of subtlety. But I've never considered it as a kind of bounding of the self, and this is what Virilio, I believe, finds a little disturbing. All these discussions about redesigning the body are my speculations or probes about what might happen if one was able to redesign the body more radically. In his article included in *Escape Velocity: Cyberculture at the End of the Century*, Mark Dery cites a medical doctor who criticizes this idea of synthetic skin. Of course, holistically, you can't just simply alter a part of the body without altering everything else about it. But there is something thought-provoking in speculating about what might happen if we could just simply construct a synthetic skin with several capabilities like, for example, permeability to oxygen and an ability to function in a sophisticated photosynthetic way. There is no practical medical, surgical way of doing it at the moment. These are meant to be tentative speculations that generate some kind of discourse rather than serious medical proposals to presently alter the body's make-up. So, in summary, what I'm really interested in is what happens when disruptions and transgressions occur – *not* devising utopian or social engineering schemes for some kind of dogmatic agenda. And none of my own writings have been anything more than poetic speculations. They're not elaborated, they are not academically examined, I don't use extensive citations. That doesn't mean that I haven't read Virilio, Baudrillard, Lyotard, Derrida, and a lot of other theorists. It doesn't mean that I haven't inadvertently appropriated some of their ideas. But these ideas can only be authenticated through the performances that I do and they only have meaning when generated by these performances. So that's the reason I write the way I do, and don't academically cite the writings of others.

J.Z. and G.H.: Referring to your bodily experiments such as the Movatar and the Stomach Sculpture, you claim that the hollow body becomes a host. Is this kind of intervention based on violence? Or can it be seen as a form of hospitality (i.e. of welcoming 'the other' within the self)?

Stelarc: I would hasten to add that it's more generous than violent; more an opening up of the body. A hollow body can be a better host – either for technology or for remote and virtual agents. A lot of these performances, like the STOMACH SCULPTURE, have been physically difficult. First, the sculpture was about 50 mm in length and 15 mm in diameter. This was the largest rigid object that we could push down the oesophagus without scraping it badly. When it got into the stomach cavity, this object opened to about 50 mm in diameter and 75 mm in length – the size of a small fist. Of course, this object could have been made smaller but I wanted to construct something that filled up the stomach cavity, that had interesting operations, and that could be retrieved afterwards. The sculpture was made of titanium, stainless steel, gold and silver – biocompatible materials that weren't going to react to the stomach fluids. I got this idea for an internal sculpture when a friend of mine, Tony Figallo, sent a clipping for proposals for the Fifth Australian Sculpture Triennial, whose theme was site-specific works. I'd never contributed to a sculpture triennial before, even though I'd been trained as a sculptor. So I thought, instead of doing a sculpture for a public space, why not construct a sculpture for an internal space? This conjured up all sorts of problems: How do I safely insert it into the body? How do I get it out again? How can I make it operational? If it's got a flashing light and a beeping sound and it moves – how am I actually going to do this? When you're amplifying body signals and sounds like brain waves, heartbeat, blood flow, and you're hearing them outside your body, your body in a sense morphs from this humanoid space to a gallery space and you have this sensation of emptying out your body. This was my first experience of a hollow body. As it was when I made the video probes. A hollow body is a host body. So in this way the body is not simply a site for a psyche but becomes a host for a sculpture. In the performance FRACTAL FLESH for Telepolis, people in other places could remotely access and actuate a body. People at the Pompidou Centre in Paris, the Media Lab in Helsinki and the Doors of Perception Conference in Amsterdam were connected to my body, located in Luxembourg. We had video screens at either end, so I could always see the face of the person who was programming my body movements, and they in turn could always see the result of their choreography. These images were always superimposed so we could see each other. That created a kind of intimacy without proximity and it gave you the sense of being 'possessed' by that remote agent. In the other Internet performances, PING BODY and PARASITE, issues of telematic scaling of the body were explored. The body is activated, is animated, not by people in other places but by Internet data and images. The Internet becomes a kind of crude external nervous system, optically stimulating and electrically actuating the body. It's never been an issue of control (actually in most of these performances what is explored is the alternative, the involuntary). That's another thing that is always brought up in relation to new technologies and, more specifically, my own work: 'Who is going to control you?' There's this kind of Foucauldian focus on control, on constraint. But what is more meaningful is to see this not as a master–slave relationship with issues of control, but rather as issues of access and of actuation, of hosting and of multiple agency.

J.Z. and G.H.: It only works in this scenario when we believe that we control the body beforehand and then technology comes and takes over.

Stelarc: That's right. But one can look at it not so much as an issue of control as an issue of complexity. What we're really constructing are more and more feedback loops between the body and other bodies and its environment, whether technological, cultural, social or whatever, and this makes for a much more interesting extended operational system. And that's another way of seeing the cyborg. Not as a kind of *Terminator 2* body, a medical military model, but rather as a system, as a multiplicity of bodies, spatially separated but electronically connected with the Internet as a kind of external nervous system, being able to perform remote functions and transmit images and information in intimate and intense ways. And if we see the issues of the involuntary body and remote stimulation as issues of body complexity rather than body control, then there's no dilemma. As you said, it's only a problem if you maintain these very distinct boundaries, if you make these distinctions – and I don't.

J.Z. and G.H.: The metaphor of connectivity seems to be a recurrent motif in your work. It also serves as something of a guiding thread for this book, which brings together work on both Orlan and yourself. With this in mind, do you see any points of connection or convergence between Orlan's performances and your own?

Stelarc: What I've always admired about Orlan is that she takes the physical consequences of her ideas. That's the difference between performance and the other two-dimensional arts. If I wanted to suspend my body, I had to cope with the physical difficulty of inserting hooks into the skin. If I wanted to insert a sculpture inside my body, I had to take the medical consequences of scraping the oesophagus and the uncomfortable feeling and the trauma of transgressing the body in that difficult way. If I wanted to explore six-legged insect-like loco-motion, I had to come up with DM 75,000 to construct such a machine and then cope with having to navigate this powerful and heavy robot. You have to take the physical consequences of these projects and Orlan does that. I really found the idea of appropriating these archetypal facial features and incorporating them into one physical body seductive. She's very much a postmodern performance artist, more so than myself. In general, what we have in common, with a lot of other performance artists before us, is that you are dealing on a human scale with the biological body, with its physiology, and you have to put up with the physical difficulties involved.

But I suspect we make very different metaphysical assumptions as to what we mean by the obsolete body. The body is obsolete in form and function. But we cannot operate disembodied. We cannot discard the body. It is not the object manipulated by a subject. I think for Orlan, she speaks of herself as a kind of psyche encapsulated in a physical body. Of course, language makes it difficult to speak without referring to an 'I'. But when this body speaks as an 'I', it understands that the notion 'I' in the English language is a simplification of a much more complex relationship between bodies, between the body and its culture and social institutions, between the body and its technologies. Our language tends to reinforce Platonic, Cartesian and Freudian constructs of internal representations, of essences, of egos. I think we have to get away from these notions and try to construct a body that is not simplistically a split mind and brain. This body is not in a kind of Cartesian theatre of 'I' as opposed to 'my physical body'. This body doesn't simplistically store images and information inside its head. Rather, the brain can be seen as a soft neuronal tissue that quivers and communicates with electrical signals. It conjures up images and ideas through a constant feedback of stimulation from its environment and words from other bodies and cultural histories, cultural inscriptions. It's wrong to talk of the 'I' as a kind of essence which possesses information and images of the world, and which navigates its body in order to perform certain actions. I suspect that when Orlan speaks of 'giving her body to art', she's taking a metaphysical stand that's somewhat Cartesian. That might be a misrepresentation. But this body considers itself a body without a mind in a traditional metaphysical sense, a hollow body which becomes not only a host for miniaturized technological components but also a body of multiple agencies remotely interacting with it, a body that has a much more fluid sense of self: not so much a split self from a body but rather a self that is extruded. I like the word 'extruded' because it visualizes the extension into the environment but doesn't produce a Cartesian split. So, at certain times, this body feels; it intimately exchanges words and emotions. At other times this body communicates remotely; it images itself as an evolutionary object.

When I talk about the obsolete body I don't mean that we should discard bodies altogether, but rather that a body with this form and these functions cannot operate effectively in the technological terrain that it has created. The obsolete body is not about a loathing of the body; it's not about discarding the body altogether. It's rather about speculating on how the body has evolved and, in a technological terrain that it has created, how the body has problems coping with the sort of intense information that is really alien to its own sensory apparatus, how it measures bits of information in scales that it can't experience. And then technology often outperforms the human body and acceler-ates the body so that it escapes from the gravitational pull of the Earth and finds itself in alien environments. So in these ways the body becomes obsolete. The question is not so much whether we discard bodies but rather how to rethink the design of the body: is this an adequate architecture for perpetuating intelligent life in a technological realm and in an extraterrestrial environment? These notions are not about science fiction or a kind of New Age, West Coast *Wired* culture yearning to transcend the body. What irritates me is people who see the Internet and virtual reality systems as strategies of escaping the body. You don't escape the body; you function differently with the interfaces that produce these immersive and interactive effects. You construct an extended operational system that functions beyond the biology of the body and beyond the local space it inhabits.

J.Z. and G.H.: Isn't this 'obsolescence of the body' you speak about also, to some extent, about the end of a certain notion of technology (at least, that which positions technology as extrinsic to human nature) as only an instrument of knowledge?

Stelarc: I think we're constantly re-evaluating the notion of what it means to be a body, what constitutes our humanity. An intelligent agent has to be embodied and embedded in the world; you can't have an intelligent entity without some kind of physical interface to a complex environment. In fact, recent experiments and research into artificial intelligence are no longer limited to studying artificial intelligence and artificial life as computer models, as entities in a virtual world, because you just can't model the complexity of the real world in a virtual environment. So what people are doing now is building simple robots, placing them in the real world and then seeing what sort of emergent behaviour occurs. These simple robots might have only three or four sensors such as proximity, touch and light sensors. What they're finding is that these artificial life forms with neural nets are capable of basic learning, like how to avoid obstacles, how to maximize their lifespan and charge their batteries, how to cooperate in gathering tasks. They develop simple social and flocking behaviours. It's really important to understand what it means to be an intelligent agent. At the moment we don't know how a disembodied intelligent agent could interact in any way with images and information that enable it to communicate and to develop social and cultural histories. Now of course how the intelligent agent is embodied might mean that a purely biological entity is inadequate. Perhaps having only a robot body is equally inadequate and that it's only through the hybridization of these two operational systems that we can perpetuate intelligent life. But there are also other possibilities, other scenarios – for example, that post-human life may no longer reside in bodies and machines but in intelligent, operational and autonomous images sustained on the Internet. In other words, viral bits of code that morph, mutate, replicate and proliferate on the Internet function in much faster and more complex ways than even human bodies and machines might. But, of course, that's predicated on the notion that the Internet becomes increasingly a much more complex environment. I think there is no longer a simplistic scenario of machines replacing bodies or becoming totally disembodied within the electronic space of the Internet. What we have are multiple possibilities which are equally interesting as scenarios, and these scenarios enable us to probe what it means to be a body, what it means to have a body, and whether it's meaningful any more to consider having a mind of our own.

J.Z. and G.H.: A number of art reviews of both Orlan's work and your own have been devoted to 'determining' whether this kind of perform-ance 'deserves' to be perceived as art. It's a similar kind of anxiety to that we talked about before, one that seems to be generated by your writing. What is it that these guardians of aesthetic standards are most afraid of, or disturbed by, in your work? What kind of challenges do Orlan and yourself pose to the traditional idea of art?

Stelarc: Oh, what determines whether it is art is dependent on a rather complex set of assumptions, expectations and of course what artists produce – whether they be objects or performances. Art already has a tradition of exposing, undermining and developing alternative strategies and aesthetics. Nothing new here in what Orlan or I do. And if my writing does generate uncertainty, anxiety, if it makes these small disruptions and creates these little slippages, that sounds good to me. The performances aren't meant to be illustrative and self-explanatory. When I come and see a work of art, I want to go away asking questions, not feeling satisfied or entertained. Art is a means of opening up the world, opening up to the world. It is not about closure, it is not about comfortable reassurance. A problem about the postmodern is that it becomes incestuous in its discourse through its strategies of appropriation and juxtaposition. It deconstructs, but it does not escape its own self-referentiality. The seductiveness of technology is the seductiveness of providing alternative possibilities, of new strategies in both conceptualizing and visualizing the arts. With technologies we get the new aesthetics of computer animation, of morphing, of interactive and immersive virtual reality environments, of remotely interacting with other bodies, of the Internet itself as a medium of expression, allowing us to use search engines to construct meta-narratives. This is a very powerful new approach in the arts and it's able to employ this vast rhizomatic bank of information and images. That's how I see the seduction of technology.

Coming back to Orlan, people have pointed out differences and similarities between us. One is that what Orlan does to her body is pretty much a permanent change: if she does an operation to change the shape of her face, it stays changed. If I put on a third hand, I can detach it; I can in a sense live a normal life outside my performance activity.

J.Z. and G.H.: But what about the Extra Ear?
Stelarc: The EXTRA EAR is different. It is seen as a soft prosthesis. And similarly to Orlan, this will be a permanent construction on my body – a soft prosthesis. And it goes beyond the realm of cosmetic surgery. All my performances explore the notion of the prosthetic body, whether the body has bits of technology attached to it or, as with the MOVATAR, the body itself becomes a prosthesis for manifesting the behaviour of an intelligent avatar in the real world. The six-legged walking machine and the EXTRA EAR are two different approaches to a prosthesis. The EXOSKELETON is the largest prosthetic extension of the body that I've been involved with, while the STOMACH SCULPTURE, as an insert, is the smallest. The EXTRA EAR becomes a kind of soft prosthesis constructed from the skin and cartilage from the body. It'll need to be pinned to the cranium using titanium pins. The EXTRA EAR has been designed to be a permanent facial feature.

In fact, the THIRD HAND was also originally designed as a semi-permanent attachment to my body; I was supposed to be wearing it as much as I would wear my clothing. The reason why it did not happen was that the hand was never built out of carbon fibre. I had to resort to using aluminium, stainless steel, Duralamin and acrylic – materials that were more easily scratched or damaged or fractured. Also, the electrode gel where the muscle signals were picked up and preamplified irritated the skin, and so the THIRD HAND then became more a performance object.

So the notion of permanent prosthetic attachments was always a possibility with my work. The problem of the EXTRA EAR being a permanent attachment is not thought of as an issue. The difficulty is that it goes beyond cosmetic surgery. It's not just a matter of me having enough money to pay for an operation, because this involves more than one kind of medical practitioner. It's going to involve reconstructive surgery, skin stretching, some orthopaedic work and perhaps some micro-surgery. And because it's an issue of excess, it becomes more and more a problem of medical ethics. Although cosmetic and plastic surgery is now considered a part of conventional medical practice, to construct extra body parts would just not be allowed ordinarily in a tightly regulated medical profession.

J.Z. and G.H.: A lot of your concern, in recent years especially, has been with technology, or technical strategies, that take machinic form: bionics, robotics, etc. – hence your Third Hand, the six-legged walking machine of Exoskeleton, etc. Even your Stomach Sculpture/Hollow Body performance consisted of the insertion into the body of a sculpture in the form of a machine or device. We know you've talked elsewhere about the relation between electronic technology and bio-technology, and the way the one in many ways led to the other as a result of greater programming power (Stelarc, non-pag.). But why this concentration on technology in this form as opposed to, say, things at the more micro end of the scale, such as biotechnology, genetics or cloning? Would you consider experimenting with microtechnologies, with genetics, hormones, viruses, bacteria, etc.?
Stelarc: That's a good question. Having grown up in the late sixties, early seventies, this was a time when people dropped acid, chewed mushrooms and experimented with brain chemistry. Timothy Leary stands for that kind of exploration of body and brain chemistry. I was at Carnegie Mellon University three years ago. They have a good biology department there, and I was really interested in the idea of growing muscle cells and experimenting with involuntary muscle movements, but on a smaller, isolated scale. However, I discovered that even though I could grow muscle cells, they didn't form actual muscle fibre. There are lots of things that you can't do yet. For example, with embryonic stem cells, we can now theoretically grow any organ in its full complexity, and steps are being taken to do this. But it probably won't be for fifty to a hundred years that we can really

grow organs. Of course, there are all sorts of ethical issues to begin with there as well. How do you acquire these stem cells? From aborted foetuses?

As an artist I want to be able to construct something that's an actual interface that I can experience directly. So I guess I've been more interested in technological augmentation or extension because you can deal with that as a component part rather than in a more fuzzy and uncontrollable way, like taking drugs. Genetic intervention will not radically alter the parameters of the body anyway. I think we are caught up in a period of time when we're talking about cloning and embryonic stem cells, growing organs and all these sorts of genetic intervention, but in reality we are not going to be able to do this in any meaningful way for a while yet. Other artists, though, like Eduardo Kac, have found ways to incorporate genetic techniques into art.

J.Z. and G.H.: When talking about the transformation of the body through the intrusion of nanotechnologies (or microminiaturized robots, as you call them), you say that 'the body becomes the landscape of machines' (Stelarc, non-pag.). Is the transformation of the body the way you envisage and stage it coupled with the change of its environment?

Stelarc: This is a very significant event in human history. At the same time that we're landing satellites on other planetary bodies, technology is landing on the human body. Initially, technology is seen as external and proliferating in the human landscape, but as technology becomes more and more microminiaturized it is also more and more human in scale. It can then constitute a component of the body, not simply to be attached but also to be implanted. Technology becomes increasingly more biocompatible. With nanotechnology we get to a scale of technology that is even below our sensory level. We may not be able to see or feel these microminiaturized machines, yet we can conceive them recolonizing the human body, augmenting our bacterial and viral populations. Biocompatibility that comes from microminiaturized scale is one of the significant events to have occurred in the twentieth century. Instead of containing the body, machines now become a component of the body. One can conjecture that a lot of future technology will be invisible because it will be contained inside the body. This kind of flip of the relationship between the body and its machines leads to a possibility of hybridization we didn't anticipate before. We thought of the cyborg as the sci-fi version of the body plugged into a robotic superstructure. Here you have a situation where biological bodies might survive with their form and functions but as hosts to microminiaturized machines. Of course, microminiaturized machines might serve medical purposes, surveillance purposes and other operational purposes within the body environment. At the moment, the design of the body is deficient in internal surveillance. But maybe in the future we'll be able to detect cancerous growths or blockages in our circulatory systems or pathological changes in temperature or chemistry early enough with these surveillance systems inside the body.

J.Z. and G.H.: To round off our discussion, perhaps you could say a few words about one of your more recent projects, the Movatar.
Stelarc: Originally I thought of the MOVATAR as an inverse motion capture system driven by a muscle stimulation interface. The seduction was the idea that an electrical flow would be created from the intelligent avatar into the human body. Muscle stimulation is quite smooth and produces fairly humanlike movements contracting muscles. I decided instead to go with a motion prosthesis, which is a pneumatically operated device with six degrees of freedom that wraps around the upper torso and arms and actuates the body with giff-like actions. It allows you to perform very precise and fast movements resembling basic computer animation. It will result in a kind of split body situation. It can be thought of as a kind of viral agent. The MOVATAR stays dormant but when it's connected to a host body it becomes active and it can actuate the body. Like a virus, it lies dormant, but when it's coupled with the host in the right environment then it can come alive. And so the MOVATAR is a kind of viral life form which will evolve in its interaction with the body. It doesn't have its own virtual environment; its environment is this interface with the real world through the physical body. In a limited sense it learns from previous experience. It will have evolutionary or genetic algorithms that allow its behaviour to be modified continuously and independently

of the human body. Also, when the physical body moves, it will generate the pneumatic sounds of compressed air, of relay switch clicks, of other sampled sounds of the motion prosthesis. These sounds will be fed back, or looped back, into the MOVATAR's program. In effect, the MOVATAR has an ear in the world, it will be affected by the sound the physical body produces, while the sound that's fed back to the MOVATAR produces a kind of startle response, so there's feedback from the real world. We're thinking also of the vision system that monitors the leg movements instead of sensors, and in that case the MOVATAR would have a kind of eye in the world as well that would allow it to process information back from the real world and incorporate it into its evolving program. These visualizations are just 3-D computer simulations indicating how this six-degrees-of-freedom motion prosthesis would function and what kinds of movements it would be able to create.

J.Z. and G.H.: It's interesting to think in what way the Movatar project challenges and pushes the whole problem of agency.

Stelarc: In the MOVATAR, you blur the distinctions between the virtual and the actual. We're doing this already with motion capture systems. If I have position/orientation sensors on my body, these allow the computer to monitor and map my movements onto a computer body, onto a virtual entity, and I can choreograph that virtual body from the real world. But here we have an inverse motion capture system, so the opposite occurs. What happens if an avatar which is imbued with artificial intelligence, which is increasingly autonomous and operational, wants to perform in a real world? It can do so by possessing a physical body. In my previous performances the body had prosthetic bits and pieces attached to or implanted inside it, but here the body itself becomes a prosthesis for the manifestation of a virtual entity's behaviour. I think it's an interesting new possibility. And since MOVATAR will be a VRML entity on a Web site, theoretically anybody anywhere can log onto it. And, provided they possess such an exoskeleton interface, the MOVATAR could perform with anybody in any place, either sequentially, one body at a time, or simultaneously with clusters of bodies, spatially separated from it but electronically

JOANNA ZYLINSKA AND GARY HALL

connected to it. So you have this virtual choreography of physical bodies, of possessed and performing bodies. I just find that a very beautiful concept.

WORKS CITED

Ansell Pearson, Keith. 'Life becoming body: on the "meaning" of posthuman evolution'. *Cultural Values* 1:2 (1997): 219–40.

Dery, Mark. *Escape Velocity: Cyberculture at the End of the Century*. London: Hodder & Stoughton, 1996.

Stelarc. 'An interview by Yiannis Melanitis'. *Arc: Journal of Research and Critical Curating*, <http://a-r-c.gold.ac.uk/reftexts/inter_melanitis.html>.

130

CHAPTER 8

Para-Site

GARY HALL

Parasite *n* useless person who lives on the resources of others. (*Penguin English Dictionary*)

. . . the parasite both belongs and does not belong to what it inhabits: breaching and compromising the identity of the body or host which it inhabits, its 'own' identity is of a different order, being at once *para-* ('beside') and *non-para-*, inside and outside, coming to figure what is at once the same as and different from itself. (Nicholas Royle)

I mean, technology, I think, comes from the Greek word '*tekhne*' meaning 'skills', so technology is not just about hardware but rather a way of skilfully manipulating, a way of technically modifying, a way of electronically constructing . . . (Stelarc)

*The following was produced as part of an experiment in developing written works specific to the digital medium. In modifying the text for publication here I have endeavoured to retain as much as possible the marks of its original form. Itself a text on the relation between art, writing and new technology in the work of the performance artist Stelarc, 'Para-Site' was originally devised as a Web site, and was intended to act as a supplement or shadow to Stelarc's own Web site, <**www.stelarc.va.com.au**>. The Stelarc 'Para-Site' was constructed by weaving together passages of text using hypertext links (indicated here in **bold** and by the use of numbers and 'go to' signs) to form a kind of textual web between its various component parts, each passage functioning as an electronic gateway to a number of other digital locations 'within' the site.*

*Additional hypertext links (again indicated in **bold**) were then used to interweave this textual web with texts and images on the artist's own Web site, with still further links being made to some of the other texts by Stelarc available on the Web. (In the 'paper' version published here, the relevant references and URLs are provided in a section of 'Notes'.) In this way the Stelarc 'Para-Site' was designed to enter into both a prosthetic and a parasitical relationship with its 'host': augmenting, extending, modifying and reconfiguring it, but also invading, disturbing, contaminating and infecting it.*

1. APORIA

How are we to understand the impact of the new, digital communications technologies on the way in which we think about and experience the world? Can the effects of CDs, VCRs, DVDs, cell phones, computers, printers, faxes, digital televisions, teleconferences, communications satellites, the Internet, the World Wide Web, hypertext, email, the e-book, Bluetooth, etc. be interpreted using the frameworks and methods of analysis that are already at our disposal? Is it not these very modes of critical interpretation that CDs, cell phones, computers, and the like challenge and bring into question, with their alterations in the divisions between subject and object, public and private, fact and fiction? Do these new communications technologies therefore require the invention of new forms of knowledge and new techniques of analysis? To approach them with anything else is to risk overlooking what is radically new about these technologies, confining them instead to a known and recognized past. And yet there is a danger that any such 'new' approach will itself leave the analysis of such technologies tied to the past, not least by ignoring the way in which they are themselves based upon, and therefore intricately bound up with, far older forms – one just has to look at the continuing print-based aesthetics of the Internet and World Wide Web, as indicated by terms such as Web *pages, folders, files, documents*, to see that. It is this radical critical **aporia** [go to 17] that the performance artist **Stelarc** [go to 2] confronts, and confronts us with [go to 15].

17. THE ETHICS OF NEW TECHNOLOGY

Of course, the **aporia** [go to 1] between the 'invention that finds what was already there and the one that produces new mechanisms or **new spaces**' [go to 13] could be said to lie at the heart of all analysis and interpretation. However, it is highlighted by the new communications technologies, which have the effect of alienating the normal and the usual, estranging it, and thus forcing us to see it again, as if for the first time, to account for it and to judge it anew. Following J. Hillis Miller, we might call this responsibility which is imposed upon us by these inventions something like **the ethics of new technology** [go to 11].

13. REINVENTING INVENTION

Jacques Derrida has observed that the task that confronts us when it comes to understanding **developments in technology** [go to 1] is to rethink the relation between those forms of analysis that merely find what is known and familiar, and those that contain the possibility of discovering that which is new, strange and previously unseen:

> . . . we have to rethink the relations between knowing and acting, between constative speech acts and **performative speech acts** [go to 14], between the invention that finds what was already there and the one that produces new mechanisms or **new spaces** [go to 22]. In the undecidable and at the moment of a decision that has no common ground with any other, we have to **reinvent invention** [go to 11] and conceive of another 'pragmatics'. (Jacques Derrida)

11. 'THE ETHICS OF HYPERTEXT'

A hypertext . . . offers the reader the necessity of deciding which path to follow through the text, or of letting chance choose for him or her. Nor is there any 'right' choice, that is, one justified objectively, by a pre-existing meaning. A hypertext demands that we choose at every turn and that we take **responsibility** [go to

19] for our choices. This is **the ethics of hypertext** [go to 17]. (J. Hillis Miller)

2. THE OBSOLETE BODY

Stelarc is perhaps best known for his thesis of the **OBSOLETE BODY**. This consists of a narrative of **human to 'post-human'** [go to 3] development in which the natural, metaphysically and biologically given body is presented as having become inadequate and as no longer being able to cope with 'the precision, speed and **power of technology**'. Consequently, the old, ego-agent-driven biological 'psycho-body' has been, or is soon going to be, replaced by a redesigned body, one that will take the form of a human/machine 'cybersystem'. The result, for Stelarc, will be a radical redefinition of what it means to be human: 'we will end up having significantly different **thoughts and philosophies**'.

3. HUMAN, ALL TOO (POST-)HUMAN

By experimenting with prosthetics, robotics and medical procedures, Stelarc is able to offer a direct challenge to fixed and unified notions of bodily identity and human selfhood. Yet despite the way in which it is often perceived (and, indeed, presented), Stelarc's thesis that **'THE BODY IS OBSOLETE'** [go to 2] is not reducible to a straightforward teleological narrative of human to post-human bodily, technological and philosophical development. Such an evolutionary to post-evolutionary trajectory is simultaneously constructed and placed in **suspension** [go to 16] in his work.

16. SUSPENSIONS

• The **'obsolete body'** [go to 2] does not represent a rejection of the human. The 'post-human' body can in fact be defined only by virtue of its *difference* from, and therefore its relation to, the 'natural' body. Hence 'it is only when the body becomes aware of its present position that it can map its **post-evolutionary strategies**'. The 'post-human' 'cyber-body' is thus entirely dependent on the biological 'psycho-body' for its identity.

Plate 6 STRETCHED SKIN/THIRD HAND, Monoral Station, Ofuna.
Photo: S. Hunter, © Stelarc

- It is also the 'natural' human body which constitutes the starting point for these performances. It is this body, rather than some machinic post-human hybrid, which is Stelarc's '**object for re-design**' [go to 4] and which acts as a template for his experiments. The body may be obsolete. 'But we cannot operate disembodied. We cannot discard the body.'
- And just as the 'post-human' body is neither entirely human nor entirely post-human, so is the 'natural' body. It too is defined in terms of its **relation to technology** [go to 5].

4. REDESIGNING THE BODY

How can Stelarc's concept of the '**obsolete body**' [go to 2] be reduced to a linear teleological narrative, a narrative in which the biologically given human body is abandoned in favour of some post-human cybersystem, when it is the former that constitutes the starting point and basis for all his experiments? It is the **natural human body** [go to 5], after all, that is his 'object for redesign' (rather than of desire) when Stelarc uses 'medical instruments, prosthetics, robotics, Virtual Reality systems and the Internet to explore alternate, intimate and involuntary **interfaces with the body**':

> It is the natural body which is augmented with hardware prostheses such as his **THIRD HAND** and **VIRTUAL ARM**, and **EXOSKELETON**, a 'six-legged, pneumatically powered walking machine'.

> It is the natural body which is augmented with **skin** [go to 8] prostheses including his proposed **EXTRA EAR**: a surgically constructed ear, positioned as an additional facial feature next to the real ear and 'able to amplify Real Audio sounds to augment the local sounds heard by the actual ears' and perhaps to 'whisper sweet nothings to the other ear'.

> It is the natural body which acts as a host for remote agents and even, as in **PARASITE** [go to 12], to the stimulations of the Internet itself.

> It is the natural body which can be redesigned so that '**TECHNICALLY THERE WOULD BE NO REASON FOR DEATH**', and whose parts need not be repaired but replaced.

> It is the natural body which in **MOVATAR** – INVERSE MOTION CAPTURE SYSTEM – 'animates a 3D computer-generated virtual body to perform in computer space or cyberspace'.

The '**post-human**' body [go to 18] can thus never be arrived at: it is always dependent for its realization on the **'natural' human body** [go to 3], a body which cannot be **left behind** [go to 6]. 'You don't escape the body.'

18. PHANTOM BODY

The body of Stelarc's experiments is *neither* human *nor* post-human. It is **suspended** [go to 16] (as he makes clear with regard to his twenty-five body **suspension events**, 'suspension means **between two**

states'): between old and new, presence and absence, proximity and distance, **human and machine** [go to 6], actual and virtual, self and prosthesis. This is indicated by the very term '***post*-human**' [go to 3], the hyphen of which acts as a link or hinge, both joining and separating the 'human' and that which comes *afterwards*, but which, **paradoxically** [go to 5], comes *before*, too. As with another important figure for Stelarc, the **zombie** [go to 23], the post-human body is neither alive nor dead. It is spectral, a **PHANTOM BODY** which, like communism and democracy, is 'always still to come'.

6. THE END OF TECHNOLOGY

The traditional, Aristotelian view is that technology is extrinsic to human nature as a tool which is used to bring about certain ends. Technology is applied science, an instrument of knowledge. The inverse of this conception, now commonly heard, is that the instrument has taken control of its maker, the creation control of its creator (Frankenstein's monster). (Timothy Clark)

Somewhat paradoxically for an artist so closely associated with the latest developments in technology, if Stelarc's art is not about the end of the human or the body in any simple sense, it *is* about the end of technology – or at least a certain conception of technology which, as **Timothy Clark** [go to 11] points out, 'with a few notable exceptions – has dominated Western thought for almost three thousand years'. For while Stelarc uses technology to augment and enhance the body, he also performs a rethinking of the **boundaries of the body** [go to 8] and its relation to technology – a rethinking in which technology is presented significantly as *neither* instrument *nor* controlling creation.

8. FRACTAL SKIN

In **FRACTAL FLESH**, muscle stimulators attached to the skin are used as a means of connecting and coupling remotely with other bodies via the Internet. Whereas usually the **skin** [go to 5] of the human body is perceived as a barrier that divides the internal meat and flesh from the external world, thus helping to generate a stable notion of bodily identity, the self and the soul, Stelarc's FRACTAL FLESH, like his **STOMACH SCULPTURE**, demonstrates that the '**skin no longer signifies closure**' . . . or not *just* closure. Like the **mouth** [go to 7] and the **ear**, the **skin** [go to 6] is also one of the points where identity is put at risk through the opening up of the self and the body to 'external' agents [go to 21] and to the world 'outside'.

7. STOMACH SCULPTURE: HOLLOW BODY/ HOLLOW SPACE

In **STOMACH SCULPTURE**, an art work, consisting of 'an extending/retracting structure, sound-emitting and self-illuminating' and operating in the stomach cavity, is inserted into the body. Brain waves, blood flow and muscle signals are amplified and broadcast, and the inside of the lungs, stomach and colon are filmed and screened – all of which serves to highlight and place in question 'distinctions between **public, private and physiological spaces**' as the inside of the body is revealed to be at once **both internal and external** [go to 6].

21. ALIEN ENCOUNTERS

Not only is the body augmented and invaded by, attached and acting as host to, technology, the body itself is revealed as foreign, automated, alien, other. The physicality of the body is split. The **natural body** [go to 5] is experienced as 'alien to itself'.

> Glove Anaesthesia and Alien Hand are pathological conditions in which the patient experiences parts of their body as not there, as not their own, as not under their own control – an absence of physiology on the one hand and an absence of **agency** [go to 11] on the other. In a **Stimbod** not only would one possess a split physiology, one would also experience parts of oneself as **automated, absent and alien**. (Stelarc)

5. 'TECHNOLOGY IS WHAT DEFINES BEING HUMAN'

What Stelarc repeatedly demonstrates is that technology is both fundamental to, and a disturbance of, our sense of the human. The body's relation to technology is not therefore one of opposites, in which an original, unified and distinct human self or identity comes into contact with an external, foreign, **alien** [go to 21] technology (something which is perhaps implied by his use of the term '**hybrid**'), the **skin** [go to 8] acting as a boundary line to divide and separate the two. Technology is not simply external. '**Technology is what defines being human.** It's not an antagonistic alien sort of object, it's part of our human nature. It constructs our human nature.' Which means that, to borrow the words of Jacques Derrida, 'there is no **natural originary body**' [go to 10], since

> technology has not simply added itself, from the outside or after the fact, as a foreign body . . . this foreign or dangerous supplement is 'originarily' at work and in place in the supposedly ideal interiority of the '**body and soul**' [go to 18]. It is indeed at the heart of the heart.

10. HERE BE MONSTERS

To say that '**technology . . . constructs our human nature**' [go to 5] and that there is no natural, metaphysically and biologically given human body is not to suggest that the relation between technology and the human is always and everywhere the same. Different technologies make possible different ways of conceiving this relation at different times. Nor is Stelarc's only function to render visible what Richard Beardsworth, following Bernard Stiegler, has termed the 'originary technicity' of the human. This would be to reduce his performances to an endless repetition of a past, and a future, that is always the same. What Stelarc performs with his investigations into how different developments in technology (robotics, the Internet, virtual reality systems, prosthetics, medical instruments and procedures) alter our conception of the human, and of the human body, is the way in which technology escapes the control of its inventors to produce unseen and unforeseeable changes and possibilities; and thus a future – for the self, the human, for the body and for technology – that can be neither **programmed nor predicted** [go to 11].

11. THE CYBORG EXPERIMENTS

To conceive technology as a prosthesis that alters the very nature of its seeming user is to be reminded how technical inventions have always been in excess of their concepts, productive of **unforeseeable transformations** [go to 10]. This deconstruction of the **Aristotelian system** [go to 6] enables each invention to be seen as an irruption of the other, the unforeseen disrupting the very criteria in which it would have been captured. . . . The advent of the other, interrupting reason and the possibility of calculation, calls for judgement precisely to the extent that its status is undecidable. This legislative moment involves a necessary and unavoidable nego-tiation with what one can't or doesn't know and puts in crisis the concepts whereby knowledge could have secured itself. It chal-lenges, for instance, the very concept of invention, for an invention has been that which is assignable to a human subjectivity, individual or collective, responsible for the discovery and production of something new and publicly available. . . . An 'invention of the other' exceeds both determined producer and recognizable object. As the double genitive already indicates ('**invention _of_ the other**') [go to 13], it produces **undecidability** [go to 12] as to **agency** [go to 23]. (Timothy Clark)

12. PING BODY

In what sense are Stelarc's gestures in his **PING BODY** performances _his_? Do they belong to him? Or are they a result of the '**external ebb and flow of data**' on the Internet? Perhaps, as Adrian Mackenzie has said, it is '**impossible to decide**' [go to 15]?

23. A FEAR OF ZOMBIES

We've always been afraid of **zombies** because seemingly they have no mind of their own, they perform involuntarily, they may be controlled by someone else. We also are very anxious about the idea of the **cyborg** [go to 2], which is a body that is increasingly automated, mechanised, so we fear the **zombie** [go to 18], we fear the **cyborg** [go to 11], but we actually fear what we have always been and what we have already become [go to 5]. (Stelarc)

22. PERFORMANCES

The constant experimentation with '**alternative, intimate and involuntary**' [go to 4] interfaces with the body is one feature of Stelarc's attempt to explore and come to terms with the effects of **new technology** [go to 10]. His experiments with **writing** [go to 14], and with the form of the text, are another. These too can be regarded as performances.

14. LANGUAGE IS A TECHNOLOGY, TOO

With their unusual style and appearance – the use of short blocks of text, the bold declarative style, the incorporation of technical diagrams, the lack of elaboration and explicit academic references, quotations or citations, the BLOCK CAPITALS – Stelarc's texts refuse to 'claim to ground [themselves] on **pre-existing knowledge or established tradition**' [go to 19]. They experiment with new strategies and alternative possibilities for writing about technology – strategies and possibilities that are **suspended** [go to 3], undecidably, 'between knowing and acting, **between constative speech acts and performative speech acts**' [go to 17].

15. PARASITE TEXT

As with the **new communications technologies** [go to 1], in order to **understand** [go to 13] Stelarc's artistic and textual **performances** [go to 22] we have to **invent** [go to 11] a form of analysis that is more than a mere 'repetition of a program of understanding and action **already in place**' [go to 19]. We have to create 'a space for an encounter with, even intrusion of, what is radically different from the self'. And we have to rethink the boundaries of the text accordingly. Since we cannot know the consequences of our probing of bodily, authorial and textual identity **in advance** [go to 19], we, too, must risk causing uncertainty, anxiety and offence.

19. MADNESS

Responsibility [go to 13] . . . must be, if it is to exist at all, always excessive, always impossible to discharge. Otherwise it will risk being the repetition of a program of understanding and action **already in place** [go to 22]. . . . My responsibility in each reading is **to decide and to act** [go to 11], but I must do so in a situation where the grounds of decision are impossible to know. As Kierkegaard somewhere says, 'The moment of decision is madness.' The action, in this case, often takes the form of teaching or writing that cannot claim to ground itself on **pre-existing knowledge or established tradition** [go to 15] but is what Derrida calls 'l'invention de l'autre' **[the invention of the other**] [go to 14]. (J. Hillis Miller)

NOTES

'[T]he parasite both belongs and does not belong'; Nicholas Royle. 'Foreign Body'. *After Derrida*. Manchester: Manchester University Press, 1995. 147.

'I mean, technology, I think, comes from the Greek word "*tekhne*"'; Stelarc, in 'Stelarc: interview by Yiannis Melanitis'. *Arc: Journal of Research and Critical Curating* November 1999, <http://a-r-c.gold.ac.uk/reftexts/inter_melanitis.html>.

13. Reinventing invention
'[W]e have to rethink the relations between knowing and acting'; Jacques Derrida. 'No apocalypse, not now (full speed ahead, seven missiles, seven missives)'. *Diacritics* Summer 1984: 23.

11. 'The ethics of hypertext'
'A hypertext . . . offers the reader the necessity of deciding which path to follow through the text'; J. Hillis Miller. *Black Holes*. Stanford, CA: Stanford University Press, 1999. 137.

2. The obsolete body

OBSOLETE BODY, Stelarc, 'The Obsolete Body', <www.stelarc.va.com.au/obsolete/obsolete.html>.

'the precision, speed and power of technology'; Stelarc. 'The Obsolete Body', <www.stelarc.va.com.au/obsolete/obsolete.html>.

'[W]e will end up having significantly different thoughts and philosophies'; Stelarc in Paolo Atzori and Kirk Woolford. 'Extended body: interview with Stelarc'. *CTheory* 6 September 1995, <www.ctheory.net/text_file.asp?pick=71>.

'THE BODY IS OBSOLETE'; Stelarc. 'The Obsolete Body', <www.stelarc.va.com.au/obsolete/obsolete.html>.

16. Suspensions

'[I]t is only when the body becomes aware of its present position that it can map its post-evolutionary strategies'; Stelarc. 'The Obsolete Body', <www.stelarc.va.com.au/obsolete/obsolete.html>.

'object for redesign'; Stelarc. In Robert Ayers. 'Obsolete body/alternate strategies: listening to Stelarc'. *Live Art Letters* 3 (February 1998): 8.

'But we cannot operate disembodied'; Stelarc, in this volume, Chapter 7.

4. Redesigning the body

'medical instruments, prosthetics, robotics, Virtual Reality systems and the Internet to explore alternate, intimate and involuntary interfaces with the body'; 'Biographical Notes', <www.stelarc.va.com.au/biog/biog.html>.

THIRD HAND, Stelarc, 'Third Hand', <www.stelarc.va.com.au/third/third.html>.

VIRTUAL ARM, Stelarc, 'Virtual Arm', <www.stelarc.va.com.au/virtarm/virtarm.html>.

EXOSKELETON, Stelarc, 'Exoskeleton', <www.stelarc.va.com.au/exoskeleton/index.html>.

EXTRA EAR, Stelarc, 'Extra Ear', <www.stelarc.va.com.au/extra_ear/index.htm>.

PARASITE, Stelarc, 'Parasite: Event for Invaded and Involuntary Body', <www.stelarc.va.com.au/parasite/index.htm>.

'TECHNICALLY THERE WOULD BE NO REASON FOR DEATH', Stelarc, 'The Hum of the Hybrid', <www.stelarc.va.com.au/hybhum/hybhum.html>.

MOVATAR, Stelarc, 'Movatar', <www.stelarc.va.com.au/movatar/index.html>.

'You don't escape the body'; Stelarc, in this volume, Chapter 7.

18. Phantom body
'suspension events', Stelarc, 'Suspension', <www.stelarc.va.com.au/suspens/suspens.html>.

'[S]uspension means between two states'; Stelarc. In Paolo Atzori and Kirk Woolford. 'Extended body: interview with Stelarc'. *CTheory* 6 September 1995, <www.ctheory.net/text_file.asp?pick=71>.

PHANTOM BODY, Stelarc, 'Phantom Body', <www.stelarc.va.com.au/phantbod/phantbod.html>.

'always still to come'; Jacques Derrida. *Specters of Marx: The State of the Debt, the Work of Mourning, and the New International.* London: Routledge, 1994. 99.

6. The end of technology
'The traditional Aristotelian view is that technology . . .'; Timothy Clark. 'Deconstruction and technology'. In *Deconstructions: A User's Guide.* Ed. Nicholas Royle. Basingstoke: Palgrave, 2000. 238.

8. Fractal skin
FRACTAL FLESH, Stelarc, 'Fractal Flesh', <www.stelarc.va.com.au/fractal/index.html>.

STOMACH SCULPTURE, Stelarc, 'Stomach Sculpture: Hollow Body/Hollow Space', <www.stelarc.va.com.au/stomach/stomach.html>.

'Skin no longer signifies closure'; Stelarc. In Paolo Atzori and Kirk Woolford. 'Extended body: interview with Stelarc'. *CTheory* 6 September 1995, <www.ctheory.net/text_file.asp?pick=71>.

'ear', Stelarc, 'Extra Ear', <www.stelarc.va.com.au/extra_ear/index.htm>.

7. Stomach sculpture: hollow body/hollow space
STOMACH SCULPTURE, Stelarc, 'Stomach Sculpture: Hollow Body/Hollow Space', <www.stelarc.va.com.au/stomach/stomach.html>.

'an extending/retracting structure, sound-emitting and self-illuminating'; Stelarc. 'From psycho-body to cybersystems: images as post-human entities'. In *Virtual Futures: Cybernetics, Technology and Post-Human Pragmatism*. Ed. Joan Broadhurst Dixon and Eric J. Cassidy. London: Routledge, 1998. 120.

'distinctions between public, private and physiological spaces'; Stelarc, 'Stomach Sculpture', <www.stelarc.va.com.au/stomach/stomach.html>.

21. Alien encounters
'alien to itself'; Stelarc. In Robert Ayers. 'Obsolete body/alternate strategies – listening to Stelarc'. *Live Art Letters* 3 (February 1998): 9.

'Glove Anaesthesia and Alien Hand are pathological conditions'; Stelarc. 'Parasite visions: alternate, intimate and involuntary experiences'. In *Art and Design: Sci-Fi Aesthetics*. Ed. Rachel Armstrong. London: Academy, 1997. 67.

5. 'Technology is what defines being human'
'hybrid', see Stelarc, 'The Hum of the Hybrid', <www.stelarc.va.com.au/hybhum/hybhum.html>.

'Technology is what defines being human'; Stelarc. In Paolo Atzori and Kirk Woolford. 'Extended body: interview with Stelarc'. *CTheory* 6 September 1995, <www.ctheory.net/text_file.asp?pick=71>.

'[T]here is no natural body'; Jacques Derrida. *Points . . . Interviews, 1974–1994, Jacques Derrida*. Ed. Elizabeth Weber. Stanford, CA: Stanford University Press, 1995. 244–5.

10. Here be monsters
'originary technicity'; Richard Beardsworth, 'From a genealogy of matter to a politics of memory: Stiegler's thinking of technics'. *Tekhnema* 2 (Spring 1995), <http://tekhnema.free.fr/2Beardsworth.htm>.

11. The cyborg experiments
'To conceive technology as a prosthesis that alters the very nature of its seeming user'; Timothy Clark, 'Deconstruction and technology'. In *Deconstructions: A User's Guide*. Ed. Nicholas Royle. Basingstoke: Palgrave, 2000. 250–1.

12. Ping Body
PING BODY, Stelarc, 'Ping Body', <www.stelarc.va.com.au/pingbody/index.html>.

'external ebb and flow of data'; Stelarc, 'Ping Body', <www.stelarc.va.com.au/pingbody/index.html>.

'impossible to decide'; Adrian Mackenzie. *Transductions: Bodies and Machines at Speed*. London: Continuum, forthcoming.

23. A fear of zombies
'We've always been afraid of zombies'; Stelarc. In 'Stelarc: interview by Yiannis Melanitis'. *Arc: Journal of Research and Critical Curating* (November 1999), <http://a-r-c.gold.ac.uk/reftexts/inter_melanitis.html>.

'a space for an encounter with, even intrusion of, what is radically different from the self'; Joanna Zylinska, in this volume, Chapter 14.

19. Madness
'Responsibility . . . must be, if it is to exist at all, always excessive'; J. Hillis Miller. *Black Holes*. Stanford, CA: Stanford University Press, 1999. 491.

PART 3

Self-*hybridation*

CHAPTER 9

Morlan

FRED BOTTING AND SCOTT WILSON

BUMPS AND NOSES

At a dinner party in the USA attended by a number of society ladies, Orlan noticed a degree of disdain towards her appearance, her nose in particular. She eventually registered the reason for their hauteur, and 'suddenly realized what had motivated their ostensibly unwarranted reactions – they all had the same nose!' (Hirschhorn, 118). Orlan's nose offended the ladies' aesthetic sensibilities not only because it failed to conform to their standard of plastic proboscial beauty, thereby eliciting their contemptuous pity, but also, Orlan suspected, because her difference disclosed the banality of their own sameness: their hostility arose, in part, as the effect of a frisson of horror rippling among the ladies, as if they had all been caught wearing the same designer dress.

Orlan has frequently stressed that she has nothing against plastic surgery, but remains antipathetic towards the 'standard criteria of beauty that cosmetic surgery imposes on female and male bodies' (*South Bank Show*). In the face of the noses of her companions at dinner, Orlan contended that 'we need to ensure that we aren't constantly confronted with the same faces, with people looking like clones, with implants always inserted in exactly the same way, in the same position, and with the face always stretched in the same way' (*South Bank Show*). For Orlan, plastic surgery provides a means of self-portraiture that decisively breaks with the forms of representation that have dominated the genre hitherto. Self-portraiture is no longer, for Orlan, the representation of her face, body and trousseau in some other medium; it is the artistic (re)construction of that face through the manipulation of skin, bone, blood, tissue and the addition of prosthetic implants. In art, the gap sustained by all forms of representation between image and face is therefore closed, just as, in fashion, the relation that subjects women and men to a particular dominant 'look' is collapsed. Orlan clearly abhors sameness, challenging any conformity to an 'imposed' platonic idea or 'image of beauty supposed to be applicable to everyone alike' (*South Bank Show*). One of the problems of the mediatized ideal image is that actual human bodies always fail to live up to it and are found wanting. However, Orlan's evocation of the clone-like products of the mechanized surgery of the cosmetics industry (her disdainful dinner companions) implies a desire directed by something other than an attainment of conventional ideals.

All images are the products of a material process of imaging (i.e. production and reproduction) taking place either in the brain or through other technical means, and are therefore subject to a prior logic of reproduction. Images are bound up in an originary iterability necessary to their imaging or imagining. Orlan's notion of a singular look, of a self-authorizing beauty, is itself an impossible 'ideal' that both depends on, and is an effect of, reproduction. It is actually the clone-like identical plastic noses of the US society ladies that more radically collapse the space between body and image: image becomes body and body becomes image in all its technological reproducibility. In contrast to Orlan's rather bourgeois, nineteenth-century idea of individual creativity and artistic transcendence, her female dinner guests are the living silk-screens of a Warholian world of industrialized artistic production. It could of course be argued that, after Jackie Kennedy and Monroe, the Britney noses and Bassinger lips (or whatever is currently favoured in fashionable circles) betray an all-too-conventional or banal image of beauty, even if there is a certain *Unheimlichkeit* in the redoubling of the same. That, nonetheless, is an inevitable effect of the repetitive logic determined by the iterability and technicity of the image, not an index of its subservience to an external standard or metaphysical ideal of beauty.

Another anecdote concerning Orlan's attendance at a different society event in the USA illustrates the iterability of the image perfectly. At a celebrity party in San Francisco hosted by a famous art collector, Orlan was invited into a special room filled with his friends. These men were, according to Orlan, 'sadomasochistic homosexuals, all clad in leather with chains and zips, tattoos and lots of body piercing'. They were also, clearly, big fans of the French artist. 'We think you are the most important artist of our time,' they chimed, surrounding her,

> and we'd like to pay a tribute to you: we'd like to pay you to organize our surgical operations. You can do whatever you like in the operating theatre, with music, texts, and sound, etcetera. We'd like to get your surgeon from New York to come and create the same bumps that you've got, because we're going to start a new trend: after body piercing we're going to start 'bumping' and very quickly, in a few years or so, it'll catch on in Europe! (Ayers, 180–81)

The artist was not impressed by the tribute, nor was she enthused by the prospect of rooms full of fashionable people sporting identical Orlanean 'bumps' along with their latest tattoos and piercings. Even though she is not against tattoos and body piercing, the prospect of her look being appropriated in this way clearly made her furious. Orlan argued that those who adopt S/M chic, like followers of any other fashion, 'believe that they are liberating themselves from the dictates of a certain society, but in fact it all boils down to the same thing because they are conforming to the dictates of a smaller, mini-society' (Ayers, 182).

The ambiguous tribute reinforced Orlan's unease about becoming less an interrogator of fashion and more a trendsetter. No sooner had she recovered from the operation to have the bumps inserted in her forehead than catwalk models were being made up with the look (Ayers, 180). The facility between Orlan's self-portrait and the fashion industry is consistent with the fact that Orlan's art has always been a kind of haute couture (or haute coupure): '[my] first works were done with the fabric of my trousseau' (Orlan, 'Conference', 84). This and subsequent works like *Baiser l'artiste* (1977), in which she is clothed in, or veiled by, a life-size photograph cut-out of her naked body, play with the interchangeability of trousseau, skin and body as different yet equivalent surfaces. In a similar way, *Baiser l'artiste* also plays with the relation between art and business, as different yet equivalent practices, selling her kisses to anyone willing to pay the price. In her later works, such as the surgery performance *Omnipresence*, the skin is treated as a fabric to be cut, shaped and stitched into a new look, body and trousseau, again becoming one and the same. Further, Orlan has never abandoned the conventional, though shifting, canons of beauty that are represented in the history of art and fashion, taking references from images of Diana, the Mona Lisa, Botticelli's Venus, Gerard's Psyche and so on. This is not, as she says, because she wants to resemble them, any more than a fashion designer would want to reproduce a fourteenth-century costume, but because they serve as an 'inspiration' so that 'their images can resurface in works that I produce, with regard to their histories' (Orlan, 'Conference', 89).

Orlan, then, has always depended on traditional canons of beauty as an inspiration for her self-portraiture, and she has always remained beautiful. Further, the surgery that she undergoes in her performances literally deepens her beauty, disclosing that, as a surface, it goes more than 'skin deep'. The beauty of her face is precisely heightened and eroticized (to the point of horror) even as it is peeled off live for the cameras, revealing the raw flesh beneath. As the scalpels, wielded by medical staff in haute couture outfits, cut into her face, Orlan's bruised and fragile beauty is technologically reproduced and relayed around the world by satellite to be viewed on video by audiences in art galleries: captured, multiplied, marketed.

Orlan's beauty remains, much as Princess Diana's indestructible beauty remained in the midst of the carnage of the Paris car accident in the 'crash photos' that circulated in press rooms and on Internet sites in the aftermath of her death (see Scott Wilson, 42–3). This indestructible beauty disclosed the Sadean nature of the relationship between Diana and the electronic media. Like those of Sade's heroine Justine, depicted in his novel *The Misfortunes of Virtue*, the sufferings of Orlan also never diminish her beauty, nor do they lead to her total dismemberment and destruction. For Jacques Lacan, the object of Sadean torture 'is to retain the capacity of being an indestructible support':

Analysis shows clearly that the subject separates out a double of himself who is made inaccessible to destruction, so as to make it support what, borrowing a term from the realm of aesthetics, one cannot help calling the play of pain. For the space in question is the same as that in which aesthetic phenomena disport themselves, a space of freedom. And the conjunction between the play of pain and the phenomena of beauty is to be found there, though it is never emphasized, for it is as if some taboo or other prevented it, as if some prohibition were there. (*Ethics*, 261)

Under local anaesthetic, Orlan's image directs 'a general pain' (Adams, 142) as it is opened outwards, its interior externalized in the flux of electronic images, towards a mass of anonymous looks in different galleries around the Western world. Her performances induce pain in the spectators: Barbara Rose notes the visceral effects and sensory overload of watching the operation (125); the performance slices through comfortable modes of viewing, representing a body in pain and causing a painful disturbance in other bodies.

This pain is the correlate of another level of discomfort, a cognitive disturbance affecting the capacity to interpret and analyse:

What's difficult in my work is that it's uncomfortable in every sense. So far as the operations are concerned, it is physically uncomfortable for me and for those who look at the images. But it is also uncomfortable to make sense of it. (Ayers, 180)

For Rose, Orlan's performances raise questions beyond the art work, and provoke uncertainty about art itself: unsure of the legitimacy of aesthetic intention, Rose asks 'whether we are dealing here not with art but with illustrated psychopathology' (125). As Lacan suggests, at the conjunction between the play of pain and the phenomena of beauty a point of incomprehensibility emerges that is manifested as taboo. At the limit, Orlan discloses the Thing where electronic continuity is experienced as pain shared by performer and spectator (Lacan, *Ethics*, 80). This Thing, around which signification is organized and suspended, is also a No-Thing, a taboo and a gap, a hole. As gaps are cut in the flesh, holes are punctured in the gaze of spectators and tears produced in the aesthetic framework.

Holes form the (absent) centre of Orlan's productions, gaps in vision and cognition inducing a visceral dissolution of boundaries and an exposure of spaces that should be covered over. During *Baiser l'artiste*, where Orlan sold her kisses behind a cut-out of her naked body, no money exchanged hands, but coins were inserted in a slot below her throat and fell to a moneybox situated at her genitals. Money dropped into a willing hole as the relationship between art and commerce was crudely exposed and entwined with images of tra-ditional feminine roles. Orlan exposes the holes in body, vision and culture that serve to articulate relationships that are usually occluded. In this way, she brings the spheres of art, femininity and business into proximity and discloses them as spaces of exchange and consumption, of the circulation and exploitation of images, bodies and looks. At the *Head of the Medusa*, performed in Aachen in 1978, viewers entering a booth were asked to confront the space of femininity and their position in relation to it. As Orlan describes it,

> Using a large magnifying glass to show my vagina (the pubic hairs on one half were painted blue) during my period, a video screen showed the head of the man or woman who was about to see, another showed the head of the men and women who were looking, and at the exit, Freud's text on the head of the Medusa was distributed. It read: 'At the sight of the vulva, the devil himself flees'. (Sarah Wilson, 11)

But even as the devil flees, a million consumers click onto digital images hoping to get a glimpse of a similar 'horror', a horror whose endless, pornographic reproduction has always been at the vanguard, or the avant-garde, of technologically innovative modes of reproduction from the printing press to photography, film to the Internet. Similarly, even as one winces and turns away from the video of her surgical performance, 'the dominant effect' of which 'at least for this viewer is horror' (Adams, 143), one turns to look again. And then again, looking for 'the pain of jouissance'. One looks again and again, hoping to be 'confronted with the horrifying spectacle of the rawness of passion, of the jouissance of the body as such, the jubilation of the meat' (Adams, 156). Oh Oh Oh Orlan!

MORLAN

With Orlan, the excess of femininity is not staged as an aesthetic fulfilment of spectatorial pleasure, a reconstitution of objects and meanings in the (symbolic) field of vision, but as a consumption taken to unbearable extremes. The jouissance evoked by Orlan's operation is destructive, an expenditure that evacuates rather than fills the corporeal and symbolic spaces it opens up. By disclosing that 'the image is a mask and that there is nothing behind it', by 'emptying out' the object of vision, a gap is created in the ruination of habitual space: 'the emptying out of the place of the object means that the structure of representation has collapsed' (Adams, 153–6). No Other holds the object in place or fills the space emptied of sense in an excess of horrifying sensation: 'an unfillable gap opens at the moment that the face is lifted' (158). The evacuation, according to Adams, offers the subject an opportunity to make sense and create new meanings. But the evacuation of structural integrity of inside and outside, subject and object, highlights the gap pulsing beneath the image: 'unfillable', it demonstrates that 'the series of images is in principle without end', having 'the effect of opening onto, or rather circulating, a void' (159). In the collapse of the structure of representation, the Other's lack comes to the fore in an economic rather than subjective dimension: 'lack is not a deficit but a structure of a wish-to-complete which includes the denial of incompleteness. It is an economic rather than a phenomenological reality' (152). Lack, loosened from the structural frame of subject and Other, is generalized as the hollow centre of an economy of desire, the space that calls out for, and endlessly consumes, more.

A strange liberation and generalization of desire emerges here. Unanchored and undirected by a symbolic frame, the pulsation of desire/lack is generated in Orlan's work, as series and as circulation, by a void: no object or image arrests its momentum, no structural opposition stems its flow. The movement is one of in-exhaustion, desire/lack generated and consumed in incessant expenditure, more and more objects and images to fill and be expended in the space of consumption. The trajectory of this economy of unanchored desiring accords with the principle discovered by the villain of Angela Carter's *The Infernal Desire Machines of Dr Hoffman*:

'All things co-exist in pairs but mine is not an either/or world.
Mine is an and + and world.
I alone have discovered the key to the inexhaustible plus.' (206)

Carter, writing in the wake of the social and sexual liberations of the 1960s, injects a sceptical note to this celebration of desiring without end through her reluctant and near-exhausted hero, Desiderio: 'He might know the nature of the inexhaustible plus but, all the same, he was a totalitarian' (207). Orlan, however, reiterates the principle of the 'inexhaustible plus' in a delineation of her project:

> [O]ur whole culture is based on the 'or' – for example, good or bad, private or public, new technology or painting, etcetera, etcetera. This forces us to condemn one element and choose the other. All of my work is based on the notion of 'and': the good and the bad, the beautiful and the ugly, the living and the artificial, the public and the private – because during my operations images of me are transmitted by satellite, so you've got them there at the same time. (Ayers, 184)

From the uncomfortable conjunction of conventional pairings, it is a small step to conjoin more: the good and the bad and the beautifully ugly. The space of the inexhaustible plus, a space of projection and desiring, also informs popular video game characterization: Lara Croft's appeal lies in an amalgamation of signs to produce a bizarrely bosomed figure 'whose very blankness encourages the (male or female) player's psychological projection', and hence the character becomes 'inexhaustible' (Poole, 164). Projection conjoined with desiring opens the space of inexhaustion to an endless sequence or series. It follows the metonymic pattern of desire and signification associated by Lacan with the displacements of the dreamwork as it avoids censure (*Écrits*). Without the prohibitive power of metaphor to arrest displacement, the associative conjunctions proliferate, linking life and artifice, publicity and privacy, in a procession no longer constrained by symbolic law. In the absence of any regulative paternal metaphor, as Baudrillard observes, the logic of 'transversality', a 'viral' traversal of all boundaries and limits (*Transparency*, 8–9), holds sway.

From O-O-O-Orlan to Mmm-more-lan, the excess of femininity comes close to the expenditures of consumer enjoyment. It is in terms of its relationship to consumption that Orlan's work, though in many ways comparable to that of Stelarc, can be differentiated from the latter's performance art. Orlan, indeed, makes the comparison herself:

Like the Australian artist, Stelarc, I think that the body is obsolete. It is no longer adequate for the current situation. We mutate at the rate of cockroaches, but we are cockroaches whose memories are in computers, who pilot planes and drive vehicles that we have conceived, although our bodies are not designed for these speeds. We are on the threshold of a world for which we are neither mentally nor physically ready. ('Conference', 91)

This statement certainly agrees with Stelarc's manifesto on the need for technological reconfiguration to enhance the biological inadequacies of the human body ('From psycho to cyber strategies'). Orlan's work too paves the way for technical supplements by opening up the body to surgical interventions and media relays: 'By stating that the body is obsolete, Orlan is preparing the destruction that is needed before the more ample work of reconstruction can begin.' 'Her work opens up abysses, digs fathomless potholes' (Onfray, 39). Hollowing out the body is also crucial to Stelarc's project. His proposal to develop a 'Stimbod' – in which he is wired up so that all his movements are operated by a computer program – is intended to construct 'a hollow body, a host body for the projection and performance of remote agents' (Stelarc, 'Parasite visions', 121). For Stelarc, the evacuation of the body and its reassembly in dispersed machinic networks corresponds to the anti-Oedipal models of desiring charted by Deleuze and Guattari: the Body-Without-Organs is 'synchronized . . . with the "hollow body"' (Farnell, 132). Discussing Orlan's relationship to the same theoretical frame, Michelle Hirschhorn sees the 'dismantling' of the organism as 'a way of opening the body to connections that presuppose an entire assemblage' (121).

But Stelarc and Orlan, for all the proximities of their projects, occupy different positions within the generalized locus of contemporary production–consumption. Stelarc hollows the body in order to fill it, arguing that the hollow body serves as 'a better "host" for packing more technology inside' (Farnell, 132). Stelarc's work, developed in conjunction with industry and corporate technicians, is oriented by the goals of hyperproduction: optimization, speed and efficiency. For him, 'to be alive means more to be operational', and ageing 'generates malfunctioning memory and inability to perform effectively' (Farnell, 132). A test pilot of new working machines and corporate interfaces, Stelarc probes the limits of technological enhancement in a productive direction, closing the gap that separates the obsolete human form from the hyper-efficient cyborg machine worker. In contrast, Orlan discloses the position of the consumer, the body becoming a site for consumption rather than work: 'in future times we'll change our bodies as easily as our hair colour', she says (Lovelace, 13–14). Orlan's project is not delimited by work. It involves a play of images and a consumption of resources and energy, as is indicated by her own comparison of her testing of bodily limits to those of 'a high-level athlete. There is the training, the moment of the performance where one must go beyond one's limits – which is not done without effort or pain – and then there is the recuperation' ('Conference', 92). In exhausting herself, Orlan draws the abject to the surface: 'in spectacular representation she offers her body as meat and pre-packages her photographic image for consumption by the art community' (Clarke, 189). Where Stelarc uses the meat to enter the matrix of technological and post-human becoming, Orlan exposes its excess, its jouissance, its consumption.

Orlan's performances interrogate the intimate embrace of art and commerce, engaging with (religious, psychoanalytic, medical) institutions of paternal authority and their representations of femininity and formations of the body with a postmodern playfulness in which stereotypes are subverted and aesthetic boundaries questioned. But in the affirmation of feminine corporeal and artistic resistance in the plasticity of the surgically remade body there is an insistence on the body's perpetual inbuilt obsolescence in which the consuming immateriality of the image comes to the fore. As a result, identities become plural, iterable and exchangeable but not necessarily commodified. The enmeshing of identities, cultural positioning and the multifaceted and polyvalent trajectories of Orlan's performances make it difficult to celebrate an uncomplicated and comfortable radicalism in the projects she undertakes. It does not seem enough to understand her work as a problematization of 'the traditional gendered relationship' governing artistic production (Hirschhorn, 111), to see it as 'a feminist polemic dramatizing the unimaginable lengths women will go to to achieve an ideal of beauty defined by men' (Lovelace, 13), or even to consider the 'trenchant edge' of claims about bodily obsolescence in terms of a denaturalizing of the way women 'are trained to see themselves as totally identified with and determined by their embodiment' (Goodall, 152). It is brave for a critic to claim that the body on which Orlan's art insists serves to rehabilitate 'matter forsaken, execrated and soiled by the market' and that the medical scene of artistic production invests 'plastic surgery with a festive, demiurgic role' when the market also renders the body a site of so much enjoyment and consumption, and when plastic surgery is already directed towards cosmetic and not strictly useful ends (Onfray, 33–4).

Much of the critical opinion on Orlan's work comes from the artist's own statements of intention. Her work, she notes, 'has always interrogated the status of the feminine body, via social pressures', so that 'the variety of possible images of my body has dealt with the problem of identity and variety' in order to 'pose questions about the status of the body in our society and its evolution in future generations via new technologies and up-coming genetic mutations' ('Conference', 84, 88). But Orlan's declarations on art, for all their claims to the subversion of bourgeois conventions and habits, see the power of resistance they advocate slide easily into a promotion and even generation of postmodern capitalism:

It [art] must challenge our preconceptions, disrupt our thoughts; it is outside the norms, outside the law, against bourgeois order; it is not there to cradle us, to reinforce our comfort, to serve up again what we already know. It must take risks, at the risk of not being immediately accepted or acceptable. ('Conference', 85)

What this rather nineteenth-century aesthetic radicalism ignores is the political and economic transformations of the 1980s. The libertarian leaders of the Western world made few concessions to 'cradling', 'comforting' or nannying in their avid imposition of free-market values on every aspect of social life. In the name of economic growth, they refused the models of bourgeois caution and conservatism in the hunt for innovation and profit. Indeed, already without traditional norms and laws, the 'order' Orlan contests is very much akin to what she represents: in the postmodern economy the entrepreneur assumes the role of creative artist in the risks, speculation and innovation s/he takes. As Jean-Joseph Goux notes, it is

> precisely at the moment when the entrepreneur must think himself into the model of the most advanced artistic genius, at the moment when the avant-gardist strategy of innovation at any price becomes the paradigm of dominant economic practice, that the avant-garde necessarily loses its difference, its marginality, its deviance-value. ('General economics', 218)

Where no grand narrative organizes the credulity of rational subjects into an ideological order of masculine norms, no paternal metaphor presides over an Oedipal economy delimiting subjective desire. Instead, an unregulated desire invests in the marginal, metonymically linked differences in which a quick profit may be made. This desiring economy is generated by those marginal differences produced by artistic, technological innovation, that can be quickly reproduced and supplied on a mass scale. In this context, Orlan's bumpy individualism becomes an instant of differentiation, authenticated by its self-author-izing avant-gardism, upon which anyone can speculate in the fashion market.

For Goux, Western civilization is distinguished by the dominance of the economy over every other sphere of life: 'the market (the economic) and not the contract (the political), to say nothing of obedience (the religious), becomes the sole regulator of all social life' ('Subversion', 37). 'Crystallized in the general equivalent – a thing that is not a thing', social power 'opens on a virtuality of relations, on the infinity of commutations' (39). The contemporary conjunction of aesthetic postmodernity and neo-conservatism manifests 'a new, extremely powerful form of legitimation that summarizes this moment of exhaustion of the utopias of modernity by their apparent, and even spectacular integration' (41). An 'objectivized and autonomized medium of exchange has created its own order' (48). The proletarians, women and artists that for Comte represented the hope of the human social realm against the incursions of economic modernity are absorbed as indices of an 'irreducible alienation with respect to the general equivalent, freed now in its pure symbolic function, which produces meaning, desire, surplus, and play, all of which would be dried up by any attempt at reappropriation or transparency'. The system declares that 'we are all, structurally and ontologically, proletarians, women, and artists' (49). Orlan's identities as woman, artist and worker (in respect of her avowed anti-bourgeois stance) distinguish, then, a particularly resonant conjunction of positions in contemporary culture. The economy of more circumscribes the world of Orlan's art, the world in which, to which, though not explicitly for which, she performs.

ÜBERBARBIE

I grew up on a farm, and I was very, very bored, and I didn't have any female role models. . . . I didn't want to be a farmer's wife; I didn't want to work in a factory; I didn't want to be a teacher. So I took an inanimate object and gave it its own personality, and that's what I brought to life when I grew up. (Cynthia Jackson, cit. Rand, 133–4)

Cynthia Jackson, speaking on *The Jenny Jones Show* in 1993, describes how, in the 1960s, the allotted position of woman, wife or worker was not enough for her. The route she took on her flight out of Hicksville was the same as Orlan's: artistic self-creation via plastic surgery. While Orlan turned to the canons of fine art and mythology for images to bring to life and flesh, Jackson chose a plastic doll. Jackson underwent nineteen operations in order to become Barbie, in an act of self-becoming at least as radical as Orlan's in the degree to which it undermines the tyranny of media representation even as it subjects itself to the traumatic bodily imposition of ideal female images. But Jackson's relation to Barbie was not one of becoming 'inanimate', as if she were a doll-like image. In contrast to a woman whose 'body dysmorphia' took the form of a desire to have both legs removed from her pelvis (so that she could be a Barbie with its legs plucked off), Jackson's becoming-Barbie involved a radical means of self-subjectification, or self-creation. This process of (re-)animation does not involve an imitation or an identification in any secondary or passive sense. Much more than superficial resemblance, Jackson's becoming Barbie involves the production of a real Barbie, or even a super-real Barbie, the Barbie that she is. Thereby, in the wake of Jackson's authentic becoming, the dolls themselves are rendered mere merchandise.

For Jackson, becoming Barbie 'expanded her possibilities' (Rand, 133). Following her plastic surgery, Jackson's life pursued exactly the same path imagined by Mattel for Barbie. Moving to London, becoming Barbie, involved adopting the sophisticated, jet-setting life that Barbie has had since the early 1960s. Later, it also involved 'changing with the times', so that Jackson 'designed for herself a career that Barbie acquired in the 1980s – she's in a rock band – and, like Barbie, too, she took up a few more careers, including professional photography' (Rand, 133). Jackson brings Barbie authentically into being in and as herself, disclosing in the process that Barbie never existed even as she makes it possible for anyone to become a real Barbie. Jackson runs a cosmetic surgery information service for others who want to become Barbie. Inventing a personality 'best expressed in outfits and accessories sold by Mattel', Jackson 'promotes herself as the anti-bimboesque beauty Mattel claims Barbie to be' (134). She believes in 'inner beauty' and has the IQ of a member of Mensa. She also, according to Rand, 'performs the corporate service of helping Mattel cast itself as the filler of needs rather than the creator of them (as in "I can't live another day without a refrigerator that has an automatic ice-cube maker")' (134).

Crucially, Jackson's becoming Barbie undermines Mattel's marketing strategy, one that precisely depends upon the difference between Barbie and real girls, real women. The message from Mattel and Barbie comics is always that girls should 'love their bodies as they are', a superegoic imperative that does little but reinforce the self-hatred that is manifested in the fetishization of the doll-like image. Given this, Jackson's actualization of Barbie performs a correlative de-idealization of that image, thereby ensuring that she 'will not be making it onto Mattel's payroll' (134).

Jackson's career, though ostensibly the very opposite of Orlan's haute-bourgeois progress through the international art scene, has nevertheless an uncanny proximity to it. Cynthia Jackson has taken Mattel's marketing strategy, its toys and images, and pushed them towards a literal excess, closing the gap constitutive of fantasy upon which the sales of Barbie dolls depend. Similarly, for one critic, 'Orlan, although seduced by the rhetoric of technology, has turned to excess as a strategy against the benign and controlled nature of the screen, and the homogenization of body images' (Clarke, 202). Countering the hyper-homogenization of technologized consumption, Orlan and Jackson seem to exceed what is already an excess of the same. Neither Orlan the artist nor Jackson the *Überbarbie* are subject to the patriarchal or phallic standard of beauty embodied by classical models such as Venus, or its kitsch Barbie doll correlates in popular culture, that attempt to regulate female bodies and the 'excess' traditionally associated with femininity. Rather, they dis-place that standard into a new order of excess that itself becomes the norm, the only regulative principle being the demand for more. In this respect, however, the strategies of self-creation and self-subjectivation employed by Orlan and Jackson are directly related to other forms of body modification – obesity and self-starvation – that are not so much responses to regulative ideal images, as effects of a general principle of excess.

Moral, rational, utilitarian and even perhaps aesthetic judgements no longer make any sense in a world palpitating with too much of everything or too much of nothing. The pathological norms of dietary excess strangely replicate the spiralling polarizations of a global economy producing and consuming beyond any regulative framework: too much affluence, too much poverty. But who can say what is too much when the imperative 'more of everything' applies? According to Jean-Joseph Goux's critique of Bataille's economic categories, 'postmodern capitalism' is defined by the inability to distinguish between useful production based on a rational measurement of human needs, and extravagant, luxurious expenditure that wastes time, goods and resources without profit or return of any kind. The erosion of the possibility of differentiation allows previously unimaginable levels of expenditure to emerge, useful and useless activity entwined to the extent that the restricted economic of production incorporates the excesses once expended in a symbolic, ritualistic and sumptuary general realm.

It is not so much a question of the absence of regulative ideals, then; more a question of the production and multiplication of marginal differences and innovations that function as the law of excess. Not only does the absence of a regulative ideal fail to arrest the momentum, a demand is made that there are always more commodities to be consumed, and more weight to be lost. Similarly, the imperative for more, and the necessity for marginal differences upon which it depends, means that there is no limit to the need for body modification and the further enhancement and development of technologies of cosmetic surgery: collagen injections, liposuction, nose jobs, neck tightening, tummy tucks, silicon breast enhancements . . . gene-splicing is surely next, and no doubt it will be accompanied by a whole new microbiological level of body redesign. There is no limit to the work that 'needs' to be done, no point where beauty is attained once and for all. The process takes over beyond the point where an ideal of beauty may once have left a customer satisfied and imaginarily complete. Beyond a return to youthful beauty, cosmetic surgery charts an exorbitant trajectory elsewhere. Difference, 'otherness' and monstrosity no longer serve as the exception guaranteeing human values; they only establish the illusion of difference and the fact of its disappearance. In the absence of a restricted economy of signifying conventions, otherness is sought out, reproduced and circulated freely: 'this liquidation of the Other is accompanied by an artificial synthesis of otherness – a radical cosmetic surgery of which cosmetic surgery on faces and bodies is merely the symptom' (Baudrillard, *Crime*, 115). The synthesis of otherness, of course, exerts the magnetic pull of the same which assimilates strangeness, a 'hypostasis of the Same' drawing the subject into increasing proximity with self-image.

In facial traits, in sex, in illness, in death, identity is constantly 'altered'. There is nothing you can do about it: that's destiny. But it is precisely that subjection to an arbitrary, fatal destiny that must be exorcized at any cost through an identification with the body, through an individual appropriation of the body, of your desire, your look, of your image. If the body is no longer a place of otherness [*alterité*], a dual relationship, but it is rather a locus of identification, we then reconcile to it, we must repair it, perfect it, make it an ideal object. Everyone uses their body like a man uses woman in the projective mode of identification described before. The body is invested as a fetish, and is used as a fetish in a desperate attempt at identifying oneself. The body becomes the object of an autistic cult and of a quasi-incestuous manipulation. And it is the likeness [*ressemblance*] of the body with its model which then becomes a source of eroticism and of 'white' [fake, virgin, neutral, . . .] self-seduction to the extent that this likeness virtually excludes the Other and is the best way to exclude a seduction which would emerge from somewhere else. (Baudrillard, 'Plastic surgery')

Beyond an ideal of self-identification and an exorcism of destiny, however, the body is given over to an economy in which sameness and otherness are artificially recreated and exceeded. There is something one can do about destiny's incessant alteration of identity: 'though we cannot make our Sun / Stand still, yet we will make him run'. Assume destiny and accelerate the process of alteration, taking control of – and simultaneously giving in to – an artificial destiny. Autoaffection, exposing the absence of otherness as it spirals inwards and evacuates all resistance, precipitates the imminent implosion of the selfsame, a final neutralization. It thus demands a countervailing pull against implosion, a repetition or reinvention of difference that goes beyond ideals and self-identity in a deforming procession of synthesized monstrosities in turn rendered the same. And so on.

Faces and bodies require incessant adjustment not just because they are subject to an implacable regime of ideal images, but because they are in competition with images that constantly readjust their look. Hollywood stars who feel their employment threatened by ever thinner human actresses also have digital rivals whose size, shape and features are not limited by corporeal standards. Indeed, the 'lollipops', whose dramatic weight loss gives their appearance a deformed quality, with heads too large for stick bodies, strangely resemble the cartoon and virtual characters whose features are overaccentuated to the point of being 'physically deformed by human standards' (Hamilton, non-pag.). The 'deformed aesthetic' moves images of desire beyond the human: 'unearthliness is part of the charm' (Poole, 153). This is perhaps the trajectory already charted by Cynthia Jackson and her tribe of *Überbarbie*. Off the farm and out of Hicksville, the *Überbarbie* hit escape velocity right out of the human race.

And on board the next upgrade of the USS *Enterprise*, a new new generation of genetically enhanced aliens converse in the bar, their ridged noses, bumps and rippled foreheads signifying the wealth of cultural difference in the Federation's universe of the Same. The Orlaneans are there, with their French accents, their little bumps and their outré noses, still pitching Romantic ideals of individual and artistic transcendence against the scornful mercantile utilitarianism of the Ferengi.

WORKS CITED

Adams, Parveen. *The Emptiness of the Image: Psychoanalysis and Sexual Difference*. London: Routledge, 1996.

Ayers, Robert. 'Serene and happy and distant: an interview with Orlan'. *Body and Society* 5:2/3 (1999): 171–84.

Baudrillard, Jean. *The Transparency of Evil*. Trans. James Benedict. London: Verso, 1993.

— 'Plastic surgery for the other'. *CTheory* 22 November 1995, <www.ctheory.net/text_file.asp?pick=75>.

— *The Perfect Crime*. Trans. Chris Turner. London: Verso, 1996.

Carter, Angela. *The Infernal Desire Machines of Dr Hoffman*. London: Penguin, 1982.

Clarke, Julie. 'The sacrificial body of Orlan'. *Body and Society* 5:2/3 (1999): 185–207.

Farnell, Ross. 'In dialogue with "posthuman" bodies: interview with Stelarc'. *Body and Society* 5:2/3 (1999): 129–47.

Goodall, Jane. 'An order of pure decision: un-natural selection in the work of Stelarc and Orlan'. *Body and Society* 5:2/3 (1999): 149–70.

Goux, Jean-Joseph. 'General economics and postmodern capitalism'. *Yale French Studies* 78 (1990): 206–24.

— 'Subversion and consensus: proletarians, women, artists'. In *Terror and*

Consensus: Vicissitudes of French Thought. Ed. Jean-Joseph Goux and Philip R. Wood. Stanford, CA: Stanford University Press, 1998. 37–53.

Hamilton, Robert. 'Virtual idols and digital girls: artifice and sexuality in Anime, Kisekae and Kyoko Date'. *Bad Subjects* 35 (November 1997).

Hirschhorn, Michelle. 'Orlan artist in the post-human age of mechanical reincarnation: *body as ready (to be re-)made*'. In *Generations and Geographies in the Visual Arts*. Ed. Griselda Pollock. London: Routledge, 1996. 110–34.

Lacan, Jacques. *Écrits*. Trans. Alan Sheridan. London: Tavistock, 1977.

—— *The Ethics of Psychoanalysis, 1959–60*. Trans. Dennis Porter. London: Routledge, 1992.

Lovelace, Carey. 'Orlan: offensive acts'. *Performing Arts Journal* 49 (1995): 13–25.

Onfray, Michel. 'Surgical aesthetics'. In *This Is My Body . . . This Is My Software*. Ed. Duncan McCorquodale. London: Black Dog Publishing, 1996. 30–39.

Orlan. 'Conference'. In *This Is My Body . . . This Is My Software*. Ed. Duncan McCorquodale. London: Black Dog Publishing, 1996. 82–93.

—— Interview. *The South Bank Show*. Dir. David Wiles. Ed. and pres. Melvyn Bragg. London Weekend Television, 1997.

Poole, Steven. *Trigger Happy: The Inner Life of Videogames*. London: Fourth Estate, 2000.

Rand, Erica. *Barbie's Queer Accessories*. Durham, NC: Duke University Press, 1995.

Rose, Barbara. 'Is it art? Orlan and the transgressive act'. *Art in America* 81:2 (February 1993): 82–7.

Stelarc. 'From psycho to cyber strategies: prosthetics, robotics and remote existence'. *Cultural Values* 1:2 (1997): 241–9.

—— 'Parasite visions: alternate, intimate and involuntary experiences'. *Body and Society* 5:2/3 (1999): 117–27.

Wilson, Sarah. 'L'Histoire d'O, sacred and profane'. In *This Is My Body . . . This Is My Software*. Ed. Duncan McCorquodale. London: Black Dog Publishing, 1996. 7–17.

Wilson, Scott. 'Diana, the press and the politics of emotion'. In *Diana: The Making of a Media Saint*. Ed. Jeffrey Richards, Scott Wilson and Linda Woodhead. London: I.B. Tauris, 1999. 40–58.

CHAPTER 10

*The Virtual **and/or** the Real*

ORLAN

Content appears to me to be the most important factor [in art]. Lately, I was delighted to read McEvilley's book *Art and Discontent*,[1] which demonstrates the ineptitudes of Greenberg's formalism.[2]

The works of art that find most favour with me are those which are above all determined by a definite take, bias or social project, a manner of thinking. The fact that these artefacts are made with the help of either new technologies or more traditional forms of expression is of course not irrelevant, but technology is not important for its own sake.

The most important thing is that these forms and techniques do not become a prison and/or a comfortable formula in which the artist takes refuge, sending his/her thoughts to sleep.

We are still 'formatted' by Christianity, which always asks us to choose between good **or** evil; the '**or**' permits a designation of the guilty one and a demonization of the one or the other . . .

Currently the '**and**' seems to me to be the only honourable and productive choice! Today the '**and**' avoids the far too widespread Manicheanisms: 'painting **or** new technologies'; 'the foundry **or** video'; 'sculpture **or** the Internet', etc., which I've often come across in the art school where I teach and in many other places.

In my work the '**and**' keeps cropping up: 'the past **and** the present', 'the public **and** the private', the 'supposedly beautiful **and** the supposedly ugly', 'the natural **and** the artificial', 'satellite transmissions **and** the drawings made with my fingers and my blood during the surgical operations/performances', 'the reliquary sculptures with my flesh **and** the works conceived with CAD, morphing . . ., produced in collaboration with the other side of the world thanks to email', etc. . . .

Of course I use new technologies, but not systematically, not at any

168

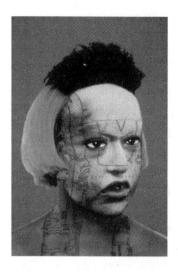

Plate 7   Orlan, *Self-Hybridation*, 1998.
Technical aid: P. Zovilé. Courtesy of
Espace d'Art, Yvonamor Palix Paris–Mexico

price, nor in order to obtain the best definition of the image with the most sophisticated machine and software, but in order that a certain way of using new technologies creates meaning and is the most appropriate for revealing the quality of the underlying idea of the art work, the idea that precedes the fabrication of the images.

Sometimes I do an art work **and/or** a performance that permits me to highlight my critical distance in relation to new technologies. For example, the performance I did at the ICA in London in 1995, 'Woman with a Head **and** Illusion, Simulation, Virtuality', was inspired by an observation: new technologies promise to get rid of the body, they promise a dematerialization, but for a mortal body like mine, that remains inaccessible. I consequently used a conjuring trick dating from 1893 thanks to which it is possible to pretend to be just a head placed on a table for the audience and oneself, not to have a body but just to be a talking head, just like my cyberware clone. However, that didn't stop me from also using for this performance new technologies in the form of videos **and** images of my head recorded in cyberware.

On the other hand, I have to say I am always surprised by the isolation of art events from new technology forums and their write-ups in the magazines. (In Italy, Francesca Alfano Miglietti tries to bring them together in her journal *Virus*.) It is rare for artists associated with 'new technologies' to be regularly invited to museums, galleries, biennial events and events hosted by art journals (except for video artists such as Bill Viola, Gary Hill, Tony Oursler).

Those artists working with the virtual, the Internet and up-to-date technologies find themselves alone and they don't know – in the majority of cases – the names of the other artists (and vice versa). Cross-over points are rare and it is absolutely necessary for that to change as soon as possible (George Rey at the Museum of Contemporary Art at Lyon is one of the ferrymen).

It is certain that a traditional plastic artist can be very disoriented when confronted with the repercussions of the artwork using new technologies. It causes problems of authorship rights (the artwork is the product of a whole team), distribution (which is immediate and to a large number of spectators), and its reproducibility (the works are easily duplicated, in particular on the Web).

Here is a very short history of art:

- For thousands of years, art was a source of social cohesion. When it kept in step with the sacred, with religion, we can say that it was also a form of propaganda.
- A long time afterwards, art set itself problems of definition and asked how reality could be represented with precision (new technologies are currently at this stage). Of course, this is a period that does not greatly interest me.
- Then art began to talk about art for art's sake.
- Then there was the market boom, where most artists adapted themselves to society and overadapted to the art market.
- Then came the market crash, which provoked an even deeper crisis, a total discrediting of art and artists (we all have, or almost all, some responsibility for this). The talk of arrière-garde, of the return to order, the return to professional skills and to figuration, was able to find attentive ears ready to put into question all the freedoms that contemporary art, and art of the twentieth century in general, had taken.

New technologies can be one of the defences against this kind of talk. Other defence strategies arise when art delves into other fields (biology, medicine, AI, networks, genetics) rather than sticking to its habitual subject matters. Another defence is the integration of the real into art, engaging in questions that concern our life and each one of us, so that art is again at the heart of relations between humans, increasing its interest for the majority and not just for a minority elite. So that art finds its role again . . .

I come back therefore to my initial words about the '**and**' in order to propose the virtual **and** the real used simultaneously as new transversalities that question art and the becoming of our world.

One of my preferred mottoes is '**remember the future**'.

Translated by Diane Morgan

EDITOR'S NOTES

1. Thomas McEvilley. *Art and Discontent: Theory at the Millennium*. New York: McPherson, 1993.
2. Clement Greenberg, a US art critic (1909–94), exerted extraordinary influence over post-war North American art as a champion of both Abstract Expressionism and one of the movement's chief exponents, Jackson Pollock. He was a proponent of a formal approach to art.

CHAPTER 11

Anger, Art and Medicine: Working with Orlan

RACHEL ARMSTRONG

As a junior doctor who had been forced to leave the profession by the unreasonable demands of the UK's National Health Service (NHS), I was an angry young woman. Looking for some means of expressing this outrage, I came across a picture of an artist whose work matched the strength of my own rage and despair. It was an image of a French performance artist called Orlan, who was staging her own surgical operations. I first met her at a conference 'Seduced and Abandoned: The Body in the Virtual World', held at the Institute of Contemporary Arts in London.

Orlan's work was already seen as controversial in the art world. She had just completed her seventh, eighth and ninth performance-operations in New York with a female cosmetic surgeon, Dr Marjorie Cramer. Orlan's multimedia auto-portraits, with their technicoloured representations of body dissections, shocked aesthetes but they also managed to capture my curiosity. I was particularly fascinated by Orlan's subversion of the medical establishment.

> Skin is deceiving . . . in life, one only has one's skin . . . there is a bad exchange in human relations because one is never what one has . . . I never have the skin of what I am. There is no exception to the rule because I am never what I have. (Eugénie Lemoine-Luccioni, cited in Orlan, 88)

During her conference talk, Orlan showed a video of her work. Surgeons were running around in designer garments, while perform-ance artists and a deaf-and-dumb linguist made hand gestures behind her. In the midst of this medical chaos Orlan somberly read from philosophical texts and answered faxed questions. The result was both comic and grotesque; it resembled a circus but with the added fascination of being able to witness the artist surrender to pain, medical error or death. But it was not the blood, open wounds or facial swelling that bonded me to Orlan, but rather the perverse picture of a future operating theatre she painted.

It was 1992 and the NHS was under increasing pressure to change. The health system was expected to become 'more efficient'. In practical terms, this meant that more private work would be carried out in public hospitals. We were often required to provide medical cover for private patients in addition to our NHS duties.

Orlan's portrait was shocking because she had opened the door to a world where medical care could be specifically customized to meet a single patient's every need, provided the funding was secured. Rather than constitute a utopian environment, her idea of clinical individuality was peculiar, idiosyncratic and psychotic. There was no established order there; the clinicians and theatre staff bowed to the whims of the patient/diva. During this perverse spectacle multiple media protruded, recording and communicating its explicit narrative. Later the patient/ artist edited the sound recording and images as an artistic video. She also processed the swabs, gauzes and pieces of flesh that had been extracted and mounted them behind thick panes of glass as 'reliquaries' that she had given up for her 'art'.

Meanwhile the audience and art critics were preoccupied with psychoanalysing the theatrical gore. Newspaper and journal articles tended to focus on the details of the operation, describing what Orlan was having done to her body: liposuction, implants or hairline raising. However, in the outrage provoked by her systematic surgical reinvention, Orlan had accomplished a *coup d'état* of the surgical theatre. Orlan wanted flowers in the operating theatre, she got them! Orlan wanted photographers to be taken, no problem! Orlan wanted to wear lipstick, of course! Orlan wanted music of a particular kind to be played and her wish was granted!

Most triumphantly of all, Orlan had persuaded the surgeon to make her face and her body change to suit her own particular design. To ensure that she had been fully understood, she had even brought along her own computer-generated picture. This operation/performance was the beginning of a new phenomenon in medicine: designer anatomy.

What had happened to the sterile surgical environment, the solemn ceremony of opening the body and the hierarchical 'respect' that was paid to both staff and patient in the operational procedure? The decorum of medical practice had suddenly become a burlesque side-show, comic, hilarious and irreverent, to everyone involved. How long would it be before our medical insurance policies guaranteed us a particular ambience in the operating theatre to speed our recovery? Would some future houseman be bleeped to register a complaint about the aesthetics of the recovery room?

I sat on my hands to stop myself from interrupting the translated French of Orlan's speech, but could not keep still in my seat. I was excited and terrified by the implications of her work.

I have given my body to Art. – *J'ai donné mon corps à l'art.* (Orlan, 92)

Perhaps the idea that this outrageous experiment was being executed in the name of something other than the 'public good' was sufficiently subversive an act against the institutions of medicine for me to volunteer my 'services' to Orlan. When I followed the blue-and-white-haired woman into the foyer and left her my card, it was my emotional intelligence and not my intellect that was on autopilot.

Orlan was initially aloof and cautious. As I persisted in my communications, she began to respond to my invitations to help her with medically related contacts and ideas. One day I came home to an answerphone message left in Franglais, in which she asked me to help her in planning and promoting her work in Britain. I was only too happy to be involved but I felt I needed to understand more about where her work was leading.

Orlan told me that she was the only artist making 'Carnal Art', which she defined as a form of classical self-portraiture but realized through the technology of our time. With modern advances in anaesthesia and surgical technique, she was able to use her flesh as a canvas. She authoritatively declared that she intended to provoke questions about the status of the body in our society. Carnal Art was not just about surgery but also about other advanced techniques in medicine and biology that raised questions related to future generations, such as genetic manipulation. I was supposed to help her in 'researching' possible bio-technological projects that she could then translate into her art.

Orlan worked long hours, travelled extensively to festivals and taught at a college of fine art in Dijon. Her life was complex, chaotic and demanding. Consequently, she was efficient, direct and often tired. When Orlan was tired, she spoke in French, and so I learned to improve my basic O-level grasp of the subject. At first I tried to say things that were far too complicated for my vocabulary, but gradually I began to simplify my sentences and realize that not everything in English has an equivalent in French. We spent more time together, agreed on various projects and started to collaborate.

I began to re-imagine myself in a medical clinic, taking a 'medical history', conducting an examination and reaching some hypothesis on the basis of which Orlan's 'outcome' could be evaluated. For example, I concluded the 'bosses' or 'horns' that she had inserted on her forehead made from the largest possible cheek implants could be considered from the perspective of the ancient clinical practice of phrenology. This was a way of reading the 'mind', made popular by Sir Francis Gall, and it involved feeling the skull for specific contours. The patterns of the lumps and bumps on the person's head were thought to be indicative of their intelligence. I found it rather amusing that Orlan's artificial excess of bumps implied that she was a woman of advanced intelligence. I then thought of the same features in the context of an alien character, Mia from *Space 1999*. In this film, Mia had a band of 'bosses' in her forehead and could transform herself into any living creature in the galaxy by catching the image in her eye. Orlan's implants alluded to the possibility of her real transformation into someone with an 'alien' anatomy, or at least signified that she desired to undergo an identity change of this kind.

Orlan and I were constantly in touch via email, faxes and telephone conversations, planning and promoting her work. She was particularly interested in travelling to Britain, as she was keen to be recognized by the increasingly prestigious British art scene.

Orlan planned to have one final operation before the new millennium. This, she told me, would be an enormous nose, the largest that could possibly be made for her face, and she suspected that the best surgeons would be in Japan. I squirmed at the idea. I had seen noses broken and cartilages realigned many times, and the result left patients with spectacular bruising. Orlan had a cute 'button' nose and was frequently asked if she had had it 'bobbed' in one of her prior operations. She found this ironic and amusing. Even though I had become used to the extreme demands that Orlan envisaged as far as her appearance went, I wondered how far this operation could be taken in the real world.

There was only one way to find out. Orlan, Professor Moss (an eminent orthodontic surgeon), Professor Alfred Linney (expert in facial aesthetics), John Wyver (who specialized in arts and technology programmes) and I sat down at a Chinese restaurant to discuss the results of a three-dimensional scan of Orlan's face. During this meeting of 'medical minds and technological excellence', the subject of discussion was the possible alterations to an original virtual model of Orlan's face in which the nasal bridge had been extended by a whole 5 millimetres.

'It is not enough!' declared Orlan through her monosodium glutamate-laden chopsticks; 'I want the most enormous nose possible for me please, like this!' For one horrible moment I thought she was going to demonstrate the whole procedure using her chopsticks as blunt surgical instruments. Instead, she pointed to a place about an inch beyond the tip of her nose.

Professor Moss went pale. He was deeply concerned about the technical implications of her request. 'Promise me, Rachel,' he said, taking me to one side as we marched down Haymarket, 'that you'll advise her most strongly not to have it done. She will be left with continuous bleeding from her nose; recurrent infections, thin skin and voice change. Besides, I don't know anyone in this country that would touch this project, from a professional perspective. The risk to their reputation would just be too great!'

I had seen Orlan a couple of times when she had had infections around her silicone implants. Her cheek appeared tense and red, she was swallowing handfuls of antibiotics and her muscles were paralysed on that side. I imagined this extended to her nose – bandaged and swollen – and to her puffy, tired eyes. It was not just the operations that would take their toll on her body but the whole healing process.

How would she breathe? More importantly, she had mentioned several times that she identified more closely with her voice than her face. Now it seemed that would change too. Did everything have to be sacrificed for art?

Professor Moss shook his head and then smiled. 'Before I met her, I assumed she was mad. Now, after talking with her this evening, I think she is clinically sane but what she is doing to herself is crazy! I wish her luck!' I did not tell him that Orlan insisted that all of us did crazy things without necessarily being crazy ourselves. Athletes push their bodies to the limit, and yachtsmen and yachtswomen risk their lives to sail around the world, but this particular project had the unique potential to become a chronic affliction. Despite her intellectual intentions, Orlan was just an ordinary person, possessing a body that was designed to age, fail and die just like the rest of us.

A few words on pain. I try to make this work as unmasochistic as possible, but there is a price to pay: the anaesthetic shots are not pleasant. . . . After the operations, it is sometimes uncomfortable, sometimes painful. I therefore take analgesics. (Orlan, 92)

As someone who had trained to accept a whole variety of different bodies, faces and personalities as being essential to the human race, I did not care about the exact shape or size of her nose. Whether Orlan was a classical beauty or a 'grotesque' would not change my high opinion of her. But I was really concerned about her health if she decided to pursue this particular project. Enlarging the nose would involve months of preparation in skin stretching, grafts of bone and tissue, and extensive remodelling, literally 'cutting off her nose to spite her face'! I began to doubt her chances of healing fully without succumbing to bone infections or sepsis.

This was no longer a 'cosmetic' procedure as such; it was radical plastic surgery, more intrusive, prolonged and dangerous. I would have to reinforce Professor Moss's advice. Her project design had crossed the line of the 'superficial' parts of her anatomy and entered into the unpredictable deep body spaces.

I went home feeling uneasy. I realized that there was a point where I would not assist in her transformation. As I had come to know more about Orlan as a person, I could no longer see her as a mere 'metaphor' for my own anger against the medical establishment and the political chaos of the NHS. She was someone I cared about. Artistic and scientific rhetoric appeared to be crude post-mortem excuses for thinly disguised self-harm. The best thing for Orlan's health would be to abandon the idea of an enormous nose, but her artistic and personal success depended on the project. Something was going to have to give, so I sat on the fence, waiting for a higher authority to decide for me.[1]

'I have given my body to Art.' After my death it will not therefore be given to science, but to a museum. It will be the centrepiece of a video installation. (Orlan, 92)

EDITOR'S NOTE

1. As Kate Ince explains in her monograph *Orlan: Millennial Female* (Oxford and New York: Berg, 2000), it now seems unlikely that this concluding operation, which would involve the construction of a gigantic elongated nose, will actually take place. 'As an end-point to "Reincarnation", the construction of a phallophanic nose would have marked a reneging on the open-ended, experimental identity work which has characterised Orlan's surgical project from the outset. . . . Her change of plan illustrates the double bind of her relationship to phallocentrically organised visual images, which initially acknowledged the representational framework of the phallocentric symbolic order, but has resisted its inscription on her flesh' (77; see also 110).

WORKS CITED

Orlan. 'Conference.' *This Is My Body . . . This Is My Software*. Ed. Duncan McCorquodale. London: Black Dog Publishing, 1996. 82–93.

PART 4

*Aesthetics and Ethics:
Technological Perspectives*

CHAPTER 12

In Defence of Prefigurative Art:
The Aesthetics and Ethics of Orlan and Stelarc

CHRIS HABLES GRAY

PREFIGURATION

Art can, art must change the world, for that is its only
justification. (Orlan, 'Orlan on becoming-Orlan')

I agree completely with Orlan that art must be political (Gray, 'Art
and the future of war'). Today, since one of the greatest political
issues we face is the progressive cyborgization of humanity (Gray,
Cyborg Citizen, *The Cyborg Handbook*), art should be, and actually is, a
major source of our insights about our cyborg society ('Cyborgs'). If
we study the work of Stelarc and Orlan closely, it is clear that not
only is their art a very political reflection on cyborgization, but it goes
much further. Their work, which is themselves, is a direct attempt to
shape our cyborg future. It is prefigurative art.

To prefigure could just mean, as *Webster's Dictionary* has it, 'to
suggest . . . to picture beforehand . . . to imagine', but that is not the
sense I want. Instead, the meaning here is 'to be an antecedent . . . to
foreshadow', also from the dictionary. To prefigure in this way is to
model, to work towards, to make the future by living it. The term
'prefiguration' has not been used much in this way (or any way,
actually) in relation to art, as far as I can determine, but it is a
common idea in politics.

Prefigurative politics is the basis for much of the non-party organ-
izing in North America and Europe today. Influenced strongly by
feminism, with its slogan 'the personal is political', activists for the
past thirty years or more have stressed that the form of their politics,

even their lives, must be consistent with the goals. The debate about prefigurative politics is often in the form of 'the ends versus the means'. Disagreements about the role of violence and non-violence in social struggles are usually between those who see a direct relationship between means and ends and people with a more instrumentalist view of reality. In any event, most feminists, anarchists and ecologists practise some form of prefigurative politics, while liberals and Leninists agree with Mao (or Trotsky, or Mao and Trotsky) that you 'can't make an omelette without breaking eggs'. Except what they really mean is that you can't make a revolution without breaking heads, but the revolution somehow won't be taken over by the best head-breakers. History tells us otherwise.

So, in that diffuse but real space that can still be called the 'counter'-culture, people try to live ecologically, relate to each other ethically, govern their communities non-hierarchically, and make political change with as little violence and as much joy as is possible. There isn't necessarily any loss of effectiveness with this approach – witness the movement against corporate globalism that has proven so powerful recently in Seattle, Zurich, London and Prague – and there is also the benefit of minimizing the hypocrisy that seems inevitable with all politics, especially those that seek fundamental change.

Art, as a major part of human culture, is inevitably political, whether that is explicit or not. I know that formalists and aesthetic romantics won't accept this, but how could it be otherwise? One of the few things Aristotle got right was that community and politics are integral; they are the *polis*. If art refuses politics, than that refusal is political in itself. Every act of representation is inevitably a political act, either reifying or challenging things as they are. The best case study of this that I know of is Serge Guibaut's *How New York Stole the Idea of Modern Art*, which demonstrates how even abstract expressionism is profoundly political in its origins and effects.

So it seems obvious that, in some ways, most art is prefigurative to some extent. Art may well have started as magic in the service of wish-fulfilment: 'See, I make the grazing beast with my spear in it so I will kill and we will eat the grazing beast.' But this belief in the direct efficacy of representation has faded somewhat in the past few thousand years. Art that shows some beautiful possible future might be considered prefigurative as well, although only on an intellectual level, but the vast majority of futuristic art seems more utopian, or dystopian, than truly prefigurative. Utopia is 'nowhere', after all, and art that posits perfection can't be prefigurative, for we'll never have perfect politics. Dystopia is then not/nowhere, which could mean everywhere, but actually it refers clearly to a society that has slipped deeply over into horror. Nazi Germany would be a dystopia were it not actual history. Dystopias might happen, but who, except the evil or insane would wish to prefigure them?

It is only recently, with some works of political or environmental performance art, that we see true prefiguration involved in what is 'officially' termed art. For example, a few years ago Beulah Gordon performed a beautiful piece called *Monk of an Order of One*, where she dedicated her life to being an activist monk for peace. But such work is not common, and it seldom addresses one of the most crucial political issues humanity is now facing: the implications of our increasingly cyborged society.

This is not the place to argue that cyborgization represents the next great step in the human–technology relationship that started with *Homo faber* (the tool maker) and evolved into our culture of cities and machines (civilization). It isn't much of an argument in any event, since thanks to such technosciences as genetic engineering we are actually on the verge of producing post-human species. The real issue is what kinds of cyborgizations we will have, and art such as Orlan's and Stelarc's can play a crucial role in demonstrating, even shaping, our options. David Tomas articulated this clearly almost a decade ago when he described his work as 'a laboratory for the production and exploration of one kind of quasi-mechanized human body' (255).

Now Orlan and Stelarc are directly addressing this issue, and they are doing so with an artistic practice that takes prefiguration, politically and artistically, to a whole new level. Looking closely at their work, we can't help but notice their powerful and principled intervention into the fundamental questions of cyborg politics, and we can also discern how their work manifests the necessary, but hidden, relation-ships between aesthetics, ethics and politics.

PREFIGURATIVE AESTHETICS

Orlan's full, flowing and multiply connecting body dramatically performs, then, the grotesque cyborg that we are always becoming. This hybrid political/technological/organic body is 100% recycled material; it is the materialization of its context. (Jasmine Rault, non-pag.)

As Raymond Williams explains it, a German philosopher by the name of Alexander Baumgarten (1714–62) coined the term 'aesthetics' for apprehending phenomenal perfection (beauty) through the senses. For the Greeks, the original *aisthesis* meant all those things that could be sensed, as opposed to only thought. Attempts to reintroduce the Greek meaning pretty much failed, leaving aesthetics stranded in art's discourse (Williams). The equally important idea of not feeling at all, of anaesthetic, was captured not by art but by science, which claims to produce an absence of feeling more efficiently than even the worst art.

While a lack of feeling is clearly desired by a minority of people, intense feelings seem to be more attractive. For many it seems any intense feeling will do, while others actually seek out horror or even despair. But many search for beauty. Now, in these late days – or are they early? – do we still say beautiful? If we do, does it mean anything?

I love beauty as much as the next guy, and believe in it even, but I still don't want to judge art by the standard of beauty. I think art should do more than be beautiful. It should act on us. If I had to use just one word to judge art by, that word would be *compelling*. Art, in my opinion, is something that stimulates our senses; art compels us to think, to feel, to change. But if more than one word were allowed to define art I would also choose *utilitarian* and talk about what art does for society, for communication, for community. Perhaps this is a very unfashionable way to approach art but that's my view of it. I think it should have some use-value.

So, inevitably, I see aesthetics leading to ethics. Some artists, and many art critics, will disagree with this, but would they disagree that the work of a good lawyer should be ethical? That a good doctor or computer engineer should be ethical? A good teacher or friend?

Why should art be above ethics? Well, I don't think it can be, and pretending it can is an ethical position itself, and not a good one.

Which doesn't mean that art should be didactic or obvious. In fact, that would be bad aesthetically. If art is to be compelling it should seduce, it must be subtle or incredibly powerful, or both. The work of Stelarc and Orlan seems to be both. For example, when Stelarc and Orlan negotiate complex agreements with medical and other experts for the bloody modification of their own bodies they directly subvert the whole apparatus that limits these technologies to medical application and medical goals. Based on aesthetic considerations, their art directly changes ethical and political norms and reclaims the individual's (or at least the artist's) right to his or her own body from the professional establishment.

In the comments above about prefigurative art I purposefully left out the one major area where most art tries to be prefigurative: aesthetics. While some artists are willing to work only, as homage or nostalgia, in previous aesthetic frames, the majority of artists, and all the artists who aspire to 'high' art and success in the art establishment, see themselves as establishing new aesthetics, as being the new avant-garde. Much of this is because the art industry is in total complicity with modernism, and together they worship progress and capitalism with a special fondness for the new commodity. But it is also a reflection that the reality for many artists is that their art is about seeing the world in new ways and expressing that, with the admitted or secret desire that they can then communicate this new vision to other people.

These aesthetic progressions have always been political – sometimes overtly so, as with the exaltation of the individual in the Late Renaissance or the role of modern art in the twentieth century, though sometimes the implications of aesthetic shifts are harder to read politically. But fundamentally the 'aesthetic is political is personal' in any order you choose. The art is either compelling or not, on you and on others. Changing, or not changing, all who experience it. Which is inevitably political. This couldn't be clearer than it is in the relentlessly prefigurative aesthetics and ethics of Orlan and Stelarc:

Orlan's experiments are aesthetic: they test the possibilities for altering form and feature. They are also social, in that they test reactions to such alterations and, interestingly, it is not the effect of the experiment – the evolving look of Orlan – that generates the strongest reactions, but rather the unreadable motivation for her work. Why is she doing this? (Goodall, non-pag.)

She is doing it because she thinks we have the right to choose our own embodiment, our own future. Which is exactly the same fundamental motivation Stelarc articulates. His desire to go beyond the limits of the natural body is also expressed through his aesthetic choices. As he says, 'TECHNOLOGY INVADES AND FUNCTIONS WITHIN THE BODY NOT AS PROSTHETIC REPLACEMENT BUT AS AN AESTHETIC ADORNMENT' ('From psycho to cyber strategies', 245, original emphasis). Stelarc's cyborgization is not the remedial intervention (prosthetics) which medicine approves of. It is an enhancement, in this case, as a positive aesthetics, as art.

At least one critic, Dawn Perlmutter, has situated Orlan and Stelarc within what she calls 'sacrificial aesthetics'. She points out that today there are 'many expressions of the aesthetic that manifests itself in blood and flesh' (1). And she goes on to link together 'tattooing, piercing, branding and body modifications along with The Fetish Scene, Modern Primitives, and Vampire Culture'.

Perlmutter also argues that aesthetics are 'now ideologically freed from ethical responsibility to society' and have 'evolved into an authentic sacrificial culture inclusive of ritual murder' (1). This may, or may not, be the case for the aesthetics of some of the subcultures she discusses, but it certainly is not true for many of the artists and practitioners she has drafted into her sacrificial aesthetic, as can be demonstrated by the clearly ethical context of the art of Stelarc and Orlan.

PREFIGURATIVE ETHICS AND EMBODIMENT

Like the Australian artist Stelarc, I believe that the body is obsolete. It can no longer deal with the situation. We mutate at the speed of cockroaches, and yet we are cockroaches with their memories on computer, piloting airplanes and driving cars which we have developed even though our bodies are not made for their speeds and even though everything is going faster and faster. (Orlan, 12)

For every one as he is himselfe, so he hath a selfe propriety, else could he not be himself. (Leveller doctrine, seventeenth century, quoted in Goodall, 3)

It has been much harder for art to be prefigurative ethically than it has been for it to put forward new aesthetics. But it has not been impossible, as some of the examples given above demonstrate. The work of Stelarc and Orlan is extraordinary in this regard. Not only do they put forward somewhat different, but fundamentally allied, ethical positions towards the individual, society and the body but they also are directly involved in actually defining new ethical arrangements around cyborg medicine specifically and cyborgization in general. It is prefigurative embodiment and ethics through aesthetics. As Stelarc says, 'As a body, one no longer looks at art, does not perform as art, but contains art' ('Hollow body', 250).

Their prefigurative ethics revolve around several key cyborgian political issues: Whose body is it? Who do the technoscientific cyborgologists work for? What is the relationship between the human and the post-human?

Jane Goodall explores some of these issues in relationship to Orlan and Stelarc in her article 'Whose body? Ethics and experiment in performance art'. She makes it clear that Orlan's 'aesthetic experiments' are necessarily experiments in ethics as well.

So, whose body is it? Despite references by Stelarc, when he works, to 'the' body, not 'his' body, it is his body that is 'worked' on. No other bodies are used and nobody else owns the Stelarc body, which is a major point of his. Only he 'owns' his body, and he isn't his body. His choice of words is to demonstrate his commitment is to the individual will or personality, not the individual's body, so he proclaims 'EVOLUTION BY THE INDIVIDUAL, FOR THE INDIVIDUAL' (Stelarc, 'From psycho to cyber strategies', 242, emphasis in the original). He sees the body as so limited, so obsolete, that to be who he wants to be requires transcending the body, his body. Orlan might see the body as more useful. She is claiming her right to her body through claiming the right to remake her body and therefore herself. Both these positions are essentially political stands.

The body is political and the body in art is even more so. It was the second wave of feminism that re-established the human body as a central philosophical issue in the late twentieth century. In the masculinist Western traditions dominated by Platonism in various forms (pagan, Jewish, atheistic and Christian), the body was political only as a metaphor – the body politic – and not in and of itself. But today the illusion that the human body is not fundamental, that it is basically an epiphenomenon of mind, has been dispelled, by feminism politically and analytically (see especially Scarry, *The Body in Pain*) and by cyborgian technosciences practically.

Although Orlan and Stelarc both critique the human body for being quite limited, if not actually obsolete if it isn't modified technologically, they explicitly defend their right to their own body, echoing the Leveller argument that it is their personal property. Goodall asks in her article, 'Do we have unlimited rights over our own bodies?' and answers with the medical and scientific perspective that bodies are 'socialised and therefore are subject to regimes of care and discipline' (3).

Yet she does note that, 'Performance artists contest the regulation of bodies through calculated offenses against body disciplines and codes of propriety' (3). But art can do more than 'contest' body regulation and discipline; it can change them as well. Goodall worries that 'Almost every aspect of Orlan's work breaches medical protocol' (5). But that is the point: to change medical protocols; to allow us to experiment on ourselves. Even if Orlan's work is 'risk without benefit' in medical terms, it is risk with great benefit in artistic and societal terms. The medical frame is too small and limited to evaluate cyborgian interventions.

As it is now, most cyborgian enhancement work comes out of the military and industry, so to have Stelarc and Orlan carry out their own cyborgian enhancement programmes based on their artistic, or even idiosyncratic, desires only broadens the discourse and opens up possibilities. Artists and non-artists are now making themselves into everything from reptiles to Barbie the doll (Asma) in what can only be the beginning of a whole range of human modifications that could well end up producing post-humans who live in the sea or even in space. There is a proliferation of possibilities. Which, interestingly enough, is where Goodall ends up, after making her 'case for the prosecution' against the work of Stelarc and Orlan. In her conclusion she admits that they make us 'rethink what it means to be an agent, and how the legal, moral and ethical liabilities of the individual can be encoded' (9).

But it is more than rethinking. Through their actual artistic practices, both Orlan and Stelarc have breached the wall that doctors and scientists have put around medical technologies, and they have shown that we can choose to modify our bodies for our own goals, not just those of technoscience.

FUTURES

The image of the cyborg has historically recurred at moments of radical social and cultural change. From bestial monstrosities, to unlikely montages of body and machine parts, to electronic implants, imaginary representations of cyborgs take over when traditional bodies fail. In other words, when the current ontological model of human being does not fit a new paradigm, a hybrid model of existence is required to encompass a new, complex and contradictory lived experience. (Gonzalez, 270)

There has been a clear progression in the work of both Orlan and Stelarc from performance art, to body art, to carnal art, to what can variously be described as cyborg art or post-human art. I would like to add prefigurative art to this litany, for the reasons discussed above.

One can argue about labels, but what is undeniable is that we live in an age where change is driven by technoscience, where unifying grand stories of this God, that nation, high art and perfect science are not shared universally, even in one geographical/temporal space, and where both the human body and nature itself seem under siege.

We have the future of the human body to consider. It cannot, it does not, stay the same. It is being modified continually by militarized technoscience, consumerist manias and technological art (Gray, 'Cyborgs'). It is changing through conscious and unconscious participatory evolution. These changes are biological, technological and conceptual. And the body changes the very way we think changes. Lisa Moore and Monica Casper once told me that 'Anatomy is epistemology', which I would amend to say, so is how we think of our anatomy. In both cases it is clear that we need an open and dynamic epistemology because our bodies, and how we think of them, are changing. This is why Steven Mentor, Heidi Figueroa-Sarriera and I have proposed our cyborg epistemology: thesis, antithesis, synthesis, prosthesis, and again (Gray et al., The Cyborg Handbook).

It is based on the traditional dialectic because the dynamism the dialectic has is worth saving. But it tries to break from the inherent binary structure of only pure action and reaction ad infinitum. Things are more complicated. Reality, like our bodies, is too lumpy, changeable and contingent for any unified totalizing epistemology, so there is always prosthesis, something from outside. Hopefully, a cyborg epistemology will resist any claims that reality is purely material or ideal, or even the tepid dualism of Plato. How do we know? Through our senses in large part – aesthetically. In our minds, totally. We see, we feel and we reflect. But it is no closed march, as the Marxist materialists or Hegelian idealists would have it; it is an open and participatory process. It is like the art of Orlan and Stelarc. They both go to great lengths to involve the public: broadcasting their mortifications; even, in Stelarc's case, giving control of internal probes over to strangers on the Internet. Orlan and Stelarc manifest a cyborg epistemology in their work. Their will, their bodies, technologies, the public and traditions all react continually together with each other and against themselves, dynamically moving to new starting points.

The other similarities between these two cyborgian artists are striking. Their work is different, their goals seem different, their stances on the body are somewhat different, but they intersect in that: (1) the canvas is their own body, which meets (2) medical technoscience in (3) sites around the globe, where it is (4) enhanced, not rehabilitated, through (5) experimentation. Their approach is that (6) art must change the world; (7) the will triumphs over technology, and (8) art triumphs over science.

One doesn't have to agree with these positions to accept that they are important artists. What are artists for anyway? Are they society's canaries? Its clowns? Its conscience? Its martyrs? For me, artists are all these things. I like funny and serious canaries . . . compelling us to think; prefiguring the future.

Which means prefiguring what exactly? Cyborgs? Post-humans? Yes, in various forms, but the embodied details are not nearly as important as the process Stelarc and Orlan use. Post-human cyborgs are coming in any event, quickly. Parents are beginning to clamour for smarter babies, taller sons and daughters, cures for inherited diseases, and life, longer life, for everyone. The 'market' for post-human modifications is clearly there, and technoscience is on the verge of delivering up some of them. The crucial question is who will decide what is done to whom? There are many experts and leaders who feel that this is not a decision to be made democratically. At the best they say let the market decide; at the worst the criterion is national security. In any event, hard choices have to be made. After all, we all can't have it all.

Will this sea change offer us more choices, so that if we wish we can proclaim, as Orlan does, that 'I am a she-man and a he-woman'? (3). Or will cyborgization strip humanity of its freedom and of its chance to choose its own future, even if that future is to become post-human? This is a political question, and for some of us a big part of the answer is artistic.

One of Orlan's favourite slogans is 'Remember the future' (Orlan, 6). That is exactly what prefigurative art should do.

WORKS CITED

Asma, Stephen T. 'A portrait of the artist as a work in progress'. *The Chronicle of Higher Education* 19 January 2001: B17–B18.

Gonzalez, Jennifer. 'Envisioning cyborg bodies: notes from current research'. In *The Cyborg Handbook*. Ed. Chris Hables Gray. London: Routledge, 1995. 267–80.

Goodall, Jane. 'Whose body? Ethics and experiment in performance art', 2000, <www.cofa.unsw.edu.au/research/stanford/artmed/papers/goodall.html>.

Gray, Chris Hables. *Cyborg Citizen: Politics in the Postmodern Age*. London: Routledge, 2001.

— 'Art and the future of war'. In *The Gruinard Installation*. Ed. Mark Little and Lloyd Gibson. London: Locus-plus, 2000.

— 'Cyborgs, attention, and aesthetics'. *Issues in Contemporary Culture and Aesthetics*. Ed. Sue Golding (Johnny de Philo). Jan van Eyck Akademie department of theory, no. 12, August (2001): 132–5.

— *Postmodern War: The New Politics of Conflict*. New York: Guilford/London: Routledge, 1997.

— , ed. *The Cyborg Handbook*. London: Routledge, 1995.

Gray, Chris Hables, Heidi Figueroa-Sarriera and Steven Mentor. 'Cyborgology: constructing the knowledge of cybernetic organisms'. In *The Cyborg Handbook*. Ed. Chris Hables Gray. London: Routledge, 1995. 1–16.

Guibaut, Serge. *How New York Stole the Idea of Modern Art: Abstract Expressionism, Freedom, and the Cold War*. Trans. Arthur Goldhammer. Chicago: University of Chicago Press, 1983.

Orlan. '"I do not want to look like . . ." Orlan on becoming-Orlan'. Trans. Heidi Reitmeier, 2000, <www.cicv.fr/creation_artistique/online/orlan/women/women.html>.

Perlmutter, Dawn. 'The sacrificial aesthetic: blood rituals from art to murder'. *Anthropoetics* 5:2 (Fall/Winter 1999–2000), <www.anthropoetics.ucla.edu/ap0502/blood.htm>.

Rault, Jasmine. 'Orlan and the limits of materialization'. *J_Spot: Journal of Social and Political Thought* 1:2 (June 2000), <www.yorku.ca/jspot/2/jrault.htm>.

Scarry, Elaine. *The Body in Pain: The Making and Unmaking of the World*. Oxford: Oxford University Press, 1985.

Stelarc. 'From psycho to cyber strategies: prosthetics, robotics and remote existence'. *Cultural Values* 1:2 (1997): 241–9.

— 'Hollow body/host space/stomach sculpture'. *Cultural Values* 1:2 (1997): 250–51.

Tomas, David. 'Art, psychasthenic assimilation, and the cybernetic automaton'. In *The Cyborg Handbook*. Ed. Chris Hables Gray. London: Routledge, 1995. 255–66.

Williams, Raymond. *Keywords: A Vocabulary of Culture and Society*. Oxford: Oxford University Press, 1977.

CHAPTER 13

Ph/autography and the Art of Life:
Gillian Wearing's Ethical Realism

JAY PROSSER

A piece by Gillian Wearing called *Prelude* was for me the highlight of 'Intelligence', the 2000 exhibition of new British art. Consisting of a video installation, *Prelude* told of Lynda, a street drinker who died from cirrhosis of the liver (the work was presented as a 'prelude' to Wearing's 'portraits of street drinkers'). The video of Lynda – smoking, talking, laughing, drinking – played to the sound of her twin sister describing the loss: how Lynda died, how their mother 'didn't care', how the funeral was 'so cold' (she had never been to a funeral 'like that'); how she herself overdosed soon after the death; how the sisters had grown up talking about death. The video ran in slow motion, beautiful, grainy, real, its traumatic subject complicated through the relationship of the twins, the almost impossible demands of separating the self from the other: 'Lynda always said that if she went, I'd go with her . . . I had a dream of her and she let go of my hand . . . I feel as though I've lost a part of my body, of myself.' The media technology confused the borders even further. The difference between the subject of screen and the subject of sound at first left us unsure who was speaking and who was being spoken about. 'I will always miss her,' Lynda's sister said, and at this point Lynda turned to face the camera full on and poignantly, suddenly present, as though it were the sister, or even we the viewer, who were lost. *Prelude's* representation of real-life trauma, its interweaving of biography and autobiography, captured what we might call ethical realism in contemporary art. It not only made art out of life; it showed a consciousness about what it *means* to make art out of life.

In his *The Return of the Real: The Avant-Garde at the End of the Century*,

Hal Foster charts the return of the real in contemporary art. He sees
the real captured in two forms: in the representation of 'the violated
body and/or the traumatic subject, and [in] a turn to the referent as
grounded in a given identity and/or a sited community' (xviii). Foster's
return of the real is inscribed in a Lacan-informed notion of 'traumatic
realism'. In Lacan, the real returns as a thing of trauma. Traumatic
realism seeks a way out of the double binds of representation that
Foster thinks dominated twentieth-century representation – that is, the
binary that positions images as either referential or simulacral. According to Foster, '*This shift in conception – from reality as an effect of
representation to the real as a thing of trauma – may be definitive in
contemporary art, let alone in contemporary theory, fiction and film*' (146,
typography in all quotations as in original). While Foster's book stops
with art in the mid-1990s, his notion of traumatic realism in two
guises can account for much of the millennial art. Etymologically,
trauma means 'wound'. Performance art in particular continues to be
drawn to the broken boundaries of the violated body in an attempt to
show the real. The French performance artist Orlan, along with Mona
Hatoum, Jake and Dinos Chapman, Damien Hirst and much of new
British art, exemplifies this traumatic wounding of the body, and thus
continues the tradition of Cindy Sherman that Foster does cover. This
is perhaps why 'Britart' has been dubbed the 'New Neurotic Realism'
by its chief patron, Charles Saatchi. Britart shows the real in all its
visceral embodiment. Alongside this corporeal evocation of the real
there has been conducted an anthropological excavation of the real in
which the artist has returned to the community as ethnographer. The
anthropological turn in contemporary art is manifested less in particular
artists than in, appropriately enough, group shows and the way in
which art is displayed. In recent museum organizations and exhibitions
– most famously, the new thematic approach to twentieth-century art
taken by Tate Modern – the individuality of artists, *oeuvres* and even
historical periods is overridden in order to emphasize the collective
and continuous interests across times. In the case of Tate Modern,
galleries are (at the time of writing) arranged according to a number
of themes, including 'Still Life/Object/Real Life' and 'Nude/Action/
Body'. Individual exhibitions seek to break down the boundaries
between the artist and the community in their subject matter.

Contemporary art's engagement in the world was the subject both of the above-mentioned exhibition 'Intelligence' and 'Quotidiana: The Continuity of the Everyday in 20th Century Art', a recent exhibition in Turin. The guide accompanying 'Intelligence' explains the conception of the artist as present 'on site', as an anthropologist or sociologist: 'Many artists today can be seen as intelligence agents at large in society, gathering and transforming the raw data of our life, critically examining our environment, the way we live, and our relations with each other' (2). Anthropology appeals to both artists and art critics because culture and community life have become the subject of contemporary art. The barriers between the exhibition space and the community are being broken down not only within the exhibition space but in the community itself. Rachel Whiteread's recent *Holocaust Memorial*, built for the Judenplatz in Vienna, which translates as 'Jews' Square', is joined to the remains of the fifteenth-century synagogue. It is an example of art constructed for a community and designed for a specific location, which explains Whiteread's refusal to resite the project to another venue.

Yet these returns to the real are not without problems. Traumatizing the body, particularly in performance art, can become narcissistic. As Foster writes, 'self-othering can flip into self-absorption, in which the project of an "ethnographic self-fashioning" becomes the practice of a narcissistic self-refurbishing' (180). This observation might serve as a literal criticism of Orlan's project of surgical reconstructions, but it can also encompass the 'vogue for traumatic confessional' (180), the insistence on 'self, self, self' that we find in more conceptual artists such as Tracey Emin. The anthropological strain of realism, in turn, succumbs to inverse problems concerning the other, namely the error in which '*the other* is held to be *dans le vrai*' (177), always and automatically according truth. As a result, art becomes reduced to anthropology. If performative realism is all aesthetic, and thus unethical or at least non-ethical, the anthropological strain of realism seems to be all ethical and not sufficiently aesthetic. In his famous attack on the minimalist turn in contemporary art in 1967, Michael Fried sees these features as the twinfold flaws of contemporary art. For Fried, contemporary art is characterized and spoiled by theatricality and objecthood – which we can understand as 'performative' and 'anthropological' realism respectively. The theatrical element in contemporary art makes us conscious of the viewing process itself; it plays to an audience. For Fried, 'theater is now the negation of art' (153). Objecthood consists in art's presentation of its subject as an unmediated experience, and Fried declares objecthood, like theatre, the negation of art: '"the condition of non-art" is what I have been calling objecthood' (152). Since Fried's *Art and Objecthood*, performativity has interestingly split off from objecthood so that it is now actually seen as the way to undermine presence and objecthood. In Judith Butler's seminal work, performativity puts identity and referentiality into mediating quotation marks. Yet in spite of this deconstruction of presence, the problems of theatre and objecthood are still with us as performative and anthropological realism – though, post-Fried, in separate strands. The theatrical or performative strand has a tendency to deteriorate into 'all self', leaving the work focused on the aesthetic; while the objecthood, or anthropological strand, threatens to slide into 'all other', foregrounding the ethical in the work at the cost of the aesthetic. All the more reason now, therefore, for a realism that is conscious of its mediation aspect, and, conversely, for a representation that does not abrogate its referent.

A number of recent works have attempted to reconcile these differences. Those in photography are particularly interesting because, of all media, photography comes closest to the real, and yet, like any other medium after structuralism, it is perceived as performative in that Austinian speech act sense. The seminal theoretical work on photography, Roland Barthes's *Camera Lucida*, grasps just this doubleness of photography. In it this archetypal structuralist/poststructuralist theorist pursues his earlier declaration of photography as a 'message without a code' – that is, a denotative medium that is nevertheless shored up by the 'connotation procedures' of code ('The Photographic Message', 19, 20). Yet *Camera Lucida* progressively discards these connotation procedures and performs a palinodic retraction of the earlier formulation. Here Barthes insists on photography as real, the thing or referent itself: 'every photograph is somehow co-natural with its referent. . . . I call the "photographic referent" not the *optionally* real thing to which an image or sign refers but the *necessarily* real thing. . . . it is Reference, which is the founding order of Photography' (76–7). Moreover, Barthes's insistence on the real in photography amounts to an involution of his entire career; *Camera Lucida* is Barthes's final work, and in it he moves from the language of structuralism/poststructuralism to an expressive/autobiographical language that he claims theory had always held at a distance:

> [M]y desire to write on Photography, corresponded to a discomfort I had always suffered from: the uneasiness of being a subject torn between two languages, one expressive, the other critical; and at the heart of this critical language, between several discourses, those of sociology, of semiology, and of psychoanalysis. (8)

While ostensibly an essay on photography – *Note sur la photographie*, as it is subtitled in French – *Camera Lucida* represents in truth Barthes's autobiographical real. He uses photography to express the loss of his own real in the form of his mother; her death propelled him into writing, and the book is a love letter to her. Ending his life with the real that had gone from this life, then, *Camera Lucida* is Barthes's most autobiographical work, in spite of the official autobiography that preceded it.

Following Barthes, photography has been inextricably entangled with autobiography – for both autobiography and photography are reconstructions that nevertheless *feel like the real thing*. Academic interest in the photography–autobiography intersection has burgeoned into a field, with recent books by Marianne Hirsch, Annette Kuhn, Linda Haverty Rugg and Timothy Dow Adams. This reconceptualization of photography's realism through autobiography is paralleled in contemporary art. The performative photographs of Sherrie Levine and Cindy Sherman produced in the 1970s and 1980s and encapsulating the postmodern displacement of identity have given way to works that use photography for more realistic and autobiographical ends. Richard Billingham's pictures of his parents and himself and American photographer Nan Goldin's hasty snapshots of herself and others around her – 'tracing histories of lives' (Rothkopf, non-pag.) – are photography as ph/*autography*; that is, photography in autobiographical mode. Goldin criticizes notions of photography as performative or a 'believable fiction', in which photographers 'fail to see that there's a difference between real life and fiction in photography – that all photographs are some kind of fiction, which I don't believe'. Such people 'didn't understand that to go out and photograph from your own life has these components of risk and uncontrollable possibilities and subtext that you can't impose upon the photos; they come from experience' (Rothkopf, non-pag.). The work of more than one photographer has been marked by parallel internal shifts, from watching others to watching oneself and, interrelatedly, to modes of representation that seek to be less manifestly performative. Del LaGrace Volcano's retrospective collection *Sublime Mutations* begins by chronicling the lesbian scene and ends with the photographer living out a transgendered life. Likewise, a photographic installation by Nan Goldin simply entitled *Self-Portrait*, which was the highlight of the above-mentioned 'Quotidiana' exhibition, is a retrospective collection of photographs from Goldin's childhood to the present day in which she turns the same unforgiving eye she has used on others onto herself. We are taken from Goldin's slim and heroic youth, experimenting with S/M and leather clubs, to explicit shots of sex, to ever more 'destructive' relationships (in the words of the accompanying exhibition book), to two black eyes, to a detox clinic, to an ageing, fattening body. The photographs are shown as a series of slides at a relentless speed, as a result of which, in our experience, *Self-Portrait* really does feel like an autobiographical narrative.

Self-Portrait is overlaid with the soundtrack of Eartha Kitt's 'Don't Want to Be All by Myself'. This is less ironic for a 'self-portrait' than it might initially seem, for, as Goldin's and the new ph/autobiographical work shows – in contrast to the previous performative focus on the self – autobiography always involves the presence of an other. Theorists of autobiography have reached a similar conclusion: Nancy K. Miller writes that the self in autobiography is 'intrinsically relational' (17), and Jacques Derrida acknowledges that 'it is the ear of the other that signs. The ear of the other says to me and constitutes the *autos* of my autobiography' (51). We are speaking of others, therefore, both in the plot of autobiography and in the address of the work to an audience. This 'among others' quality is doubly useful. It breaks the *mise en abyme* circular self-referentiality of performative representations; and it draws the real closer, for the other is not fabricated but referential. In autobiography the turn to the other overcomes the impasse of autobiography as indistinguishable from fiction, not referential but, as Paul de Man puts it, an 'illusion of reference' (69). De Man famously describes autobiography not as a revelation of the face but as a 'de-facement' of the self. It is a figuring that defers the referentiality of identity. Such deferral of identity groundedness, perhaps especially in contemporary art, raises ethical quandaries. In the case of Orlan and Cindy Sherman, whose work pursues such performative notions of the self, there are no *real* others in their work. Any element of otherness is manufactured, aestheticized – it is another version of the artist's self. This manufactured otherness not only is narcissistic, but also leads to questions, in the case of Orlan, about 'how she can do it', how she can treat her self as if it were an other. These are, effectively, ethical questions. However, the obsessive focusing on the self to the exclusion of others foregrounds aesthetics at the expense of ethics. The self is only a canvass for the art, and this revelation appears to render the artist oblivious to real others around her.

In contrast, the recasting of photography as a referential medium in new ph/autographic work has gone hand in hand with a grasping of the self as situated in the midst of, but nevertheless distinct from, others. This double shift – from the performative to the real and from the self to the other – is crucial for an ethical art. Ethical philosopher Peter Singer has offered a theory of ethics that does not oppose self-interest but rather recasts it to allow for the presence of the other. In etymology the word 'ethics' is actually the plural of *ethos*, meaning nature or disposition, particularly of a culture or community. Ethics thus refers to natures or dispositions pluralized, to being among others. *Ethos* is in fact an expression of the *ethnos*, with the idea of plurality, of culture or community, and of a self that finds itself among others underlying both these terms. According to Singer, ethics consists of taking the point of view first of the other, and then of the universe; it thus involves a shift to *ethnos*. In its ideal form, ethnography, which is equivalent to today's social anthropology, not only places the self among others in order to learn more about both, but also puts others *before* the self. Such an ethnographically informed ethics is compassionate, identificatory, other-directed – and, crucially, self-aware. Lévi-

Strauss, writing of Rousseau, highlights what for him is not a paradox: that Rousseau wrote simultaneously of himself in his autobiography and of 'remote men' in the earliest form of ethnology. It is absolutely fitting that autobiography and anthropology originate in Rousseau's *oeuvre* together. Lévi-Strauss states that Rousseau's model of identification provides us with 'the only possible basis for ethics' (43): 'It lies in a conception of man which places the other before the self, and in a conception of mankind which places life before men' (37). The two-way formula – that the I is another (Rimbaud) – must be grasped alongside the conclusion drawn through ethnographic experience, 'that the other is an I' (37). 'Performative realism' gives us only the first half of this equation; 'ethnographic realism', if we're lucky, only the second. The twinfold importance of autobiography and ethnography working together, then, is to direct us forward into *ethos*, the point of view of the universe. An ethical realism in *aesthetics* would require a further awareness of the instruments for grasping the relations between the self and the other, a self-consciousness about what it means for the artist to represent the real. Photography and the visual media arising from it are the perfect media for this ethical realism. They allow us to get closer to the real, without obscuring the fact of their mediation and succumbing to naive realism. It is Gillian Wearing's emergent *oeuvre* that currently most fulfils these balances required of an ethical realism.

Wearing's art excels in its *ethno*graphy (i.e. its relation to nation, people, culture) because she goes beyond herself and those most like her. From a middle-class middle-England background herself, Wearing has progressed to two kinds of photographic subjects in her work. One is the socially extraordinary, the other marked as such. Hence among her subjects are the homeless, drunks, transsexuals. Her second subject comes to her almost by happenstance, as she takes a cross-section of society (e.g. those who respond to an advertisement she has placed) and photographs them. In both strategies Wearing puts aside the prerogative of artistic selection. In extending her subjects beyond herself to commune with strangers as part of her artistic objective, Wearing is quite different from other contemporary artists – black British artist Steve McQueen, for instance, with his videos of himself and other black men, or even Goldin, who remains among friends. As

Wearing herself puts it, 'I'm interested in people more than I am in myself' (Ferguson *et al.*, 125). The ethnographic is particularly manifested in her interest in social trauma. Indeed, *Trauma* is the title of one of her most recent works, a series of videos that collates individuals' experiences of child abuse. *Drunk*, another new work that constitutes a sequel to *Prelude*, performs a similar socialization of the experiences of street drinkers. In making a move from the performative self to the other, then, Wearing also exemplifies a move from the fabrication of trauma in the wounded body to the recording of the existent trauma in the body politic. I would question whether the central focus on the body with its violated boundaries in the artists such as Orlan, Sarah Lucas, even Del LaGrace, who continue the tradition of the traumatized bodies of Cindy Sherman and feminist art, can be described as ethical, because the boundaries they transgress are artificial while the trauma seems self-inflicted. Even if it is not explicitly unethical, their work remains trapped in the point of view of the self. Instead, Wearing's socially traumatized subjects are intrinsically other, marginal, or, to use the term of 1960s American photographer Diane Arbus, with whom Wearing has been compared, 'freaks'. But while Wearing might share subjects with Arbus, she does not share her vocabulary or her point of view: 'I don't see the people I film as freaks. . . . I am saying that everyone is different' (Ferguson *et al.*, 16). Writing about Arbus's work, Susan Sontag claims that Arbus 'was not interested in ethical journalism': her subjects 'are necessarily ahistorical subjects, private rather than public pathology, secret lives rather than open ones' (42). Wearing, in contrast, socializes her others, setting them in context and finding the I in the other according to the Rousseauian ideal of anthropology, rather than the otherness of others 'Arbus-style'.

Like the earliest anthropologists, Wearing uses photography as a tool to document others. She shows a genuine ethnographic curiosity about other people's lives. In *Interviews with People in the Street* (see Ferguson *et al.* for this and other works by Wearing not included in the reference list) she actually stops people and conducts interviews in the street. At the same time, she does not succumb to a banalization of others but uncovers the extraordinary in the ordinary, the otherness in the self. *My Favourite Track* is a row of videos simultaneously playing back individuals singing their own songs that we cannot hear in their Walkmans. The collective cacophony symbolizes the isolating experience of many of our contemporary cultural practices: 'The piece is about isolation,' Wearing says (Ferguson *et al.*, 27), yet we all do it, together. Because of Wearing's difference from her subjects, accompanied by her sympathetic, even identificatory, look, ethical questions about relations between the self and the other, about who gets to represent the other's reality, rise to the surface. The title of her early work, *Signs That Say What You Want Them to Say and Not Signs That Say What Someone Else Wants You to Say*, presents others speaking for themselves rather than being spoken for. Wearing's subject is the life in the autobiographical sense of what the subjects want to say, and her art positions her as a recipient of others' traumatic stories. In *Confess All on Video*, one subject describes his experience of making a video with Wearing as 'part of a therapeutic process'. In another video, *10–16*, Wearing reveals her presence on screen as a listener. What makes this realism ethical is that Wearing does not speak for others; she, and therefore we, are the subjects who – 'more importantly', as one of her exegetes writes (Ferguson *et al.*, 85) – listen. While Goldin gets back to the real of life in photography by crossing borders between self and real others – 'There is no separation between me and what I photograph' (Rothkopf, non-pag.) – Wearing is conscious of her distinctness. She recognizes that identification is the process of travel itself and that we cannot close the gap between self and other. She makes this process of travel her concern.

Wearing's introduction of herself into her ethnographic work serves to frame the border between self and other, and to hold off resolving their difference. At such moments, we are aware of the artist's distinctness from her subject, and therefore of our own, either by seeing her included in her work, or being made conscious of her mediating presence. In *10–16*, Wearing is also a surrogate listener for us. In order not to reproduce anthropology's alterizing structures, Wearing must demonstrate an awareness of them. Mindful of voyeurism, she remains reflexive, where 'reflexivity' is defined in Foster's words as 'parallactic work that attempts to frame the framer as he or she frames the other' (203). Wearing bypasses the idealization of the other – which amounts to an othering of the other, a confining to positions of absolute alterity in the Arbus school – by exchanging positions, by ph/autography. In *Take Your Top Off*, a series of photographs of three transsexuals, Wearing photographed herself in bed alongside her subjects, her breasts exposed like theirs. The reflexivity and self-consciousness of the work is caught by her showing the shutter release bulb in the photographs. Wearing not only reveals her body as she reveals theirs, she makes no attempt to conceal the technological process that allowed her to take the self-portrait, where she as an artist came into the making of image: 'I wanted to do something that made me feel vulnerable' (Ferguson *et al.*, 12). The ethnographic realism of these transsexual portraits is exemplary of participant observation in the Malinowskian ideal of anthropology. It is a fitting ethical corrective to anthropology's othering in colonial observation which operated in an unreflexive conception of photography.

Wearing's art can be described as autobiographical, then, and yet in the fine play of balances between the self and the other it is not narcissistic. When she takes her top off it is clear from her unsmiling and tense discomfort that she is not an exhibitionist; she is dispositionally self-conscious. Writing about her personality, interviewers often stress Wearing's shyness. There's something about the lovely paradox of the shy autobiographer that makes her the perfect, the most ethical autobiographer. In contrast to the exhibitionist's text, the self is always placed alongside others and, perhaps because of the shyness, can only be approached through, and subordinated to, others. Strictly speaking, Wearing is more of a memoirist than an autobiographer, for memoirs are stories of others narrated alongside, and often in the foreground of, the authorial self. As Donna De Salvo in an interview with Wearing nicely describes Wearing's approach to autobiography through others, 'You become a kind of story-teller, except that in telling the story you end up adding your bias, so you also become a part of that story. We don't know where you begin and they end' (Ferguson *et al.*, 24). This interrogation into where the borders of the self end and others begin, the dramatization of the self endeavouring to become the other but ultimately recognizing difference as the foundation of identification, is central to *Dancing in Peckham* and *Homage to the Woman*. Autobiographical consciousness and self-revelation give rise to and arise from the ethical problem of aesthetics, of making art from others. Seeing a woman dancing jubilantly and maniacally out of sync in a Peckham (London) shopping centre and realizing that even if she wanted to make that woman into art she would not be able to approach her without othering her, Wearing decides that she can only show herself reproducing the scene. She thus films herself.

> And I wanted to say, 'Can I have your name and address and put you in my video?' You just realize you've got to stop yourself because it would be so patronizing. Maybe I was recognizing nuances in myself as well, because I can be like that – I do actually dance quite maniacally. I had to take it one step further. . . . For me to be that interested, it's got to be something about me. (Ferguson *et al.*, 116)

Wearing's ethical hesitations about aesthetics take her fascination, her desire to make art, back to her own look. In *Homage to the Woman with a Bandaged Face Who I Saw Yesterday down Walworth Road* the ethical questions are even more serious. Wearing sees a woman whose face is covered with a mask and desires to make her a subject of her art. Again, in identifying with the woman and reproducing that identifica-tion in her art – art which is the process of identification – Wearing says, 'I was answering a lot of my own questions about how I perceive people, and the perception of someone looking at me' (Ferguson *et al.*, 30). The look comes back and she puts herself in the place of the other. 'I'm always trying to find ways of discovering things about people, and in the process discover more about myself' (Ferguson *et al.*, 132). Neither work is a performance, because, especially in *Homage to the Woman*, Wearing's own vulnerability in making herself the subject of the same look is clearly visible. Her own vision as an artist is obscured by the mask. This act of becoming the other does not amount to 'acting out' but rather to *a process of understanding*, a term Wearing uses in relation to the aims of her art. This kind of art is not only ethical; it is also compassionate art, in which the under-standing of the other in his or her situation constitutes the basis of compassion. Speaking of how Wearing's work combines two sets of contradictory elements, both the real experience and the conscious mediation of it, both the self and the other (representing what we are referring to here as ethical realism), John Slyce describes Wearing's work in terms that converge what Foster meant by 'reflexivity' and 'traumatic realism':

> Wearing frames herself as she frames the Other. This builds reflexivity into the work which helps her negotiate the contradictory status of otherness as both given and constructed, real and fantasmatic. . . . [R]ather than brushing aside the problems that arise in representing the Other, Wearing reaches out to the frustrations and the traumas that we each experience in attempting to represent that which we feel to be real, and part of ourselves. (Ferguson *et al.*, 76)

The reflexivity of self-conscious looking at the other thus brings into the frame the problems of representation, of borders and mediation that go to the heart of questions about an ethical realism. What ends *Homage to the Woman* – and what makes it so devastating for many viewers – is the failure to establish contact: the one attempt at communication is foreclosed (the garage mechanic who comes up to Wearing wants only to satisfy his own curiosity) while the masked woman is left out of the communication process altogether. As in *Dancing in Peckham*, people *notice* the other but refuse to *see* her; they remain voyeurs in their failure to make contact with her. Yet Wearing highlights her difference. As an artist she can represent the state of not being seen. Indeed, the mask – a mediating layer – may be a metaphor for Wearing herself. Russell Ferguson has noted the continuity of the use of the mask in her work, along with some other 'disjunctive elements that both separate and unify' (Ferguson *et al.*, 36) – such as lip-synching and signs. The mask is a material border between the real and the artificial, the self and the other. It also allows a self to become an other – and vice versa, as Wearing's *Confess All* testifies. In *Confess All on Video. Don't Worry, You Will Be in Disguise. Intrigued? Call Gillian*, Wearing allows confessors to choose from a selection of masks and films her subjects making their confessions on videotape, a technique she repeats in *Trauma*. As Wearing says, the masks 'would enable them to say things they wouldn't normally say' (Ferguson *et al.*, 19), or, as Ferguson puts it, 'the masks conceal only to promise greater revelation' (40), resulting in a 'visual structure [which combines] both an extreme level of authenticity . . . and an extraordinary level of artificiality' (36–7). Ferguson elaborates a Greek dramatic sense of mask at work, which obliterates superficial appearances in order to allow more fundamental truths to be revealed. It is not irrelevant that for Lévi-Strauss the mask constitutes a key anthropological object; it is a means by which many cultures enable individuals to identify and take on social roles.

There is an interesting and telling contrast to be drawn between Wearing's masks and Orlan's disfigurements. Whereas Orlan gets her face made over by the plastic surgeon in order to displace – or deface – identity, thus revealing in order to conceal, Wearing, in *Homage*, *Confess All* and *Trauma*, uses the mask to expose identity. Oddly, Wearing's putting on the dressings of another's facial treatment seems less metaphoric, closer to the real autobiographical experience of disfigurement itself, as described in Lucy Grealy's *In the Mind's Eye: Autobiography of a Face*, than Orlan's performative but nevertheless undergone facial surgeries. In *Homage* Wearing wonders what it is like to be that masked woman; in *Confess All* it is only with the face masked that identity can be revealed. In both it is impossible not to read the mask as face – there is peculiar coherence between the artificial and the real. For Orlan her identity cannot be situated in her face or, even if it is, it is as endlessly mutable as her plastic surgery. Ferguson, in his survey on Wearing, rightly states that her work is quite different from the work of Sherrie Levine, Richard Prince and Cindy Sherman in the 1970s with their 'paradigms of the embrace of multiple identities' (34). Sherman especially is described as 'paradigmatic of what might loosely be called a "postmodern" acceptance of identity as multiple and mutable' (39). Orlan's disfigurements clearly belong in this realm; they are literalizations of Paul de Man's 'autobiography as de-facement'. They enact the postmodern fictionality of the self. Each surgery produces a different self, which undermines the very notion of selfhood. Wearing, in contrast, shows 'the continuing appeal of the older idea of an integral core of authentic identity' (34). The appeal, I would suggest, is one not only of psychic reassurance but also of ethical concern. Singer's conception of ethics – 'about how we ought to live'; 'what kind of things are ultimately good?' and 'how do we decide what actions are right?' (*Ethics* 3, 10) – demands a stabilization of terms postmodernism has rendered unstable: self and other, and the borders between them; as well as the existence of the real. Ethical art, like an ethical life, reinstates a subject who knows before her actions, who seeks through her actions consciously and intentionally to improve the lot of others – that is, their real conditions in the world. A performative self appears just too desultory, just too erratic and narcissistic to effect such changes. If Orlan's face unmasks identity and reveals it to be fictional in gesture, Wearing's mask conversely allows her access to the real – just as the other, which is another kind of mask, allows her access to herself. It is the latter that constitutes the basis of ethical realism.

Nevertheless, Wearing's work does show a necessary self-consciousness about aesthetics. The mask is also a metaphor for the new visual media that constitute much of the new realism in contemporary art. Like the mask, they are mediations that nevertheless allow access to the real. Photography, photographic installations and video have now been integrated into art and combined with other technological media. In several pieces of new British art in Tate Britain, technology was used to connect to the real. Foster's term 'screen' is valuable for suggesting how visual media return the real, but only through the process of mediation (i.e. 'screening'). Visual technologies capture Wearing's Real but problematize in their technology the idea of mediation, of *tekhnē-logos* – etymologically art as knowledge or truth. Wearing says, 'I'm interested in people, but I can't bear the idea of the technology being something that represents me' (Ferguson *et al.*, 15). As Mick Gidley points out in his book *Representing Others*, the aesthetic sense of representation in the creative arts cannot be divorced from the political sense of representation as 'representing others'. This is especially the case for realism, because to claim to represent someone's reality – unmediated by aesthetics – is, as Gidley writes in the context of anthropology, to constitute that reality while concealing the mediation. It is thus a political act. Photography with its proximity to the real succumbs in particular to this illusion of reality. Wearing's use of visual technology foregrounds the problems of the real, without forgoing it altogether.

In documenting the real, photography is similar to anthropology.

The tradition of documentary photography arose from anthropological/ sociological work carried out in 1930s America. But in *Signs*, for instance, where Wearing is at her most anthropological, documenting a community, she combines photographs with other media. The inclusion of written text in the photographs foregrounds the non-realism of photography – both in the sense that the photograph does not really represent the subject and also revealing the ethical problems involved in the tradition of documentary/anthropological photography. Presenting the photograph as real, as a complete document of the subject in itself, and eliding the fact of its own mediation, both by the photographer's subjectivity and by technology, documentary photography did not 'see' the subject in an ethical sense. Wearing's *Signs* are accompanied by text as a comment on what the photograph fails to represent, which results in dissonance between the signed text and the photograph (witness the sign 'I'm desperate' held by the slick city worker). Wearing explains that although she thinks of much of her work as portraiture, her photographs are portraits in which the subject has some personal voice, 'because it's too easy for a photograph to make people look like something they're not' (Sawyer, 10). As opposed to the documentary tradition, Wearing states, 'I couldn't bear the idea of taking photographs of people without their knowing' (Ferguson *et al.*, 8), and writes of her own *Signs*, 'This image interrupts the logic of photo-documentary and snapshot photography through the subjects' clear collusion and engineering of their own representation' (Ferguson *et al.*, 96). If the photographic portrait captures the social being, the sign or the text is the inner force that disrupts this.

The documentary realism currently in vogue with fly-on-the-wall documentaries such as *Big Brother* might appear to display subjects' true lives. However, in their continuation of the documentary tradition such works are in fact highly superficial, reinscribing in voyeurism the difference between the self and others. Wearing never says her work stands for life; it is rather its edited version. As the artist herself puts it, 'It's like editing life. Nothing would ever be interesting in its real state' (Ferguson *et al.*, 119) – so Wearing's work is the *art* of life, then. The turn to signs and mediation that Foster and Rosalind Krauss chart in art in the 1970s on the back of poststructuralist theory is relevant here; Foster calls it the 'textual turn', while Krauss describes it as 'notes on the index'. What arises at this point in representation is a crisis in the sign, its non-signification that would be spun out to postmodern arbitrariness, even meaninglessness, its failure to refer to the real. This crisis has become the self-referential subject of representation. Foster speaks of 'crises of representation', while Krauss highlights particularly Barthes's earlier pre-*Camera Lucida* sense of photography as a 'message without a code' – 'a trauma of signification' (Krauss, 206). After this crisis of the sign is recognized as no longer a sufficient subject of representation, Wearing returns to the real, reconnecting representation to the real out of ethical imperatives. She avoids both the naive realism of documentary photography 'before the crisis' and the free-floating significations of the 1970s crisis in which, as Krauss writes, photography 'has increasingly become the operative model for abstraction' (210). In Wearing's *Signs*, the index reconnects, through text, the photograph to the concrete. It is the signs combined with the photographic image, sometimes dissonantly, that carry the meaning – the life/the autobiography. Ultimately they point to the non-indexicality of the photograph. After the crisis of representation, it is the Real that is returned, not the real – a point that takes us back to Barthes and Foster's traumatic realism.

Wearing is much closer to Barthes's later reconception of photography as traumatic, as speaking the unspeakable and as Real. In the palinodic shift Barthes makes in his two conceptions of photography, his earlier realist becomes a Realist. He acknowledges that his 'message without a code' was a combination of a naive realist and structuralist conception of photography. Realism 'before structuralism' held that reality was unproblematically representable. This obliviousness to mediation allowed structuralist and poststructuralist critics to dismiss realism as naive *per se*. Realism in that capitalized Lacanian sense holds that reality is *ipso facto* outside representation. In Lacan the Real is an order distinct from the Symbolic. When the Real does appear, traumatically, shockingly, it enacts a tear in the Symbolic, upsetting the very conditions of representation. For the later Barthes, it is this Lacanian Real that is behind his description of photography as not real but Real. Barthes cites Lacan's notion of the Real – 'the *tuché*, the Occasion, the Encounter' (4) that, as Lacan writes, returns 'in a form . . . of trauma' (55). Barthes's '*punctum*' in photography is this return of the Real, the puncture or wound echoing, etymologically, trauma. Not coping with the death of his mother, Barthes sees the hole in realism – and it is this hole that photography captures. Explicating Barthes's Realistic conception of photography, Foster writes that this *punctum*, this *tuché* or real, is a confusion between subject and object – 'of subject and world, inside and outside' (134).

Aware of these confusions, Wearing tries to convey the traumatic essence of photography and the way in which, as a mode of cultural knowing, or our primary mode for recording reality, photography perpetuates confusion between subject and object and captures the holes in reality. In *Confess All*, one speaker has a 'photographic memory of brother and sister snogging' that has stalled his life, making sexual relations or any other kind of intimate contact impossible. The scenes of incestuous confusion between subject and object, desire and identification have been imprinted onto his memory, freezing his life like a photograph. Capturing a real that is too Real, Wearing shows the traumatic associations of photography. In *Sixty Minute Silence*, she criticizes the way in which photography is used for surveillance, for culturally pernicious effects. Indeed, this video of a quadrille of police surveying the viewer surveying them, for which Wearing won the Turner Prize in 1997, suggests that issues of surveillance, and a conception of photography as invested in – if not causative of – trauma, are perhaps behind the shift in contemporary art from photography to the new photographic media such as video. Photography is now elongated, its moment stretched out, the past made re-present. It was this 'pastness' that for Barthes was traumatic about photography – the past had been there, 'ça-a-été,' the past was irrecoverable. The new media make photography present. Even if they are not subsumed into video, photographs in contemporary art now often involve a screening. In the case of Goldin's *Self-Portrait*, for instance, the viewer is shown the slides in rapid succession in three or four rows of seats, reached through an archway – as if he or she was in a cinema watching a film. To similar effect, Wearing slows the speed of some videos, or emphasizes that the speed of the action in the film is painfully slow anyway, as in *Drunk*, when we are forced to identify with the amount of time it takes a young man to put a T-shirt on. Wearing does not resolve the trauma of photography, but she wants us to pay attention to it. As Ferguson points out, video restores the narrative function to art, and, we might specify here, to photography. The shift to the new technologies reflects a need to construct and tell stories, to make meaning from the no longer sufficient instant of trauma. In 'Intelligence', the exhibition of new British art, video installation, combined with other mixed media such as sound, is the most prominent form.

If the new technologies tell the stories of trauma, they also foreground the process of mediation and the points at which speech or representation fails, thus averting the charge of naive realism. As Miranda Sawyer concludes in her article on Wearing written for the *Observer*, Wearing 'shows just how eloquent lack of eloquence can be' (15) – and we may recall here that Barthes does not reproduce the photograph of his mother which he insists is her reality. The new media make us aware of the ultimate screen between the self and the other, of the ways in which communication can be (is inevitably?) dubbed, misheard, drowned out, screened and mediated. In *2 into 1*, Wearing dramatizes the relational nature of identity – and the way in which these relations can fail – through swapping the speech of a mother and her two sons. Hilary's plaint about how her son Alex likes to bully her is said in her voice but lip-synched by Alex's image; Alex's criticism that she likes to be dominated by men is poignantly mouthed by Hilary. The exchanged speech, the breaking up of sound and image and the consciousness of the mediation, all heighten the interrelatedness but also the struggle towards mutual responsibility these subjects, as self and other, should have towards each other as social beings. The same technique is used in *Prelude*, but even more traumatically. When you first view/hear it, you think it is Lynda who is speaking, telling her own story, the words corresponding to the image of Lynda. You then realize with a shock that it is the twin sister's commentary on her dead sister, that the text overlies the image, in the sense of covering or silencing it, the dissonance between media bringing alive this trauma, the hole in representation that is a hole in life (death). Perhaps this is the more nuanced reason why the video is called *Prelude* and not 'Reprise', in spite of the fact that *Prelude* resurrects a dead subject (Lynda had died before Wearing had completed the video). *Prelude* returns us to the frozen moment before the loss, the past of the photograph, making the real Real.

Wearing's art is not simply realism. In some sense, her ethical realism is Realer.

Thanks to Margaretta Jolly for directing me towards Peter Singer.

WORKS CITED

Adams, Timothy Dow. *Light Writing and Life Writing: Photography in Autobiography*. Chapel Hill: University of North Carolina Press, 2000.

Barthes, Roland. *Camera Lucida: Reflections on Photography*. Trans. Richard Howard. London: Vintage, 1993.

— 'The photographic message'. In *Image Music Text*. Ed. and trans. Stephen Heath. London: Fontana, 1977. 15–31.

Billingham, Richard. *Ray's a Laugh*. Scalo, 2000.

de Man, Paul. 'Autobiography as de-facement'. In *The Rhetoric of Romanticism*. New York: Columbia University Press, 1984. 57–81.

Derrida, Jacques. *The Ear of the Other: Otobiography, Transference, Translation*. Ed. Christie McDonald. Trans. Peggy Kamuf. Lincoln: Nebraska University Press, 1988.

Ferguson, Russell, Donna De Salvo and John Slyce. *Gillian Wearing*. London: Phaidon Press, 1999.

Foster, Hal. *The Return of the Real: The Avant-Garde at the End of the Century*. Cambridge, MA: MIT Press, 1996.

Fried, Michael. *Art and Objecthood: Essays and Reviews*. Chicago: University of Chicago Press, 1998.

Gidley, Mick, ed. *Representing Others: White Views of Indigenous Peoples*. Exeter: University of Exeter Press, 1992.

Gillian Wearing. Serpentine Gallery, London. 14 October 2000.

Goldin, Nan. *Self-Portrait*. Museum of Contemporary Art, Castello di Rivoli, Turin. 29 April 2000.

Grealy, Lucy. *In the Mind's Eye: Autobiography of a Face*. London: Arrow, 1995.

Hirsch, Marianne, ed. *The Familial Gaze*. Hanover, NH: University Press of New England, 1999.

— *Family Frames: Photography, Narrative and Postmemory*. Cambridge, MA: Harvard University Press, 1997.

'Intelligence: The New British Art'. Cur. Virginia Button and Charles Esche. Tate Britain, London. 8 September 2000.

Krauss, Rosalind. *The Originality of the Avant-Garde and Other Modernist Myths*. Cambridge, MA: MIT Press, 1985.

Kuhn, Annette. *Family Secrets: Acts of Memory and Imagination*. London: Verso, 1995.

Lacan, Jacques. *The Four Fundamental Concepts of Psycho-Analysis*. Ed. Jacques-Alain Miller. Trans. Alan Sheridan. New York: Norton, 1981.

LaGrace Volcano, Del. *Sublime Mutations*. Stuttgart: Konkursbuch Verlag, 2000.

Lévi-Strauss, Claude. *Structural Anthropology*. Vol. 2. Trans. Monique Layton. Chicago: University of Chicago Press, 1984.

McQueen, Steve. *Bear*. Tate Modern, London. 8 September 2000.

Miller, Nancy K. 'Representing others: gender and the subjects of auto-biography'. *Differences: A Journal of Feminist Cultural Studies* 6:1 (1994): 1–27.

'Quotidiana: The Continuity of the Everyday in 20th Century Art'. Cur. Giorgio Verzotti. Museum of Contemporary Art, Castello di Rivoli, Turin. 29 April 2000.

Rothkopf, Scott. Interview with Nan Goldin (1999). *Harvard Advocate*. <www.harvardadvocate.com/spring99/interview.html>. 10 October 2000.

Rugg, Linda Haverty. *Picturing Ourselves: Photography and Autobiography*. Chicago: University of Chicago Press, 1997.

Sawyer, Miranda. 'Daring Wearing'. *The Observer Magazine*. 3 September 2000: 10–15.

Singer, Peter, ed. *Ethics*. Oxford: Oxford University Press, 1994.

—— *How Are We to Live? Ethics in an Age of Self-Interest*. Amherst, NY: Prometheus Books, 1995.

Sontag, Susan. *On Photography*. London: Penguin, 1979.

Tate Modern, London. 8 September 2000.

Wearing, Gillian. *Confess All on Video. Don't Worry, You Will Be in Disguise. Intrigued? Call Gillian*. Tate Modern, London. 8 September 2000

—— *Dancing in Peckham*. Serpentine Gallery, London. 14 October 2000.

—— *Drunk*. Serpentine Gallery, London. 14 October 2000.

—— *Homage to the Woman with a Bandaged Face Who I Saw Yesterday down Walworth Road*. Serpentine Gallery, London. 14 October 2000.

—— *Prelude*. Tate Britain, London. 8 September 2000.

—— *Signs That Say What You Want Them to Say and Not Signs That Say What Someone Else Wants You to Say*. Serpentine Gallery, London. 14 October 2000.

—— *Trauma*. Serpentine Gallery, London. 14 October 2000.

—— *2 into 1*. Serpentine Gallery, London. 14 October 2000.

Whiteread, Rachel. *Holocaust Memorial*. Vienna.

CHAPTER 14

'The Future . . . Is Monstrous':[1]
Prosthetics as Ethics

JOANNA ZYLINSKA

To articulate a prosthesis means, on the one hand, to bring to light the artificiality of what is supposed to emulate the real and, on the other, to bend, twist or adjust the connection between two bodily organs. The figure of what we might call 'double articulation', prosthesis has always been associated with both silence and speech. A perfect prosthesis can 'pass' for the lost bodily part it replaces, and thus remains invisible and unspeakable. But, as David Wills explains in his eponymous book on prosthesis, in its first appearance in English in 1553 the word 'prosthesis' stood for 'an addition of a syllable to the beginning of a word' (218), designating an interruption and simultaneous extension of the body of language. Focusing on the discursive arrangements around the practice of torture which depended on both bodily extensions and verbal excess, Wills draws attention to the element of violence that prosthesis inextricably entails. Physical violence is a manifestation (or an extension, a substitute, or, indeed, prosthesis) of power exerted on weak but unsubmissive bodies which are then prosthesized (extended, adjusted, bent, etc.) in an attempt to deprive them of their integrity and inviolability. But prosthesis also involves another kind of bodily disintegration: it violates the logic of

Plate 8 EXTENDED ARM, Melbourne/Hamburg. Photo: T. Figallo, ©
Stelarc

*totality that underlies Western concepts of identity
and selfhood. A prosthetic extension reveals a lack
in the corpus to which it is attached, the very need
for, or even a possibility of, such an attachment or
extension indicating an original incompleteness, or
perhaps unboundedness, of the self. It is in this
sense that prosthesis becomes an important figure in
ethical ruminations.*

PROSTHETICS AND ETHICS

Many traditional forms of ethical thinking in Western philosophy are
organized around the concept of prosthesis. As John Wild argues in his
introduction to Emmanuel Levinas's *Totality and Infinity*, 'There is a
strong tendency in all human individuals and groups to maintain this
egocentric attitude and *to think of other individuals either as extensions of
the self, or as alien objects to be manipulated* for the advantage of the

individual and social self' (12, emphasis added). But I want to suggest in this chapter that it is possible – even necessary – to conceptualize prosthesis beyond self-possession and autonomy. Looking at different ways in which the self negotiates its relationships with alterity and exteriority, I want to position prosthesis as an articulation of connections and slippages *between* the self and its others. Prosthetics will thus stand, for me, for an ethical way of thinking about identity and difference.

While I am particularly interested in changes in the concepts of identity and difference that have been provoked by recent developments in technology, I do not subscribe to the linear model of the development of the human from the 'natural man' to the 'posthuman cybernetic organism'. Samuel Weber has argued in his reading of Heidegger's 'Die Frage nach der Technik' that technology and nature are in fact two processes of *poièsis* (i.e. bringing forth, or creation) that function according to the same mechanism. However, Weber moves beyond the everyday understanding of technology as relating to contemporary advances in media, communication and medicine, to embrace its meaning of 'technique, craft, or skill'. If 'the innermost principle of "nature" is its impulse to open itself to the exterior, to alterity', technology-as-a-technique has to be seen as one form of nature, or even described as 'more natural than nature itself' (67). Inspired by Weber's argument, Catherine Waldby suggests that the very relationship between technology and the human has a prosthetic character: 'modern technics is never simply at the disposal of "Man" but sets Man up and replaces and displaces him in dynamic ways' (42). In this sense the term 'the post-human', which is frequently used in cyber-discourses, should be seen as a different view of subjectivity, one that 'thinks of the body as the *original prosthesis* we all learn to manipulate' (Hayles, 3, emphasis added), and not the next stage on the evolutionary ladder. Contemporary experiments in cosmetic and corrective surgery, organ transplants, genetics and cloning – to name but a few contentious areas where such prosthetic couplings are currently taking place – have brought to the fore the instability of the relationship between nature and technics, but they have also foregrounded their mutual interdependence. These conceptual changes are transforming the ways in which we define identity, allowing for the emergence of less bounded and more connected models of human subjectivity. They also create possibilities for reconsidering the relationship between what belongs to the self and what does not, thus calling for a rethinking of the ethical relationship between the self and its others.

In this chapter I intend to interpret this newly emergent view of the human as always already 'intrinsically other', that is, existing in relation to, and dependent on, its technology, from the perspective of Emmanuel Levinas's ethics of respect — which constitutes one of the most significant interventions into debates over ways of approaching alterity — in order to develop what I describe as the prosthetic ethics of welcome. Rather than propose a grand theory of ethics, I want to explore singular ethical moments in the practices of two artists: the Australian performance artist Stelarc and the French performance artist Orlan. Opening their bodies to the intrusion of technology and acquiring some forms of body extension, Stelarc and Orlan raise the issues of hospitality and welcome, of embracing incalculable difference, in a radical way. In this context, prosthesis can be interpreted as an ethical figure of hospitality, of welcoming an absolute and incalculable alterity that challenges and threatens the concept of the bounded self. But Orlan's and Stelarc's art will not be seen only as an illustration of a ready-made ethical theory: it is the performative aspect of their artistic practices, where 'performativity must be understood not as a singular or deliberate "act", but, rather, as the reiterative and citational practice by which discourse produces the effects that it names' (Butler, 2) that will be seen as a (necessarily precarious) legislation of an ethics of welcome. Even though neither artist defines their work as having an explicitly ethical character, I want to argue that their bodily experimentation challenges the possessive individualism that is characteristic of the capitalist model of selfhood, delineating instead the contours for what Celia Lury describes as 'prosthetic culture' (1). It is not necessarily through art that fixed identity can be challenged, but artistic practices of this kind foreground the broadly enacted performativity of identity, as well as preparing the grounds for the rethinking of identitarian relationships in our culture.

WELCOMING THE ALIEN: EMMANUEL LEVINAS'S ETHICS OF RESPECT

> *The identity of humanity is a differential relation between the human and technics, supplements and prostheses. (The seeming logic of this sentence, defining the human partly by relation to itself, works precisely to dislodge the concept of the human from any identity whose 'origin' is not always split, supplementary.) Technics and the human have to be thought on the basis of 'an oppositional différance' that necessarily displaces our concepts of both. (Clark, 247)*

The alterity that the self encounters in the world can be both animate and inanimate, material and immaterial. Whatever its form, Emmanuel Levinas – the philosopher whose writings constitute a starting point for the ethical ruminations included here – argues that

> Western philosophy coincides with the disclosure of the other where the other, in manifesting itself as a being, loses its alterity. From its infancy philosophy has been struck with a horror of the other that remains other – with an insurmountable allergy. ('The Trace of the Other', 346)

Challenging what he perceives as the totality of our culture, which unavoidably results in egocentrism and violence, in his major work *Totality and Infinity* Levinas sets out the principles of his ethical project. He describes this book as 'a defence of subjectivity'. However, subjectivity here should not be understood 'at the level of its purely egoist protestation against totality, nor in its anguish before death, but as founded in the idea of infinity' (26). For Levinas, infinity springs from 'the relationship of the same with the other' (26), a relationship that is irreducible to the terms and conditions delineated by the self. This irreducibility of the other to the self creates conditions for the emergence of an ethical moment. Of course, the sentient self can react to the arrival of the other by either welcoming or rejecting him or her. But this possibility, as well as a necessity, of responding – that is, reacting – to what Levinas defines as an incalculable alterity of the other is the source of an ethical condition (even if not a guarantee of its positive fulfilment). Refusing to assert the self's primacy, Levinas focuses on the vulnerability of the self when facing the other, who is always already 'absolutely other', and whose otherness can evoke different reactions in the self. In this sense, respect, which is one of the key terms of Levinas's ethics, does not mean that the other cannot be ignored, scorned or even annihilated, but rather that he or she has to be addressed (responded to) in one way or another. As Simon Critchley explains, ethics, for Levinas,

> is not an obligation toward the other mediated through the formal and procedural universalisation of maxims or some appeal to good conscience; rather – and this is what is truly provocative about Levinas – ethics is lived in the sensibility of a corporeal obligation to the other. (64)

Levinas terms this arrival, or apparition, of the other before the self *the face.*

To render the dynamics of this encounter, Levinas has recourse to the images of rupture and overspilling.

> The other who manifests himself in the face as it were breaks through his own plastic essence, like someone who opens a window on which his figure is outlined. His presence consists in divesting himself of the form which, however, manifests him. ('The Trace of the Other', 351)

What we experience here is an act of displacement, a breaking out of the plasticity of essence towards the insubstantiality of air. Levinas's other interrupts his own alleged completeness and separability; he amputates himself from the window which constitutes a part of his being and reaches out to the self, thus allowing for the substitution, or rather supplementation, of the apparently stable ideas of identity and alterity. It seems to me that the Levinasian encounter with the other inscribes itself in Wills's idea of a prosthetic relationship, which he defines as 'displacement, replacement, standing, dislodging, substituting, setting, amputating, supplementing', and as 'articulations between matters of two putatively distinct orders' (Wills 9–10). This encounter 'is necessarily a transfer into otherness, articulated through the radical alterity of ablation as loss of integrity' (13). In this way, ethical perspective opens up between the self and the other, even though, let me repeat, there is no guarantee that the self will respond ethically to this situation. It is 'because the self is sensible, that is 'to say, vulnerable, passive, open to wounding, outrage and pain' that, as Critchley argues, 'it is capable and worthy of ethics' (64), but, we have to remember, it is not sentenced to the performance of an ethical act. The ethical conditions arise out of this *possibility* of acknowledging and welcoming the alterity that, according to Levinas, is always already part of the self's experience.

ETHICAL CONFUSION AND 'GOOD SCANDAL': THE PROVOCATIONS OF ORLAN AND STELARC

In what follows I want to argue that the sentient self in Orlan's and Stelarc's performances is articulated (in the double sense of being expressed and connected) in a way that foregrounds its openness to 'wounding, outrage and pain'. Indeed, outrage has been a frequent reaction to both Orlan's surgeries and Stelarc's 'body shamanism'.[2] As Jane Goodall remarks,

> Both artists have achieved notoriety for taking risks in deliberately spectacular ways. They are creators of *scandal*, in the original sense of the term as σχανδαλον, a trap or stumbling block, metaphorically interpreted as a moral snare causing perplexity and ethical confusion (*OED*). Some forms of risk-taking may be scandalous, but scandal in this sense tests the moral ground and puts morality itself at risk. (153)

Interestingly, for Goodall, the scandalous nature of Orlan's and Stelarc's work does not erase the possibility of reading it in an ethical context. Instead, she describes their bodily experiments as a 'good scandal – one which generates complex confusions around high-intensity issues and cannot be resolved through the simple assertion of precepts' (154). I would not like to treat the notion of a good scandal as a positively valued state of events, dialectically opposed to the 'original', bad situation of moral confusion. Its 'goodness' results for me from the impossibility of providing a consistent, totalizing narrative about the events in question. In this sense, Orlan's and Stelarc's performances inscribe themselves in the logic of the *differend*, which Jean-François Lyotard defines as 'a case of conflict between (at least) two parties, that cannot be equitably resolved for lack of a rule of judgement applicable to both arguments' (*Differend*, xi). For Lyotard, differends, which are born from encounters between phrases of heterogeneous regimens, are unavoidable in our everyday life. The occurrence of differends in discourses about art, nature, politics, ethics or morality – something that is so vividly manifested in different, irreconcilable responses to Orlan's and Stelarc's work – is also a guarantee of the emergence of an ethical dimension; that is, a need to respond to the often uncomfortable 'otherness' of their performances. This ethical dimension can be either embraced and explored from the perspective of respect for what often seems shocking and incomprehensible or absorbed by the totalizing logic which yearns for the undisturbed unity of the self without the other.

The scandal the two artists often provoke can be attributed to the obligation they put on otherwise complacent selves, making them face the unspeakable and thus challenging them in their self-knowledge and self-sufficiency. Inspired by Levinas's philosophy of respect for the alterity of the other, Lyotard explains the nature of this scandal as follows:

[O]bligation should be described as a scandal for the one who is obligated: deprived of the 'free' use of oneself, abandoned by one's narcissistic image, opposed in this, inhibited in that, worried over not being able to be oneself without further ado. (*Differend*, 109–10)

Acknowledging further that these doubts can only be voiced by a 'far too human, and humanist' self, Lyotard goes on to ask the following question: 'Can we begin with the dispersion, without any nostalgia for the self?' The scandal of an ethical relationship as illuminated by

Levinas consists for him in the recognition that '*The ego does not proceed from the other; the other befalls the ego*' (110, emphasis in original). Here, the alterity of the other presents itself as, first, irreducible to the I, to my dreams, fears and expectations, and second, as arriving unexpectedly and taking the I by surprise, thus depriving it of mastery and self-possession. The identity of both Orlan's and Stelarc's 'performing I' is always prosthetic, foregrounding and enacting the 'radical recontextualization' of the self through the processes of artificiality and contrivance (see Wills, 45). It is the way in which Orlan and Stelarc expose the non-mastering relationship of the self to alterity (see Wills, 26), a relationship that calls us to respond in one way or another to this scandal of heterogeneity, dispersal and confusion, that I want to investigate in the next two sections of this chapter.

'I IS AN OTHER': ORLAN'S PROSTHETIC SELFHOOD

The work of the French performance artist Orlan, who is remodelling her face over and over again to conform with different standards of beauty and thus problematize their 'natural' character, is an example of such a non-mastering relationship with alterity. In her most recent project, *Self-Hybridation*, Orlan is digitally constructing a series of portraits, 'adorning' her face with elements from the pre-Columbian cultures, which, as the artist herself says, 'have a relationship with the body which is particularly disturbing for us, which completely challenges us and which is very intense. . . . This is the idea of entering into the skin of the other' (Ayers, 177). The photographs representing Orlan's face equipped with the large nose of King Wapacal or carrying a superimposed Olmec mask, the production of which involves skull deformation, as well as scar-like drawings, can be seen as a continuation of the artist's earlier project *Interventions*. Initiated in 1990, *Interventions* consisted of a series of cosmetic surgeries by means of which Orlan self-mockingly modelled herself on selected mythological figures: she acquired the nose of Diana, the mouth of Boucher's Europa, the chin of Botticelli's Venus, and the eyes of Gerome's Psyche. However, the final result was no more important than the actual operation-performance, conducted by 'surgeon-sculptors' (Armstrong, 4) in cooperation with the artist herself.

Plate 9 Orlan, *Self-Hybridation*, 1998.
Technical aid: P. Zovilé. Courtesy of
Espace d'Art, Yvonamor Palix Paris–Mexico

But Orlan objects to having her work reduced to the problematics of identity.[3] In interviews and conferences she asserts the directedness and vocation of her artistic I, which she sees, in a somewhat Mephistophelean fashion, as involved in a 'struggle against the innate, the inexorable, the programmed, Nature, DNA (which is our direct rival as far as artists of representation are concerned), and God!' (Orlan, 91). She announces further, 'My work is blasphemous. It is an endeavour to move the bars of the cage, a radical and uncomfortable endeavour!' (91). In this way, Orlan inscribes her project in a certain teleology of liberation, facilitated and authorized by the artist as an agent of social change and a source of moral anxiety. During her surgeries Orlan is only partially anaesthetized, which allows her to maintain control and direct the performance from her operating table. And yet, the boundaries of her carefully contrived 'I' suddenly open up with her announcement that 'I is an other' (*'Je est un autre'*) (91).

Interestingly, a number of interpreters of Orlan's *oeuvre* display a similar ambiguity regarding the artist's identity and its possible concep-tualization. Sarah Wilson, for example, claims that ever since Orlan's series of *tableaux vivants* staged in 1968 and parodying the Venuses of Manet and Velasquez, the artist 'was always, insistently, herself' (10). Wilson does not question Orlan's intention of single-handedly challeng-ing God, Nature and DNA: indeed, the declaration of prosthetic selfhood, translated into English by Wilson as 'I am (*sic*) an other', becomes for her the realization of the dream of ultimate fulfilment and plenty. Seen in this way, Orlan not only fights God, she becomes God, 'sacred and profane, Alpha and Omega' (Wilson, 16). And yet Wilson's article, significantly titled '*L'Histoire d'O*, Sacred and Profane' opens with an assertion, 'Orlan is O, "The O in open. *The O of the other*"' (8; emphasis added). Michel Onfray, in turn, interprets Orlan's surgeries as springing from a desire 'to bridge the abyss between what one feels oneself to be and what, in reality, one shows'. According to him, Orlan manages to 'correct and transcend' human alienation 'by making the inside and outside match' (35). Orlan's totalization of identity, her de-prosthesization of selfhood, signifies for Onfray an ethical undertaking of attempting to overcome the fragmentation that is characteristic of 'our nihilistic, postmodern age' (34). Making 'the signifier, the face, coincide with the signified, the soul' (35), Orlan's work is turned here into a magic cure against 'this spreading desert, void of intellectual resistance'; it is elevated to the position of a moral agent who will cleanse 'matter forsaken, execrated and soiled by the market by invoking the possibility of sculpting it as only an artist can'. Stefan Morawski, author of *The Troubles with Postmodernity* and exponent of the thesis of the 'aestheticisation of everyday life', shares Onfrey's diagnosis of our contemporary ailments, but offers a completely different reading of Orlan's work. In 'A symptomatic case of self-mystification', Morawski asks, 'What is the sense of her art?', only to conclude that in our 'Tower of Babel', 'the values have vanished and lay [*sic*] entangled on the scales' (203). Since, according to Morawski, Orlan attacks 'both culture, metaphysical needs and nature (which, after all, is the basis of sexual differences and identity)' (199), the possibility of identifying an ethical dimension in Orlan's work is for him totally foreclosed.

What emerges from the above discussions is that Orlan's work can always be simultaneously interpreted as a 'good' and 'bad scandal', revealing a differend (itself a prosthetic figure, a figure of 'double articulation') between the heterogeneous discourses employed for its analysis. I do not intend to resolve this conflict here. I am more interested in the very possibility of continuing to comment on Orlan's performances without attempting to close off the differend by 'usurping' her work for some pre-defined purpose (e.g. salvation or castigation). At this point I would like to return to Orlan's declaration 'I is an other', and to relate it to Jacques Derrida's interpretation of the relationship between selfhood and otherness as delineated by Levinas. My reason for turning to these two thinkers is that the questions concerning identity, alterity and their possible (ir)reconciliation which I am discussing here in relation to Orlan have been addressed in a most rigorous and provocative way in their work.

The ethics of welcome and hospitality, a recurring thread in Derrida's work, is based on the disavowal of the subject–object distance upon which Western philosophy has based its understanding of alterity. Derridean hospitality – delineated as an *extension* of Levinas's ethics of respect for the alterity of the other – implies the possibility, and danger, of the intrusion of the unpresentable, of what we cannot yet know or name, into the confined territory of the self. Instead of protecting itself against the unknown, the self extends a prosthetic invitation to the always already monstr-ous (in the sense of 'showing itself as something that is not yet shown') other, and thus recognizes the necessary doubling – but also splitting – of identity. However, as Derrida observes, for any action, any decision, to take place, 'it must be made by the other in myself' ('Hospitality' 67; cf. *Adieu*, 23). A decision made by the self which does not have any doubts regarding its rightness and which is fully in control of what it is doing is not a decision: this kind of decision has already been, in a way, pre-decided. The self, the host awaiting the arrival of the other, is at the same time 'a hostage insofar as he is the subject put into question' (*Adieu*, 56).

From this perspective, Orlan's attempts to 'move the bars of the cage' through her performances – even if enveloped in the rhetoric of self-liberation – become a simultaneous attack on the idea of the self that maintains a fantasy of autonomy and solipsism, a self that sees itself as separate from the innate, from Nature and from DNA. Orlan's fight against the self's components (which are here projected as its absolute 'others') and her attempts to de-prosthesize selfhood in order to achieve a state of perfect closure work only when this self is opened to the intrusion of incalculable alterity. Significantly, one of the operations Orlan underwent for her *Interventions* series involved inserting two cheek implants onto her temples, 'giving a sort of naughty Pan "horned" look' (Millard, 52). By shifting the corporeal boundaries in this way, Orlan makes us realize that 'Nothing "fits" any longer. . . . The inside no longer lies patiently within the outside, contained and stable, and a guarantee that the world is just the world' (Adams, 156–7). I do not interpret Adams's conclusion as a reinforcement of the evolutionary narrative of technological development, but rather as an acknowledgement of the idea that selfhood can only come from 'the other' (both human – i.e. spectator audience, a surgeon-intruder; and non-human – i.e. a cheek implant, an anaesthetic injection), and thus is intrinsically prosthetic. By allowing for this sort of bodily intervention Orlan embraces the possibility of the unpredictable trans- formation that inevitably 'explodes' the humanist discourse of identity. Perhaps even against herself, and in contradiction to her modernist concept of artist as public conscience and scandal-monger, Orlan performs what Timothy Clark calls a 'deconstruction of the Aristotelian system', where technology is perceived as 'extrinsic to human nature as a tool which is used to bring about certain ends' (238). By allowing 'the unforeseen [to disrupt] the very criteria in which it would have been captured' (Clark, 250), Orlan enacts what we could term 'the exhaustion' of the discourse of 'identity without difference' which is not able to convey the unforeseen and the 'not-yet'.

This sense of unpredictability and 'not-yet' is clearly visible in the open-endedness of Orlan's project, which always involves the possi- bility of an accident and failure. As Barbara Rose observes,

> each time she [Orlan] is operated on, there is an increased element of risk. She insists on being conscious to direct and choreograph the actions, so the operations take place under local rather than general anaesthesia. The procedure, known as an epidural block, requires a spinal injection that risks paralysing the patient if the needle does not hit its mark exactly. With each successive surgical intervention and injection, the danger is said to increase. . . . To at least some degree she risks deformation, paralysis, even death. (82–7)

The recognition of this dimension of mortality in Orlan's work has important ethical consequences. I am not primarily concerned here with the issue of medical ethics, which is frequently raised in the context of surgical interventions into the body, their scope and justification, but rather with the ultimate performance of the ethics of hospitality in this particular artist's body. If, as Levinas argues, 'I am responsible for the other insofar as he is mortal' (quoted in Derrida, *Adieu*, 7), Orlan can be said to instantiate what Levinas terms 'the passage to the ethical'. By embracing mortality as an unavoidable part of the performance, Orlan undertakes responsibility for the other *in* her, for her death *and* life. Undermining the perception of death as a 'termination of life', she foregrounds death as an unavoidable element – perhaps also the most significant incarnation – of the self's relationship with incalculable and infinite alterity. Her sacrifice goes beyond the logic of capitalist spending, which depends on the equal calculation of gains and losses. But it is only in the light of the possibility of deformation and annihilation that her decision of self-offering gains an ethical character. Its ethicity follows neither the Judaeo-Christian tradition of martyrdom as part of a redemptive project (even if the artist does actually resort to the rhetoric of self-sacrifice when announcing that she is 'giving her body to art') nor the sacrificial economy of biovalue which designates some bodies as less valuable than others (Waldby, 52): it is death *as such* (i.e. the unpresentable, rather than 'a passage to eternity', as 'the end-product of life', etc.) that needs to be responded to and chosen. Through the extension of her body towards absolute alterity, Orlan challenges the confinement of moral agency to an autonomous and bounded self.

'THE INFORMATION IS THE PROSTHESIS': STELARC'S BODILY EXTENSIONS

PHANTOM LIMB / VIRTUAL ARM

Amputees often experience a phantom limb. It is now possible to have a phantom sensation of an additional arm – a virtual arm – albeit visual rather than visceral. The Virtual Arm is a computer-generated, human-like universal manipulator interactively controlled by VPL Virtual Reality equipment. Using data gloves with flexion and

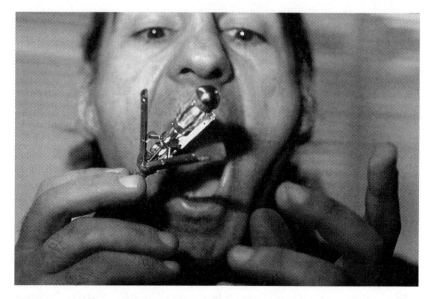

Plate 10 STOMACH SCULPTURE, Fifth Australian Sculpture Triennale. Photo T. Figallo, © Stelarc

> *position-orientation sensors and a GESTURE-BASED COMMAND LANGUAGE allows real-time intuitive operation and additional extended capabilities. (Stelarc Web site)*

Stelarc's performances have always focused on the idea of prosthesis: from external bodily extensions such as the Third Hand or Extended Arm, to internal prostheses such as the Stomach Sculpture, where the body 'becomes a host not for a self or soul, but simply for a sculpture' (Stelarc Web site). His experiments have most recently culminated in the development of the Movatar project – that is, an avatar taking over the human body, which then functions as a prosthesis for this avatar. As the artist himself explains,

> Motion Capture allows a physical body to animate a 3D computer-generated virtual body to perform in computer space or cyber-space. . . . Consider, though, a virtual body or an avatar that can access a physical body, actuating its performance in the real world.

If the avatar is imbued with an artificial intelligence, becoming increasingly autonomous and unpredictable, then it would become more an AL (Artificial Life) entity performing with a human body in physical space. (Stelarc Web site)

While differing as to the degree and scale in which the body is extended, augmented and transformed, all these performances seem to have been inspired by the idea of openness, of welcoming the unpredictable and the unknown. This kind of transaction, intended to 'explore alternate, intimate and involuntary interfaces with the body' (Stelarc Web site), does not come without a loss; but what Stelarc renounces in his prosthetic performances is not agency as such – that would only reinforce the humanist, agent-driven notion of selfhood, a notion to which he does not subscribe – but rather *the idea of the self* as an autonomous agent. Stelarc's declarations that accompany his artistic practices do not share Orlan's language of self-sacrifice and artistic vocation. By dispassionately referring to his body as 'the body', Stelarc foregrounds the 'originary prosthecity' of selfhood and its situatedness in the network of relations that criss-cross the envelope of the skin.

This abandonment of the idea of self-as-agent, as skin-bounded and will-controlled, creates an ethical opening in the discourse of subjectivity which traditionally singles out the individual at the cost of suppressing an incalculable alterity it might encounter. However, Stelarc does not announce this withdrawal of agency in advance, but rather performs it through his prosthetic manoeuvres. His performances connect, divide, transmute and cut across the strict conceptual boundaries on which the discourse of 'identity without alterity' has relied. Stelarc's prostheses do not merely extend the body perceived as a bounded whole: the Extended Arm or the Movatar make the real arm or the neural system look like prosthetic devices. 'ALTERING THE ARCHITECTURE OF THE BODY RESULTS IN ADJUSTING AND EXTENDING ITS AWARENESS OF THE WORLD' (Stelarc Web site). As a result, the body is seen here not as an envelope for a soul or agency but rather as a sequence of co-dependent additions and replacements. In fact, the metaphysical perception of the self as a sum of bodily parts plus 'something else' (psyche, soul, practical reason) can itself be described as a prosthesis, an extension of the corporeal towards the spiritual, a bridge between materiality and ideality. Howard Caygill argues that

> The redesign that Stelarc envisages entails a thorough reconsideration of prosthesis. Instead of regarding the prosthesis as a supplement to the human body, it is now seen as already an integral part of its organisation and consequently as a site for its potential reorganisation. (48)

What I have termed here the 'originary prosthecity' of Stelarc's performances is a reworking, in the context of technology and experimentation, of the idea of 'originary alterity' that underpins Levinas's ethical thinking. As Joanna Hodge explains,

> Originary prosthecity is the thesis which declares the unjustifiability of theses, except in terms of carrying the discussion from where it starts to where it ends in a way which lends it sense and significance and which shows the necessary polemical nature of any determination of meaning and order. (192)

This notion of discussion mentioned by Hodge inscribes itself in the logic of Lyotard's differend referred to in the earlier part of this chapter. From the perspective of the differend, the ethical character of Stelarc's performances will never be unambiguously asserted or denied, but it does not mean that we cannot — or even should not — follow our polemical path (which does not actually arrange itself into the kind of provisional linearity Hodge has delineated) to consider the possibility of ethics erupting within artistic discourses, especially those that often lend themselves to negative and accusatory readings. Levinasian ethics supports what Hodge calls 'the unjustifiability of theses', and therefore cannot be enclosed in a book of conduct. It does not consist of rules and regulations, which should not lead to a conclusion that his ethics is unfounded: it springs precisely from the recognition of, and respect for, the other, whose alterity cannot be reduced to the ideas elaborated and mastered by the self. The self is not for Levinas a 'microcosm in miniature'; it emerges only in contact with, or as a response to, the other, who is both a stranger and 'in all essential aspects like me'. It can thus be concluded that ethics is here an *inevitable* consequence of this recognition of the 'thereness' of the other. Its inevitability does not mean that the other cannot be annihilated or devoured, rather that it is necessary to respond to alterity in one way or another. Indeed, this pervertibility of ethics is also its first and foremost condition. '[T]his pervertibility is the positive condition (to be affirmed, then) of all the "positive" values (the Good, the Just, and so on) ethics enjoins us to seek' (Bennington, 72). Stelarc's performance of prosthetic self hood can thus perhaps be described as the abandonment of the idea of self-possession and self-mastery. It creates a space for an encounter with, even intrusion of, what is radically different from the self and yet what remains, paradoxically, in some sort of relationship with the self. By denying the mastery of the self (of the artist, *auteur*, creator, demiurge), Stelarc does not give up what he previously possessed; he rather resigns from a certain idea of not only the performance artist but also the human as *only singular* and autonomous. His 'hospitality' – to borrow Derrida's term, which he employs to describe precisely this kind of ethical opening – should not, however, be interpreted as an act of goodwill but rather as a compulsion to respond to the inevitability of ethics and a decision not to commit violence against it.

Stelarc himself willingly embraces the rhetoric of hospitality in his performances, describing the body as a 'host – not only for technology, but also for remote agents' ('Parasite visions', 66). His Stomach Sculpture project, in which a dome capsule built of high-quality metals was inserted into his body and then arrayed with switches on the control box and documented by means of video endoscopy equipment, is one example of such unconditional hospitality. As the artist himself puts it,

It is time to recolonise the body with MICROMINIATURISED ROBOTS to augment our bacterial population, to assist our immunological system and to monitor the capillary and internal tracts of the body. . . . SPECK-SIZED ROBOTS ARE EASILY SWALLOWED, AND MAY NOT EVEN BE SENSED! At a nanotechnology level, machines will inhabit cellular spaces and manipulate molecular structures. ('From psycho to cyber strategies', 248–9)

This interpenetration between human and machine is for Stelarc a promise of new forms of hospitality and intimacy: 'The body has been augmented, invaded and now becomes a host – not only for technology, but also for remote agents' ('Parasite visions', 66). Opening his body to the intrusion of technology and thus shifting the locus of human agency, Stelarc renounces the possibility of knowing the consequences of his connected performances in advance. By abandoning the desire to master the house of his own body and opening himself to the (perhaps hostile) intrusion of the guest, Stelarc performs the most ethical act of what Derrida terms 'unconditional hospitality', where

> unconditional hospitality implies that you don't ask the other, the newcomer, the guest, to give anything back, or even to identify himself or herself. Even if this other deprives you of your mastery of your home, you have to accept this. It is terrible to accept this, but that is the condition of unconditional hospitality: that you give up the mastery of your space, your home, your nation. ('Hospitality', 70)

But this openness towards alterity is not a passive enterprise. Even though the self cannot rely on a book of laws and rules for its conduct, the welcome it extends towards the other – to retain its openness and not to fossilize into a predictable and measurable 'gift' – has to be constantly revisited. In this sense, Stelarc's continual rethinking of the ways in which prosthetic relationships can be recast in his performances can be interpreted as a responsible response to ethics itself, a response that arises out of the duty towards unassimilable difference. Geoffrey Bennington confirms that

> an ethical act worthy of its name is always *inventive*, and inventive not at all in the interests of expressing the 'subjective' freedom of the agent, but in response and responsibility to the other. . . . I can in fact 'express myself', exercise my freedom, only in this situation of response and responsibility with respect to the always-already-thereness of the other text as part of a 'tradition' to which I am always already indebted. (Bennington, 68)

Stelarc's inventiveness leads him constantly to run up against the limits of the physical and the corporeal in search of its possible extension and of what he terms 'the telematic scaling of subjectivity'. Perhaps we could go so far as to suggest that his performances enact a kind of 'connected Levinasianism', one that arises out of a specific historical moment in the development of technology that embraces the everyday in numerous ways. As email communication, online shopping and virtual friendships are becoming a prominent part of many people's lives, Stelarc proposes a way of encountering the alterity of technology which moves beyond both technophilia and technophobia. Recognizing a certain unavoidability of prosthetic connections facilitated by the Internet and cyberspace, he predicts that 'bodies will generate phantom partners, not because of a lack, but as an extending and enhancing addition to their physiology' ('Parasite visions', 69). Exposed to the multiplicity of agents, the body has to develop a kind of 'fluid and flowing awareness that dims and intensifies as they are connected and disconnected' (69). An ethical response of this kind presents itself as a non-hysterical acceptance of a necessity.

'A SPECIES FOR WHICH WE DO NOT YET HAVE A NAME'

Orlan's and Stelarc's performances not only foreground the originary prosthecity of identity but also embrace the intrinsic monstrosity of the human that becomes ever so visible in 'the technological age'. To describe their artistic projects as 'monstrous' does not amount to reducing them to 'bad scandal' or horror. A monster, according to Derrida, 'shows itself [elle se montre] — that is what the word monster means — it shows itself in something that is not yet shown and that therefore looks like a hallucination, . . . it frightens precisely because no anticipation had prepared one to identify this figure' ('Passages', 386). The prosthetic ethics of welcome cannot thus be learned in advance, because an encounter with alterity (which we can supplement — even if not substitute — here with prosthecity or monstrosity) is always singular and irreplaceable. But its uncertain occurrence and unpredictable form do not diminish our responsibility to respond to what shows itself as incalculably different. As this alterity transcends our discursive mastery, the ethical moment of being faced with incalculable difference, with 'a species for which we do not yet have a name', presents itself as inevitable.

NOTES

1. In the interview with Elizabeth Weber titled 'Passages – from traumatism to promise', Jacques Derrida, whose words I have borrowed for the title of this chapter, explains the 'monstrous' character of the future as follows: '[T]he figure of the future, that is, that which can only be surprising, that for which we are not prepared, you see, is heralded by species of monsters. A future that would not be monstrous would not be a future; it would already be a predictable, calculable, and programmable tomorrow. All experience open to the future is prepared or prepares itself to welcome the monstrous *arrivant*, to welcome it, that is, to accord hospitality to that which is absolutely foreign or strange, but also, one must add, to try to domesticate it, that is, to make it part of the household' (386–7).
2. For an interpretation of Stelarc's work in the context of shamanism and Western ritual, see Marsh (96–140).
3. When discussing her recent project *Refiguration / Self-Hybridation* with Robert Ayers, Orlan explains that 'Here we're quite a long way from the problem of identity. These are images that I put before the public, which could find takers in our society, and which, in the end, present themselves as being "acceptable" as a type of face that doesn't, strictly speaking, refer to identity. Of course there's an inference in relation to what *I* am, but no, this isn't work concerned with identity. You could put it like this: it's simply the idea of saying that beauty can take on an appearance that is not usually thought of as beautiful' (Ayers, 180).

WORKS CITED

Adams, Parveen. *The Emptiness of the Image: Psychoanalysis and Sexual Difference*. London and New York: Routledge, 1996.

Armstrong, Rachel. 'What is sci-fi aesthetics?' *Art and Design: Sci-Fi Aesthetics*, 12:9/10 (September/October 1997): 3–5.

Ayers, Robert. 'Serene and happy and distant: an interview with Orlan'. In *Body Modification*. Ed. Mike Featherstone. London: Sage, 2000. 171–84.

Bennington, Geoffrey. 'Deconstruction and ethics'. *Deconstructions: A User's Guide*. Ed. Nicholas Royle. Basingstoke: Palgrave, 2000. 64–82.

Butler, Judith. *Bodies That Matter: On the Discursive Limits of 'Sex'*. London: Routledge, 1993.

Caygill, Howard. 'Stelarc and the chimera: Kant's critique of prosthetic judgement'. *Art Journal* 56 (1997): 46–51.

Clark, Timothy. 'Deconstruction and technology'. In *Deconstructions: A User's Guide*. Ed. Nicholas Royle. Basingstoke: Palgrave, 2000. 238–57.

Critchley, Simon. *Ethics – Politics – Subjectivity*. London: Verso, 1999.

Derrida, Jacques. *Adieu to Emmanuel Levinas*. Trans. Pascale-Anne Brault and Michael Naas. Stanford, CA: Stanford University Press, 1999.

— 'Hospitality, justice and responsibility: a dialogue with Jacques Derrida'. In *Questioning Ethics: Contemporary Debates in Philosophy*. Ed. Richard Kearney and Mark Dooley. London: Routledge, 1999. 65–83.

— 'Passages – from traumatism to promise'. In *Points . . . Interviews, 1974–1994, Jacques Derrida*. Ed. Elizabeth Weber. Stanford, CA: Stanford University Press, 1995. 372–95.

Goodall, Jane. 'An order of pure decision: un-natural selection in the work of Stelarc and Orlan'. In *Body Modification*. Ed. Mike Featherstone. London: Sage, 2000. 149–70.

Hayles, N. Katherine. *How We Became Posthuman*. Chicago and London: University of Chicago Press, 1999.

Hodge, Joanna. 'Forays of a philosophical feminist: sexual difference, genealogy, teleology'. *Transformations: Thinking Through Feminism*. Ed. Sara Ahmed *et al.* London: Routledge, 2000. 182–95.

Levinas, Emmanuel. 'The trace of the other'. Trans. Alphonso Lingis. *Deconstruction in Context*. Ed. Mark C. Taylor. Chicago: University of Chicago Press, 1986. 345–59.

— *Totality and Infinity: An Essay on Exteriority*. Trans. Alphonso Lingis. Pittsburgh: Duquesne University Press, 1969.

Lury, Celia. *Prosthetic Culture*. London: Routledge, 1998.

Lyotard, Jean-François. *The Differend*. Trans. Georges Van Den Abbeele. Manchester: Manchester University Press, 1988.

Marsh, Anne. *Body and Self: Performance Art in Australia 1969–92*. Melbourne: Oxford University Press, 1993.

Millard, Rosie. 'Pain in the art'. *Art Review* (May 1996): 52–3.

Morawski, Stefan. 'A symptomatic case of self-mystification'. Trans. M. B. Guzowska. *Magazyn Sztuki/Art Magazine* 10:2 (1996): 196–203.

Onfray, Michel. 'Surgical aesthetics'. In *This Is My Body . . . This Is My Software*. Ed. Duncan McCorquodale. London: Black Dog Publishing, 1996. 30–39.

Orlan. 'Conference'. *This Is My Body . . . This Is My Software*. Ed. Duncan McCorquodale. London: Black Dog Publishing, 1996. 82–93.

Rose, Barabara. 'Is it art? Orlan and the transgressive act'. *Art in America* 81:2 (February 1993): 82–7.

Stelarc. 'From psycho to cyber strategies: prosthetics, robotics and remote existence'. *Cultural Values* 1:2 (1997): 241–9.

—— 'Parasite visions: alternate, intimate and involuntary experiences'. *Art and Design: Sci-Fi Aesthetics*. 12:9/10 (September/October 1997): 66–9.

—— Web site, <www.stelarc.va.com.au>.

Wilson, Sarah. '*L'Histoire d'O*, sacred and profane'. In *This Is My Body . . . This Is My Software*. Ed. Duncan McCorquodale. London: Black Dog Publishing, 1996. 7–17.

Waldby, Catherine. *The Visible Human Project: Informatic Bodies and Posthuman Medicine*. London: Routledge, 2000.

Weber, Samuel. *Mass Mediauras: Form, Technics, Media*. Ed. Alan Cholodenko. Stanford, CA: Stanford University Press, 1996.

Wild, John. Introduction. In *Totality and Infinity: An Essay on Exteriority*. By Emmanuel Levinas. Pittsburgh: Duquesne University Press, 1969. 11–20.

Wills, David. *Prosthesis*. Stanford, CA: Stanford University Press, 1995.

Name Index

Note: 'n.' after a page number refers to a note on that page.